FAMILY SECRETS

FAMILY SECRETS

WHAT YOU DON'T KNOW

CAN

HURT YOU

JOHN BRADSHAW

BANTAM BOOKS
NEW YORK • TORONTO • LONDON • SYDNEY • AUCKLAND

FAMILY SECRETS

A Bantam Book / May 1995

Library of Congress Cataloging-in-Publication Data

Bradshaw, John, 1933–
    Family secrets : what you don't know can hurt you / John Bradshaw.
        p.   cm.
    Includes bibliographical references.
    ISBN 0-553-09591-9
    1. Family—Psychological aspects.   2. Secrecy—Psychological
aspects.   *3. Mental health.   I. Title.*
HQ518.B73   1995
155.9'24—dc20   94-49196
                                                                  CIP

Published simultaneously in the United States and Canada

Bantam Books are published by Bantam Books, a division of Bantam
Doubleday Dell Publishing Group, Inc. Its trademark, consisting of
the words "Bantam Books" and the portrayal of a rooster, is Regis-
tered in U.S. Patent and Trademark Office and in other countries.
Marca Registrada. Bantam Books, 1540 Broadway, New York, New
York 10036.

PRINTED IN THE UNITED STATES OF AMERICA

BVG   10   9   8   7   6   5   4   3   2   1

CONTENTS

v

PART THREE

GETTING BACK TO KANSAS

DO YOU KNOW A SECRET LIKE THIS?

Five-year-old Stanley runs up to four-year-old Bobby and screams, "I know a secret that you don't know." Bobby starts to cry and runs away.

Secrets give us power over those who are not in the know. They can make us special and important. They can also protect us from harm. Secrets are an integral part of human life. Not being in on a secret can be a source of misery and pain. And sometimes being in on a secret can cause us consternation and confusion. See if you relate to any of the following secrets. These and many others are the stuff of family secrets and form the subject of this book.

BILLY is puzzled by his father's strange behavior. On the day after his eighth birthday, his mother tells him that his father has a sickness in his mind called paranoid schizophrenia. She also tells him that he must never discuss this with anyone. Billy feels very scared. He's afraid his father will get worse. He's afraid to bring a friend home from school for fear of what his father might do. Most of all, he's afraid that he might become mentally ill someday.

HARRIET feels pressured by Hogarth to be frugal about money. He seems to resent every cent she spends. Harriet skimps and saves in every way possible. She never buys anything for herself. She does, however, secretly stash money she's received from birthday and Christmas presents. She has also made some extra money from sewing and using food coupons. Harriet lives in constant fear that Hogarth will find her secret stash.

JULIANNA is confused about a woman her mother calls Aunt Susie, who is often at her house when she comes home from school and leaves before her father gets home in the evening. Once when she came home, Aunt Susie and her mother were in her mother's bedroom with the door locked. Julianna got very frightened because it sounded like her mother was being hurt. When she banged on the door, she was told everything was okay and to go and play. Aunt Susie is very sweet to Julianna and often brings her toys and treats. Julianna's mother has told her that Aunt Susie is their special secret, and she has made Julianna swear never to tell her father about her.

BUTCH sees his brother, Corbet, hanging out with a well-known drug dealer at school. A week later he finds drug paraphernalia hidden in the cellar of their house. On Saturday night Corbet comes home early and then sneaks out again and doesn't come home till six in the morning. It is obvious to Butch that Corbet is on drugs. Butch tries to talk to Corbet about the dangerous life he is leading, but Corbet is hostile and tells him to mind his own business. Their parents are both busy with careers, and they don't seem to notice what is happening. Butch wants to tell them about Corbet, but he feels like he would be a rat if he did.

PEGGY's childhood was truly joyous. The family had everything that money could buy. Her father was very mysterious and glamorous to her. He traveled quite a lot, but when he was home, he didn't have to go to work like her friends' fathers. He was fun and spent lots of time with her. One day when she was thirteen, the police arrived at the door with a warrant for her father's arrest. He was accused of being a hired gunman who had killed several people. Peggy's world fell apart at that moment.

MARKUS has always longed to go on hunting trips with his dad and his dad's buddies. Now that he is fourteen, his father has invited him to come along. He discovers that the men have hired prostitutes to go with them. The first night out his dad sends one of them to sleep with

Markus, telling him that it's time he became a man. Markus is so excited that he ejaculates prematurely. He is the butt of the group's jokes for the whole weekend. Besides the shame and guilt, Markus feels like he has betrayed his mother.

MYRTLE's mother was in bed most of her life. She had a "nervous breakdown" when Myrtle was four, and she was sick a lot of the time after that. She never left the house and suffered from many physical symptoms, especially an acute heart condition.

Myrtle walked on eggs throughout her entire childhood, and she spent her adult life protecting her mother from any upset.

When Myrtle was forty-five, her mother was diagnosed with terminal cancer. She lived much longer than was predicted, and the doctor kept remarking on the strength of her heart. Myrtle is now questioning every aspect of her mother's illness.

GRETCHEN has just finished her third visit to a therapist. After describing her many symptoms, her therapist asks her if she has any memories of sexual abuse. Gretchen says no, but leaves the session feeling very troubled and upset. She has always felt that something troublesome happened to her in childhood, and she has already experienced a series of sexually abusive relationships. She is afraid to go back to see the therapist for fear of finding out that something terrible happened to her in childhood. She wonders if it is necessary to know what happened in order to go on with her life.

Every family has secrets. Some are benign and constructive, protecting the family and/or its individual members and aiding in their growth and individuality.

Other secrets are toxic and destructive, destroying trust, intimacy, freedom, personal growth, and love. What you don't know can really hurt you!

PROLOGUE

All men by nature desire to know.

ARISTOTLE

The unexamined life is not worth living.

SOCRATES

When I was eleven years old, I experienced my first dark secret, the kind this book is about. I liked to sneak into my parents' room and open closets, boxes, and drawers to see what I could find. One day while rummaging through my dad's socks, I spotted a tin box with a key. When I opened the box, there were mounds of silver dimes shining like buried treasure. My dad was rarely home. Somehow finding his dime collection gave me a bond with him. Now I knew about his secret hiding place. I opened the box periodically as if to have a chat with him and to see how his collection was growing.

One day I took two of the dimes. I carried them around for several days, carefully guarding them lest my sister and brother find out. Then one afternoon when I was alone, I went to the grocery store and bought four candy bars. I pigged out on them in a vacant lot near my house. The guilt was awful. I knew I had broken one of the Ten Commandments and that I would fry for it. Still I returned to the tin box several times to steal dimes, taking a few more each time. Once I took several dollars' worth. I took the bus downtown and had my first spending spree at the five-and-ten-cent store. I spent the dimes with the reckless abandon of a drunken pirate celebrating a conquest.

A few days later I heard my dad asking my mom if she had taken some dimes out of his collection. I knew the jig was up, but when my father asked me whether I had taken any, I lied vociferously. I kept this secret until it gradually faded into the fabric of shame and guilt that came to dominate my sense of identity.

What I remember most is how much anxiety the secret created. I couldn't even enjoy the toys I bought at the five-and-ten-cent store. I had to hide them in the vacant lot and be on my guard when I went to play with them. My siblings had no new toys and would surely want to know where I had gotten these, and most assuredly they would tell my mother about them.

One Saturday when I went to my secret hiding place, I was shocked to find that my toys were gone! Someone had found them. I cried for a long time, but I couldn't tell anyone or get any solace for my grief. Dark secrets often bring this kind of pain.

Our Mysterious Families

My childhood curiosity about my parents' world seems to be shared by many. We have an innate urge to know about things, especially our roots. Our family is the clan from which we come, part of our fate, and in many ways that which shapes our destiny.

I'm still interested in understanding my family. Over the past fifteen years, I've learned a lot about the dynamics of how families operate. I've been on a kind of psychic archaeological dig in relation to my own family, and I've made some valuable transforming discoveries about family secrets.

Deciphering family secrets takes us into the heart of the family's mysterious power to impact our lives. I call this journey into the family's secret world *soul*-searching.

Soul-searching attempts to go deeper into our family's reality than we have ever gone before. Soul-searching means seeking our family's *essence*—that which makes it most what it is. Soul-searching asks us to *think* about things pertaining to our family that we've never thought about before. It asks us to listen to our family's stories without our previous judgments and habituated ways of understanding. Expanding our awareness about our family gives us a new opportunity to access the strengths and vulnerabilities we have developed as a result of adapting to their dark secrets. Expanding our awareness about how our family's dark secrets have impacted our lives helps us imagine new possibilities and new choices for our lives.

As a child, I was told, "What you don't know won't hurt you." That was a potentially damaging statement. You may have heard it too. It has kept children from thinking about their family's secrets for generations. But what we don't know can cause devastation in our lives.

In the pages that follow you will read about many people who consciously believed they were living their own lives, while in reality they were acting out their families' dark secrets.

Some secrets the family *knows* it's keeping; a lot of conscious energy is expended on hiding the truth. But some of the most painful relationships and some of the most traumatic and shameful events get repressed. They become unconscious. Like our timeworn sayings, the shameful, painful aspects of family life become the stockpile of secrets hiding in the rubble of the unconscious. The farther back these secrets go, the deeper and more dangerous they become. As our ancestors learned to avoid the truth, avoidance became a way of life. Rules were set up to insure avoidance. Over time family members learned to avoid their avoidances. Layers of unconscious secrets developed that finally resulted in "collective amnesia"—a multigenerational trance. All long-standing groups have some degree of this trance. Families have their own distinct brand of it. If you don't know about all this, it can hurt you—sometimes very badly.

What I will show you in this book is that families are paradoxical. The dark secrets that are so carefully guarded get revealed and uncovered because the children act them out—if not in this generation, then in the next, or the next. The Bible tells us:

Whatever is hidden away will be brought out into the open and whatever is covered up, will be uncovered. (Mark 4:22)

I don't know if the biblical writer had family secrets in mind, but I do know that the secrets are revealed in many forms—ranging from having idiosyncratic and seemingly weird feelings, thoughts, and behaviors to openly expressing a secret by repeating it in one's own life.

I have a far greater respect for the family's power to impact our lives than I did in 1984, when I made the PBS television series *Bradshaw On: The Family*. Real families defy our theories and abstractions about them, and often the very problems that we try to change are what makes the family most human. I have also updated my understanding of the nature of shame and what a crucial part natural shame or modesty plays in our lives. Modesty allows us to accept the limits of our own ability to understand our family.

To grasp your family's dark secrets soulfully, I will ask you to make a decision to discipline yourself. Soul-searching demands a kind of moral courage and a commitment to discovering the facts no matter what. Buddhists call this kind of discipline *beginner's mind*. I describe what this means in Chapter 4.

Going into the depths of your family requires that you look for patterns that have persisted for several generations. In spite of the mystery that surrounds the family, there are certain guides that can help us through the maze. I have found the work of psychiatrist Murray Bowen to be helpful in giving my family experience a certain coherence and meaning. I will use the Bowen Theory as a roadmap on our journey.

A Trip to the Land of Oz

This journey will be hard, but it will also be soulful. That is why I have also chosen the story of Dorothy and the Wizard of Oz to guide us. I've always loved this story, and somehow it has stood the test of time. Perhaps this is due to the movie version and Judy Garland's unforgettable performance as Dorothy. But on a deeper level, I think it is because the story embodies something that is unconsciously shared by everyone.

Dorothy is surrounded by secrecy. Her real parents are a dark secret. She is an orphan. She lives a bleak and joyless life with her Aunt Em and Uncle Henry. Dorothy's dream describes her journey to find herself, her true home. When she leaves she is a displaced person, and when she returns she is at peace with herself. She discovers that in order to find home, you have to leave home. She also discovers that there will be allies (the Scarecrow, Tin Man, and Cowardly Lion) on the journey, as well as grace.

Grace is a free gift. When the good witch Glinda gives Dorothy the silver slippers (they are ruby only in the movie), she tells her that they will protect her from ultimate harm.

Dorothy, like all of us, fails to recognize this gift of grace while it is operating in her life. (We usually become aware of it only in hindsight.) And like all of us, Dorothy encounters many obstacles along the way, the greatest of which is traversing the Haunted Forest to kill the Wicked Witch of the West. She survives this task because of the combined power of the community of friends that she has created and because of the intelligence, love, and courage they bring to their quest.

After she traverses the Haunted Forest, Dorothy has to face the ultimate disenchantment. The very source of power she has struggled toward—the Wizard of Oz—has no magical powers.

Like Dorothy, all of us have to leave the magical world of childhood and grow up. Our parents are not gods who can save us from suffering and death. We may have to face other disappointing things about them, too, like their dark secrets.

All in all, the story tells us that there is no magical answer to a problem called life. We never find out the secret of Dorothy's origins. All we know is that when she leaves home, things are bleak and empty, and when she returns, she is at peace. All of us have the power we need within us. Dorothy had what she was looking for all along. By the end of her story, her color-tinted glasses have fallen off and she's lost her magical slippers, but she is happy to be home.

I've entitled Part One of this book "Finding Home by Leaving Home." In it I will discuss the nature of secrets, distinguishing healthy secrets from unhealthy ones. I also will show the power that dark secrets have over us. I will then examine what is most paradoxical about family secrets: the fact that we somehow *know* them unconsciously and act them out. I will try to show you how that is possible.

In Part Two, entitled "Traversing the Haunted Forest," I will offer you a kind of Rosetta stone—a family chart that clinicians call a *genogram.* Using it as a guide, I will take you step by step, helping you to make a three-generational family map. I will also give you some other tools for deciphering your ancestors' and your parents' dark secrets.

Part Three is called "Getting Back to Kansas." In this section I will offer you some suggestions about what to do with what you have discovered, including how and when to tell family secrets and how to deal with their impact on your life. I'll ask you to look at your own dark secrets and be aware of the energy it takes for you to maintain them, as well as the ways they limit and constrict your life. And I'll suggest ways you can reconnect with your family or stay safely connected with it.

Finally I'll suggest that you explore the secret self that is yet to be, the potentialities and untapped possibilities that are uniquely yours. I call these your *soul secrets.*

My earnest hope is that you traverse this dark forest and that while touching your family's hidden side, you also touch its beauty and strength.

PARABLE

The Secret History of Dorothy

On a stormy winter night ravaged by high winds, a beautiful little girl was born in a small town in Kansas. Tragically, her teenage mother died in childbirth, and it was not certain who her father was.

She was adopted by her Aunt Emily and Uncle Henry, a poor farm couple who were rigid and stoic in their religious beliefs. They named the little girl Dorothy.

As Dorothy grew up, she was forbidden to ask about her real mother and father. They were in heaven, and it was considered a breach of faith to question any aspect of God's will.

Dorothy's only joy was a small dog she called Toto. She found the dog on a lonely country road one day and was allowed to keep him as long as she did all the chores Uncle Henry set before her and was perfectly obedient.

Uncle Henry secretly resented Dorothy. She was another mouth to feed, and he judged her real mother a terrible sinner. Henry scrutinized Dorothy's every move, scolding and shaming her terribly if she made a mistake. He often threatened to give Toto away.

Dorothy was terrified of Uncle Henry. She stuttered and acted inept and awkward when she was around him.

Dorothy came to believe that there was something very wrong with her. She thought she was stupid and selfish and felt afraid of her own shadow.

One day when she was ten years old, she found an old photo album while rummaging around in the attic of the farmhouse. When she looked through it, she found a picture of a woman who looked something like Aunt Em, only much younger. On the back was a note that said, "To my dearest sister, Love Amy." All at once Dorothy knew that this was her mother. Her heart began to pound as she stared at the picture. Her mother was so beautiful. She was wearing a real dress-up dress, and Dorothy imagined it must have been red, her favorite color. Further along in the album she found another photo of her mother with a somewhat older man who had his arm around her. The man was too young to be her grandfather, and anyway she had once seen *his* picture in Aunt Em's chiffonnier drawer. But the man in the photo was vigorous and handsome, and Dorothy felt that he might be her father.

After a while Dorothy started to feel guilty. She knew she shouldn't be looking at these pictures and longing for her mother and father. God would surely punish her if she persisted. So she closed the album and put it back in the old black trunk where she had found it. She vowed never to look at it again, and she never did.

But she did think about the pictures. And when she was doing her boring farmyard tasks or being scolded by Uncle Henry, she would see her mother's beautiful face and long for her to come and take her home.

When Dorothy reached her early teens, she started to have a recurring nightmare. All she could ever remember about it was that she was lost and she could see her mother's face calling to her and reaching out her hand, but Dorothy somehow couldn't quite reach her.

One stormy night when there were reports of twisters in the area, Dorothy dreamed that her house was picked up by a huge twister and landed on a wicked old witch, killing her. She awakened to find herself surrounded by the most curious people she had ever seen. Also standing before her was a good witch named Glinda, who wore a sparkling ruby red dress and looked just like the picture of her mother in the album. "Mother, take me home, take me home!" Dorothy cried. But Glinda did not gather Dorothy into her arms, as the little girl hoped. She was kind, but she firmly told Dorothy that the journey home was difficult and that she would meet many obstacles along the way.

If you have read L. Frank Baum's book *The Wonderful Wizard of Oz*, you know this part of the story.

But Baum left out one detail. When Dorothy and her friends finally met the Wizard, he looked exactly like the man in the photo that Dorothy thought might be her father.

When Dorothy woke up the next morning, she felt better about herself, although she was confused about the meaning of her dream. After school that day she asked her favorite teacher about it. Her teacher told her that every part of the dream was a part of herself. The Scarecrow's brains were hers, and so was the Lion's courage and Tin Man's heart full of love. The teacher said the dream was telling her that she was a wonderful young woman.

Then her teacher said, "The tough part is that you, like all the rest of us, must learn that no one has any magical powers to save us. Our parents are only men and women, not witches and wizards."

Dorothy was deeply moved by all of this and remembered it always. When she turned eighteen, she left her aunt and uncle's farm and got a job. She put herself through college and became a newspaper reporter. She ultimately found out much more about her real mother, Amy, who had died when Dorothy was born. She also found out that the older man in the picture was a teacher at her mother's high school who had left under hushed-up circumstances. She came to believe he was her biological father, but she never tried to trace him.

Dorothy later married and had two daughters and a son of her own. I can't exactly say she lived happily ever after. She and her husband had fights like all of us, and her children disappointed her in some ways, just as most kids do their parents. At times she was bored and even depressed. But on the whole she found life worthwhile and often enjoyable.

As Aunt Em grew older, she softened a bit and was willing to talk about her younger sister Amy. When Dorothy and the children visited the farm one summer, Em spent hours at the kitchen table with her going over the old family album. Uncle Henry was still gruff, but Dorothy let him know that his days of shaming her were over. He never said much to the children, but he let them come with him to the barn "if they keep quiet." Somehow they liked to go along.

PART ONE

FINDING HOME
BY
LEAVING HOME

Secrecy is as indispensable to human beings as fire and as greatly feared. Both enhance and protect life, yet both can stifle, lay waste, spread out of all control. Both may be used to guard intimacy or to invade it, to nurture or to consume.

SISSELA BOK

CHAPTER 1

WHEN SILENCE IS GOLDEN

With no control over secrecy and openness, human beings could not remain sane or free.

SISSELA BOK

Silence and secrecy are worth as much as gold when used in the right way.

ROSEMARIE WELTER-ENDERLIN

When I was in the seventh grade, a Boy Scout leader came to our class and gave an inspiring lecture on the virtues of scouting. I was already a Cub Scout, and I wore my uniform with pride. I was very committed to the Cub Scouts' philosophy of honest citizenship and loyalty to the American Way. I signed up for the Boy Scouts without hesitation.

My first scout meeting was great, with the announcement of a wiener roast picnic and bonfire on the weekend. The weekend came, and the picnic started out fine, with all the hot dogs you could eat and lots of ice cream and cake for dessert.

The bonfire was also fun. We gathered next to the football field, sang songs, pledged allegiance to the flag, and felt exhilarated to be part of the troop. I felt like I was growing up. All the older eighth-grade guys were there, and they were acting really nice to us younger kids.

And then it happened—the beginning of a true nightmare. The scout leader announced that he was leaving and that the older boys had some special initiation activities for us newcomers. I had an immediate feeling of danger. An older kid named Feigle was grinning at me. So was George Morales. They were known for their dislike of seventh graders. Then it started. We were told there was to be a contest—a race in which we were to hop blindfolded with our ankles tied together. That didn't sound too bad until Feigle announced that there were some leftover wieners and that each one of us was to take one and place it between the cheeks of his buttocks. Anyone dropping his wiener would face dire consequences.

My memory gets a bit fuzzy here. All I know is that I felt my wiener slip out on the third or fourth hop. There were four of us that didn't make it. Once again my memory gets a bit blurred. I remember being encircled by the older boys. I saw them grab James Schimek, pull his pants off, and throw them into the fire. When I saw his boxer shorts being yanked off, I bolted for the open end of the football field.

I was not fast, but I had played a lot of sandlot football and was a fair broken field runner. Feigle and Morales came after me as I raced toward the darkness at the other end of the field. Thank God I had gotten a real jump on them. I ran past the fieldhouse and into the streets near my house. I found some bushes behind a garage, and I crouched there for at least thirty minutes. After I was sure they had stopped looking for me, I ran home.

I went inside as if nothing had happened. My mother questioned me about the evening. I couldn't tell her what had happened. I mumbled something like, "It was great, but I don't have time to meet the Scouts' strenuous schedule and keep up my straight-A report card." I went to bed with my mother's voice droning on about the value of being a Boy Scout.

As I lay there, I felt great anxiety about going to school on Monday. I feared the teasing I would get and what Feigle and Morales might do to me. I felt ashamed that I wasn't man enough to take the hazing. I also felt disillusioned about the Boy Scouts—at least this one troop didn't seem like a very good advertisement for Truth, Democracy, and the American Way. I vowed never to tell anyone in my family.

When I went to school on Monday, I heard the news. A kid had gotten burned badly in the hazing. It was an accident, but all the Boy Scouts in the eighth grade were in big trouble. My escape was forgotten.

I carried this experience in the secret chambers of my heart. I knew a deep truth about myself and about my limits. I learned that I had great fear of violence, and I also learned about my sense of modesty. I hated that macho kind of violence! I still do. As the years went by, I came to respect the part of me that refused to be hazed that night in

1945. What started out as a shameful secret later became the root of what I now call my natural shame—an essential guardian of my humanity.

Secrecy as Protection, Secrecy as Power

The ability to keep things secret is an essential power that all human beings possess in order to protect themselves. Keeping my secret about the Boy Scout experience allowed me a private place in which I could come to terms with my seemingly cowardly behavior.

Over the years other events proved to me that I was not a coward. And each time I experienced being courageous, I had to rethink my running away from the bonfire. This process of secretly evaluating our life experiences is the way we learn about ourselves. It ultimately helps us form our self-identity. To have no capacity for secrecy is to be completely vulnerable to the way others see us. Had I told my secret, I would have been judged a sissy by some members of my family. My secrecy was a boundary that protected me from their judgmental eyes.

Somehow I think my mother knew that something traumatic had happened to me that night in 1945. She allowed me to quit the Scouts with almost no resistance, and she never questioned why. I was allowed to have unqualified privacy in integrating my experience.

TWO FACES OF SECRECY

I'm beginning this book with a discussion of privacy, because without an understanding of privacy you cannot grasp the two faces of secrecy. One face, privacy, is the realm of *natural secrecy;* the other face, what I'll call *dark secrecy,* is the realm necessitated by the breakdown of privacy.

By starting with privacy, I also want to challenge the notion that all secrecy is sick and that every secret must be disclosed.

I remember doing a show with Geraldo Rivera on incest and quoting a recovery saying I had heard many times: "Families are as sick as their secrets." I believed that for a long time. Our current cultural mood is to believe it. We live in an age where openness and rigorous honesty are valued, and secrecy seems to be in conflict with openness and honesty.

But I'm uncomfortable now with such an absolutist approach. If we see secrecy only as something negative, we will miss its crucial significance as an essential element in our right to privacy and freedom.

What Is Secrecy?

The dictionary gives three meanings for the word *secrecy:* intentional concealment; what is unknown; and what is yet to be discovered. I will be discussing all three kinds of secrets in this book, because all three shape our families and how we experience them.

The Latin word *secretum* means "something hidden or set apart." And although they are not present in every secret, the concepts of deception, furtiveness, lying, prohibition, intimacy, silence, and sacredness also influence the way we understand secrecy.

What I'll call the *content* of a secret can be almost anything. We may choose to hide almost any fact, feeling, or behavior. And as I will explain, this choice may itself be a secret to the person who chooses it. The intention to conceal something may be unconscious and unknown.

Another important aspect of secrecy is who "owns" the secret. This is sometimes called the *location* of the secret. A secret may be shared with no one, or it may be confided to another on the promise that it go no farther. Some secrets may be known to a whole group or they may be known to all but one or two members. This can be a crucial factor in how secrets affect families.

Secrecy can be either positive or negative—and sometimes it is both. The same secrecy that can foster a sense of brotherhood in an ethnic or religious group can at the same time fuel bigotry and hatred toward those not of the group. I'll ask you to keep this polarity in mind as we examine the range of family secrets.

However, I believe that some secrets are *always* destructive. For example, incest, battering, alcoholism, murder, and any other form of violence to another's person are always deadly secrets.

I also believe that some secrets are always constructive, such as those that protect one's dignity, freedom, inner life, and creativity.

Culture and Secrets

There is a large middle ground where secrets are neither destructive nor constructive as such but have to be judged by the way the secret is interpreted by a group, such as a family, and by how it functions in terms of the dynamic process and needs of that family system. Cultural, ethnic, and religious beliefs often play a major role here.

Growing up in my Catholic family, we believed that eating meat on Friday was a grievous sin, one that could send you to Hell. I once willingly and with conscious forethought ate a cheeseburger on Friday. This became a big secret that I guarded vigilantly. When the Catholic Church decided to change this teaching, the secret was no longer necessary.

Scientific knowledge has transformed many family secrets. Mental illness and mental retardation were once a family's most guarded secrets. Beliefs in witchcraft and demonic possession were used to castigate and institutionalize such people. We've come a long way from the nightmarish days of insane asylums and frontal lobotomies. Our modern understanding of brain chemistry and other organic factors has enabled families to openly seek the support they need.

Moral beliefs also shape secrecy. One family may be quite flexible in their beliefs about premarital sex, perhaps not openly encouraging it but giving their teenagers explicit instructions about birth control and AIDS. Such a family would have only a minimal need to keep sexual matters secret, except as a matter of personal privacy. Another family might be quite rigid and teach that any form of sex before marriage is sinful. Sexual matters would likely be a major area of dark secrecy in such a family.

Many past cultural beliefs and expectations are now seen as too rigid and moralistic. In the past, dark secrets clustered around issues pertaining to elopement, marriages where the woman was already pregnant, adoption, illegitimacy, alcoholism, divorce, and sexual abuse. These were considered to be major areas of toxic shame, moral failure, and sin.

The relativity of modern consciousness has mollified the rigidity and totalism of past morality, and its "terrible moralism" has been softened by a more enlightened understanding of the ambiguity and polarity of reality. For example, the stigma and humiliation of being an unwed mother has been greatly modified. This is not said to encourage such behavior. But it is clear that moralizing judgment has done little to change it. The label of illegitimacy itself is now seen as victimizing and punishing.

Today, too, alcoholism is understood as an illness, and some of its dark secrecy has been alleviated. I am in my twenty-ninth year of sobri-

ety, and much has changed since I took my last drink. When I began
my recovery, alcoholism was looked upon as a moral failure. Alcoholics were thought to be weak-willed and degenerate gluttons. Those
days are gone forever, and the treatment of alcoholism has advanced
considerably.

One of the greatest areas of change is in the enlightenment now
given the family members of alcoholics. Family members began to understand that if they told the secret and stopped covering it up, the
alcoholic would have to face the consequence of irresponsible behavior. The collapse of the secret-keeping system is often enough to pro-
pel an alcoholic into treatment.

The advance in the treatment of the families of alcoholics has also
led to the uncovering of one of this century's greatest secrets. In the
past we didn't realize that the toxic shame and the dark secret of alcoholism had such far-reaching effects. To the degree that the children
in an alcoholic family experienced the alcoholic's drinking, they developed a number of traits that followed them into adulthood and continued to impact the next generation. This insight also helped us to
understand the consequences of growing up in physically, sexually,
and emotionally abusing families. While there are traits specific to each
kind of abuse, the common thread that binds them all together is
childhood trauma. Many of the same traits are found in trauma victims
of any kind. The cultural understanding of this secret has liberated
millions of people.

Privacy as a Right

Recently two young girls in Houston were viciously murdered. When
they were first reported missing, I eagerly turned on the TV news to
get an update. When their mutilated bodies were finally found, the TV
reporters hounded the girls' father for a comment. The father was
grief-stricken and in shock. No words could convey his horror. He
wanted and needed to be left alone. Yet the camera stayed fixed on
him, and the TV reporter persisted in sticking a mike in his face. I was
furious at the reporter, and when several other people mentioned
having the same response, I felt we were sharing a basic truth. The
reporter was engaging in an obscene behavior.

Many of you may have watched Super Bowl XXVIII, between Dallas
and Buffalo. Thurmon Thomas, Buffalo star running back, fumbled the

ball twice, both times leading to Dallas scores. The second fumble may have been the turning point in the game. Thomas was mortified and humiliated. He sat on the bench with his face in his hands. *He was literally trying to save face.* The cameraman focused on him and allowed us to stare at him for what seemed like a full minute. Afterward the camera came back to his shameful visage several times. I felt like screaming at the director to get the TV camera's eyes off of him and leave him alone in his pain. Death, grieving, the sexual intimacies between a husband and wife, and a person's feelings of failure and shame are private matters.

The media actions I'm describing violated essential human privacy. We not only have a right to privacy, it is part of our natural endowment. *The more our natural need for privacy is respected and honored, the less deliberately secretive we need be.*

PRIVACY AND NATURAL SHAME

I believe that our need for privacy is not just a product of our culture. It is biologically based.

We are born with an emotion of natural shame that protects us from unwanted access. This emotion signals us when our sense of modesty is being violated. We blush when we feel embarrassed and unprotected in a social or public situation. We bashfully cling to our parents when we encounter strangers.

This natural shame or modesty is our innate way of *protecting ourselves,* our core boundary. It is the foundation of our freedom, self-discovery, and self-actualization. Silvan Tompkins, perhaps the leading authority on the meaning of shame, has said, "In contrast to all other affects, shame is an experience of the self by the self." Shame is natural: *it is shamelessness that is unnatural, socially determined, and learned.*

In his wonderful book *Shame, Exposure and Privacy,* Carl D. Schneider points out that one of the main reasons Americans have trouble grasping that shame is natural and shamelessness is unnatural is that we have only one word for shame in English. Most Indo-European languages have two or more words for it. Greek, for example, has five words that can be translated as "shame." The same is true for Latin. In German *Scham* means "shame as modesty," while *Schande* means "shame as dishonor and disgrace." In French *pudeur* means "shame as modesty," and *honte* means "shame as disgrace." Before we perform an action that might endanger us, we hesitate and resist—a case of *pudeur;* after an action that hurts and humiliates us, shame burns in our memory—a case of *honte.*

Shame as modesty is an innate signal that tells us we are being exposed when we are not ready to be exposed. Even newborn infants shut their eyes, turn their heads aside, and throw their hands up when they are overstimulated and need to withdraw. When we blush, or feel bashful or embarrassed, we have reached a limit. Someone or something is threatening our sense of self. We are overexposed and unprotected, and we need covering.

Modesty allows us to be hidden, covered, and protected in an appropriate way. It extends to several natural areas of life. Once we are out of infancy, we have a basic modesty about eating, eliminating, and sexual functioning. We have a sense of modesty and awe pertaining to God and prayer, also to our sense of goodness and virtue. We have a natural sense of modesty pertaining to birth and death and our personal dignity and self-worth.

Max Scheler, the German philosopher, compared these inherently private human behaviors to the roots of a tree, which, in order to generate the life of the tree, must remain buried in the ground. Just as the roots of a tree have a need for concealment, so also our psychic life has an area of profound roots that can function only in the shade of concealment.

Essential Areas of Human Experience That Privacy Protects and Makes Possible

There are at least four areas of human life that privacy makes possible and safeguards.

- Privacy safeguards much that is connected to the human life cycle, including eating, elimination, sexuality, reproduction, birth, suffering, and death.
- Privacy is needed in order to have individuality and selfhood.
- Privacy fosters the expansion of soul—that is, the *depth* of life.
- Privacy protects the realm of the sacred and holy where life's mysteries are ensconced in awe.

Without the modesty that safeguards privacy, members of a family would lose their *essential humanness.* When a family no longer has boundaries of privacy, its members either resort to dangerous isolation or defend themselves with dark secrets rooted in toxic shame.

VIOLATIONS OF MODESTY

With the exception of the Boy Scout experience, I had no privacy as a child, no right to lock the bathroom door, no room of my own where I could go and be assured some moments of peace. At one point in my life, my brother, sister, and I shared the same bedroom. At another point I slept on a rollaway folding bed in the dining room and kept my clothes in the cabinet with the silverware and the plates and saucers.

Someone was always watching me. Adult eyes were everywhere joined in guard duty, watching and waiting for me to mess up. And when they couldn't watch me, at night in my bed under the covers, God was watching me. I was viciously *overseen.* There was no place to hide, no way to relax, no place to dream. Recently I read a stanza of a poem from Robert Browning. "I give the fight up: let there be an end, / A privacy, an obscure nook for me. / I want to be forgotten even by God." I knew exactly what that meant.

Without a room of my own, I had to resort to hiding and unhealthy secrecy. My secrets protected me and allowed me some space to breathe. But the more I resorted to secrecy, the more I had to expend my energy to guard the secrets that guarded my space. Secrets beget secrets, and lies beget lies, and after many years I found myself lost in the stormy waters those lies had fostered.

The lack of privacy in my family was more or less typical of most families that I knew. Some of my friends had a room of their own because of better economic circumstances; but in my generation parents and other adults had absolute "rights" over their children, and children had no "rights." The authoritarian form of family life that I grew up in was based on a kind of ownership. A man's property included his wife and children, and parents owned their children. There is no real place for privacy in authoritarian patriarchal forms of family life.

In George Orwell's famous novel *1984,* Winston Smith fought against being totally controlled by the thought police of the totalitarian state. He hid in an alcove in his living room, where the eyes of Big

Brother's TV monitor could not see him. He wrote over and over in his diary: *Down with Big Brother.* (In case you don't remember, Big Brother was the totally controlling authority of the year 1984. Saying anything against this authority was considered a thought crime.) Winston risked being punished with years of hard labor in order to have the freedom of his *secret thoughts.* Even though he knew they would get him sooner or later, he was willing to grasp a moment of his own selfhood and autonomy by secretly writing in his diary.

DARK SECRECY AS THE PERVERSION OF PRIVACY

When privacy is prohibited, separateness becomes an act of stealth. *The less privacy there is, the more one must resort to secretiveness.* As Gary Sanders, a doctor at the University of Calgary, puts it, "Secrecy is the *necessity* of keeping something to oneself, while privacy is the *choice* of keeping something to oneself."

What I call *dark secrets* most often result from the perversion of privacy. They are rooted in the violation of modesty and natural shame. They cluster around issues pertaining to birth and death and the realm of the sacred, with its norms of good and evil and sin and salvation. Many dark secrets have to do with the psychic disguises and pretend behaviors that form our false or pseudoselves. Many others cluster around sexuality, eating, and the confusion of sexuality and bodily functions. Others relate to losing and saving face: issues pertaining to our authenticity, our good name and identity.

To clarify these areas of natural privacy and show how they can give rise to dark secrets, I'll briefly discuss each major category. Chart 1–1 lists them in outline form.

The Sacred

"Don't discuss religion with friends," I was told as a child. "It's too personal, and people get too emotional about their beliefs."

The sacred has always been looked upon as a realm of privacy. Prayer is also by nature a private act. Jesus admonishes those that pray in public, "Go into a room by yourself, shut the door, and pray to your Father who is there in the secret place." Much of TV evangelism is obscene, destroying the very nature of prayer by parading it in public.

CHART 1-1

REALM OF THE PRIVATE:
NATURAL AREAS OF CONCEALMENT

The sacred
  Prayer
  Morality
Birth
Death and dying
Intense suffering and pain
Bodily functions
  Eating
  Elimination
The dignity of the self
  Good name
  Face
  Body
Success/Failure
Tangible possessions
  Home
  Money
  Property
Intangible possessions
  Ideas
  Opinions
  Feelings
  Values
  Self-values
Intimacy
  Friendship
  Love/Spouse
Sexuality

The sacred is best experienced in silence, in the inner recesses of our being, where we listen to the "still quiet voice." When the sacred and the holy are made public, they lose their identity.

Matters pertaining to personal virtue and goodness are private. When that which is supposed to be private is made public, its very nature is defiled. Truly virtuous behavior is intended either for the good of oneself or for the good of another. When the motivation for good actions is public applause, the good behavior loses its character. Bragging about good deeds cancels out their goodness.

Birth

While our birth and parentage are matters of public record, they nonetheless belong to the realm of the private. Birth and death are profoundly mysterious. Hannah Arendt writes, "Man does not know where he comes from when he is born and where he goes when he dies." We cannot live without wondering about our origins. What was it like to be in the womb? Think of the fatefulness of being born to your mom and dad, who met each other by chance. Children often question their parentage during childhood: "Are these my real parents? Maybe I was adopted." Adopted children cannot avoid the question of their biological parents. "Who are they? Where are they? Why did they give me up? Did they do it for my own good? Did they really want me?"

Those who find that they have a sibling, usually a half-brother or -sister that they did not know about, are curious to find them and know them. A hidden sibling is usually part of a larger dark secret. Another birth secret has to do with paternity. To find out that the one you thought was your father is really your stepfather or your cousin can be devastating. Children today may face the issue of being conceived by an unknown father who sold his sperm to a donor bank.

Death and Dying

"Death," writes Silvan Tompkins, "is unique in being a universal source of shame." Death and the act of dying, with their accompanying suffering and deep grief, are human experiences that are properly hidden within the family, away from public view.

At the same time, when we die, we need our life openly honored and acknowledged for what it was. To grieve a person's death is to symbolically confirm and value their unique life.

People from other cultures are often shocked at the impersonal way death is treated in American society. They see people dying in hospitals, separated from their loved ones, reduced to data on a chart, and finally isolated with the hospital staff, for whom death means only the ultimate defeat of their knowledge and skills.

Many people carry secrets either about ungrieved deaths of family members, or in relation to a family suicide over which they feel power-lessness and shame.

There are also many family secrets around the process of dying and terminal illness that will lead to death. Many people carry secret memories of war with its faceless, anonymous, mutilated, and unmarked dead.

Intense Suffering and Pain

Although we experience the involuntary servitude of bodily existence, we guard against being reduced to mere bodily existence. Clothes conceal our bodies, covering our vulnerability. Stripping off a person's clothes is demeaning and shaming—as I instinctively knew at the Boy Scout outing. This form of defilement is used in torturing captives in war as well as in prisons.

When someone is in great pain or suffering, they need the protection of privacy. Watching the police beat Rodney King over and over again on television was disgusting and obscene. Children who watch their mother being beaten by their father are also being victimized. Any witness to violence is a victim of violence. Such abuse often becomes a dark secret.

Bodily Functions

All bodily functions belong to the realm of the private. All cultures have some practice of seemliness in relation to elimination. Exposure during the act of excretion brings on immediate shame.

Most families have their own unique language and ways of talking about private matters. Expressions for elimination can be quite creative and colorful, only to be outdone by special names for genitals. I once sat for thirty minutes listening to a male client who kept referring to his "Billy Ray Dill." It finally dawned on me that this man was talking about his penis!

We eat in public, but notice how the elaborate rules about table manners, conversation, and so on cover up the basic activity! Have you ever been the only one eating in a group? Most people do not like having others watch them while they eat. Many people are even embarrassed if they are the last to finish.

Secret eating rituals are part of the toxic shame in eating disorders.

People with eating disorders move away from mutuality and sharing and do these secret rituals in bleak isolation.

The Dignity of the Self

Good Name

Remember as a child how upsetting it was when your sibling or your playmate at school called you a name? There is tremendous power in name-calling. Great damage is done by gossiping and judgmentally discussing and criticizing another's good name.

Our name is honored by proper salutation. Our way of addressing another person may reveal the depth of our acquaintance and the degree of familiarity. Using the first name of someone with high-ranking dignity may be disgraceful to them.

Tribal people go on vision quests in order to discover sacred names that bring them new powers.

Part of the institutional degradation of prisons and prisoner-of-war camps is the practice of stripping people of their names and depriving them of their identity by giving them a *number*. Slavery was the ultimate atrocity, robbing people of their right to self-possession.

Face

Our face is inseparable from our identity. The face is the seat of modesty. It is also the seat of emotional expression. To be slapped in the face is a great dishonor. When people are ashamed, they hide their faces. We've all seen the news stories when a person taken into custody after being charged with a crime puts their hands over their face when the camera comes in for a close-up. Shame as modesty guards us against inappropriate exposure. Hiding our face, trying to save face, and losing face are the ways we often define violations and overexposure of ourselves.

God said to Moses, "My face you cannot see for no mortal man may see me and live." Violations of the sacred are often referred to as *defacement.*

Body

Our face is part of our body, and our body belongs to the realm of privacy. No one has the right to touch our body in any way that we deem intrusive. And no one has the right to tell us how our bodies should look. We are in the world by way of a body, and our body represents our selfhood. Our bodies are laden with psychological significance. There are two major areas where our bodily privacy is violated: physical abuse and sexual abuse.

Many people today still do not see physical punishment as evil, and it has been a common practice for most of human history. As democracy has deepened and we have come to understand that all human beings, including children, have dignity, equality, and the right to bodily privacy, we've come to see that spanking and all forms of physical abuse (chronic threats, pinching, pushing, throwing the child around) are primitive and rooted in cultural and religious patriarchy. Physical abuse is a misuse of power and a direct assault on the innate dignity of our bodily existence.

Today, more people understand the evil of sexual abuse. It is the ultimate invasion of the body. There is a growing awareness that sexual abuse is more about power than about sex, and that it is rooted in false beliefs about parental ownership of children.

Men and women also suffer from a cultural invasion of bodily privacy in the form of rigid criteria for sexual attractiveness. Thinness and large well-proportioned genitalia have become a holy obsession in our culture. Half of the clients I have counseled had concerns about the attractiveness of their body in general and the size of their penis, breasts, or buttocks in particular.

The Paradox of Women's Bodies

Women's bodies constitute one of the central paradoxes in women's lives, and language has been a part of the paradox.

On the one hand, women's sexuality has been suppressed. Women have not even been able to speak about their own bodies—their sexual parts have been unspoken and even misnamed. In the early part of this century, words for female body parts such as clitoris, vulva, or labia were not included in standard dictionaries. As Harriet Lerner has pointed out, the incomplete labeling of female genitals—especially those that might be a source of pleasure—has served to keep women's bodies a secret even from themselves.

On the other hand, women's sexuality and female bodies have been severely objectified and exploited by the public media. Women and girls are continually presented in demeaning and degrading pictures, their breasts exposed, their legs spread open, inviting sexual penetration. The unspoken message is that women's bodies are the property of men. Women have only recently begun to claim their basic privacy and ownership of their bodies.

Success/Failure

Success is something deeply private and personal. When we cling to someone else's definition of success, we set ourselves up for dark secrets. The private measure of success is finding the work that gives a particular meaning and sense of worth to our lives. It is internal, while the setup for dark secrets is external. Social and cultural beliefs about success often dictate how our reputation is measured. Making lots of money is considered a major criterion for success in our culture.

People often suffer greatly because they allow themselves to be measured by external standards of success. Self-worth and self-esteem are really private matters. True self-esteem can come only from the inside.

Tangible Possessions

Our possessions belong to the private sphere. They are extensions of ourselves. Tiny children identify with their toys and clothes and fight for them as if their identity depended on them. Clothes often give us our identity and at the same time allow us to belong to a group. Although we have the right to clothe our bodies with our own unique style of dressing, we often compromise this private right because of the dictates of cultural norms.

Each house has some of the unique marks of its possessor. We guard our property, put locks on our doors, maybe add alarm systems or burglar bars. Secrecy and concealment help us safeguard our property.

No one has a right to know how much money we make or to pry into our business. Yet culture often invades this realm. We may feel shame if we consider ourselves too poor or too rich, even if we would be satisfied if we didn't compare ourselves to others.

Intangible Possessions

Our possessions are not limited to tangible things. Some of our most cherished possessions are intangible and belong to the psychic realm.

These include our creative ideas, our personal dreams and ambitions, and our values. Sometimes we may choose to keep our feelings and opinions a secret.

Your self-value is your most personal and secret intangible possession. It is ultimately a matter that is formulated within yourself and cannot be dependent on public response. If your self-value comes only from the outside, it is no longer your self-value but someone else's evaluation of you.

A person with a poor sense of self-value will often create a false secret self to compensate. Our false selves are dark secrets we use to guard our inner sense of inadequacy. In Chapter 9 we will discuss the secrets about ourselves that we keep from others, and even the secrets we keep from ourselves.

Intimacy

The right of entry into the private sphere of another person is what Martin Buber called the I/Thou relationship—a relationship of participation, empathy, sympathy, and sharing. Only when both partners are willing to be exposed and vulnerable is mutual privacy created. If only one is exposed and vulnerable and the other is covered, then both are violated.

We need closeness with special friends to share and support our lives. Friends are those with whom we can be truly intimate. Building true friendships requires time and work. Most of us do not have time for more than a few good friends. We share things with them that we would not share with anyone else. Most of us also need one person in our lives to whom we matter and who matters to us in a most special way. This is our spouse or lover. We express our sexuality in our relationship with them.

Sexuality

From the ultraprudish and exaggerated modesty of our Victorian past, we have come full circle, reducing sexuality to sex—a matter of instincts, genitalia, and frequency. Dark sexual secrets are the most common of all secrets.

Perhaps in no other area of the private is modesty more important than in the realm of sexuality. Reducing sexuality, the personal meeting in desire and love between two human beings, to raw sex (the cold fuck), is pornographic, and pornography is sexual obscenity. Once shame as modesty, as the guardian of sexuality, is lost, then intimate genital bodily acts are severed from the social, emotional, and moral considerations that make human relations human.

Once shame as modesty is broken down, the individual is stripped of his protective covering, and the human significance of sexual behavior is emptied of its meaning and the persons involved are reduced to objects. As an object, one cannot participate in the human significance of what is taking place in the sex act, and once made into an object, one projects that objectification onto others. The sexual voyeur wants only to look and observe the other as an object. A man absorbed in masturbating with pornography is feeding his own curiosity and fascination with violence and power. The woman he observes in demeaning and shaming positions is a dehumanized object. The observer cannot sympathize with or participate in the woman's humanity. Sexuality, devoid of modesty and profaned in its need for privacy, is the basis of an enormous range of dark family secrets.

Max Scheler, the German philosopher, wrote poignantly about the function of sexual shame in the development of sexuality. He felt that sexual shame or modesty helped form sexual desire and helped to facilitate sexual expression in fulfilling human intimacy.

Without sexual shame libido would not be inhibited. Without such inhibition, we would remain at the primitive level of autoeroticism. We would mire ourselves in indulging our own feelings and cravings and be unavailable for sexual arousal by another. Shame as awe moves us to want involvement with the subject of our awe—the other person.

The blush that is present at the beginning of any new sexual relationship is also there when two people have had lots of sexual experience with each other. Without the blush, bashfulness, awe, and shyness of shame, sexuality would degenerate into repetition, method, and technique. For two people to truly participate in the fulfillment of sexuality, they must do more than place their bodies at each other's disposal. Both must be willing to be vulnerable and be open to receiving the gift of the other. Shame provides a pause and a hesitation that creates a space within which two lovers can discover each other.

Healthy shame is the conscience of erotic love. It opposes lust and impersonal sex. The loss of shame as awe and modesty sets up a variety of potential dark sexual secrets.

FAMILY PRIVACY AS HEALTHY SECRECY

What would families look like if they protected each person's natural right to privacy? They would be families that maintain healthy secrecy. (See Chart 1–2.)

CHART 1–2

HEALTHY FAMILY SECRETS

INDIVIDUAL

> Generative and adaptive secrets
> (related to the formation of individual identity)

GENERATIONAL

> Marital secrets
> Sibling secrets

PROTECTIVE

> Protective of the whole family
> Protective of each individual's dignity

PLAYFUL

> Aimed at surprising and bringing joy to other members
> Fun, pranks, surprise parties, and presents

A healthy family allows all members appropriate space and a sense of their own inviolability. Couples need privacy to continue their own process of self-formation. Their children need privacy to do the same. This unqualified privacy is a *basic human need.*

Individuality and self-separation were not goals in patriarchal/matriarchal models of family and society. People repressed feelings and banded together in protective unity. It was virtuous to give up one's own will and one's own thinking for the sake of family or group survival.

Today we prize selfhood and individuality and know they are not possible without some separation from our family systems. For separation to take place, we need unqualified privacy—a space or place in our physical, emotional, intellectual, and spiritual world that is inviolable.

Much of the classic ethical and legal thinking about privacy focused on family privacy, but not in the sense that I am using the term. "A man's home is his castle" was a principle that justified keeping the state or government out of private family matters. A spouse was protected against being forced to testify against a mate. By the same token, what went on within the walls of home was virtually unquestioned.

We are in a transition now. As democracy becomes internalized, we are experiencing more and more conflict between the inviolability of the family and the inviolability of individual family members. Battering fathers and husbands were once routinely left unprosecuted, because how wives and children were treated was considered a private affair.

Today we are vigorously challenging the belief that parents have a right to hit or disrespect their children's physical, emotional, and intellectual space, or that husbands own their wives and have rights over them. This battle is a long way from being won, and it raises many difficult social and political issues that are outside the scope of this book. For example, levels of privacy often conflict. We may have to violate family or generational privacy in order to protect the individual's personal boundaries.

Individual Secrets

A husband and wife may keep some secrets from one another. These have to do with the mysterious depth of self that marks their unique identity. The secrecy that preserves the central aspects of our individual identity is often called *generative secrecy*. It is generative because it allows us to grow and change. Generative secrecy begins with the first "no" and "I won't" of the toddler's self-separation. Without separation there can be no secrecy. We have to have a sense of self, no matter how rudimentary, in order to have our own secrets. My Boy Scout experience was an individual secret of this kind.

Character Needs a Darkroom

Children have a special need for concealment. They have an innate sense of limits stemming from their natural shame, but they must build and develop strong boundaries. Parents must do two things to help them build their boundaries. First they must model good boundaries themselves and secondly they must enforce firm but just limits so that their children can internalize them. Children imitate their parents by role-playing. They adapt and learn by imitative practice. And like players rehearsing for a play, they don't want to be seen until they are well rehearsed. They need protected space to play-act their life rehearsals.

Photographers must go into their darkrooms to develop their film. The child's need for inviolable privacy is like the photographer's darkroom. Josef Karsh once said, "Character, like a photograph, develops in the dark."

Generational Secrets

It is best to keep the generational lines in a family intact: families need a generation gap. It is appropriate for there to be a sibling coalition and a parental coalition. The kids have secrets that are part of a normal testing of their own limits and part of developing their own unique sense of selfhood. A first love relationship and a first romantic kiss are not things children normally want to share with their parents. Often sexual behaviors will aim at imitating grown-ups and are best shared with a child's own peer group. Sibling coalitions are most common between same-sex siblings, but it's not uncommon for brothers and sisters of nearly the same age to have shared secrets. When these generational relationship lines are crossed, secrets can become toxic and dysfunctional.

Dad's trouble at the office and his difficulty with authority figures are best kept between Mom and Dad. Mom's troubles with Dad should not be shared with the children, unless they are directly affecting their lives and they know about them.

If Mom goes on a spending spree and charges a wardrobe of new clothes and then hides them in the children's room and makes them swear never to tell their father, she is setting up a dangerous cross-generational alliance with them.

When parents cross generational lines, children are caught in a terrible loyalty bind and have their privacy violated. The same thing happens when a parent requests a sibling to spy on their brother or sister and then report back to the parent. Secret alliances or coalitions are generally symptoms of severe family dysfunction.

Marital Secrets

When Mom and Dad are working on maintaining good boundaries and show respect for each other, along with humility and modesty, the environment is ripe for the children's natural shame to be transformed into modesty, healthy secrecy, and good boundaries. Because Mom and Dad have space for themselves in their lives and in their marriage, they allow the children to have space.

Parents should make it clear through their speech and behavior that their marriage is their primary relationship. No one should be more special to Mom than Dad and vice versa. If a child becomes more important to one parent than his or her spouse, an unholy alliance is set up, and the lines of privacy are severely disrupted. Mom and Dad need the space to have their own special "pillow talk" and rituals of love and intimacy.

Mom and Dad should reserve the right to withhold certain family lore and items of value until it is appropriate to share these with their children. Mom and Dad should also reserve the right to keep certain facts about themselves and their relationship private. Mom and Dad have responsibilities as parents. Their job is to provide rules, discipline, moral modeling, and money, and these matters are age-appropriately private. In many cases they should not be open to discussion with the children.

Sibling Secrets

In healthy families siblings, especially those close in age, have special loyalty bonds and special secrets. This is healthy, and unless a child's secret endangers his safety, health, or psychological well-being, it is important that the child be given his space. Finding a suicide note in a diary, and finding drugs and drug paraphernalia in your brother's or sister's possession, are examples of secrets that need to be confronted.

In general children's privacy needs to be protected in an age-appropriate manner. It is not appropriate to allow a three-year-old to lock the bathroom door.

I use age seven as the transition age for a child's right to personal privacy. Seven is the age that marks a child's ability to think in a consistently logical manner. At this age children should be allowed to lock the door to their bedroom and bathroom, choose their own clothes, and have their own money and possessions. This right presupposes that the child is not mentally or emotionally disturbed and is developing more or less normally. Parents need to have good reasons for intruding in any of the private areas we have been talking about in their child's or adolescent's life. Parents also need to protect younger children from the intrusions and violations of their older brothers or sisters.

Sometimes poverty or economic barriers prohibit a family from having the physical space their members need in order to have adequate privacy. In such situations efforts should be made to safeguard those areas of privacy that are available.

Protective Secrets

All families need boundaries of protection to guard their unique family style and protect themselves from outside intruders.

In a community or society where privacy was loved, respected, and understood as a basic need, the whole family's privacy would be naturally honored. Instead, many families feel under siege.

Just as we hide our valuables in secret places in the house so that snoopers and burglars can't find them, so ethnicity, religious belief, economic conditions, sexual preference, and lifestyle may be facts that must be kept secret.

Sometimes this is literally a matter of life and death, as for Jews during the Nazi era. Sometimes the secret protects us from humiliation and exposure. My friend David lied about his family's Jewish background to the kids in his predominantly Christian neighborhood. Nan lied about her family's wealth. She wore drab and well-worn clothes to school to avoid being teased by the poorer children.

Gay and lesbian families often stay in hiding. Remember that it sometimes takes great courage to stay in hiding, just as it may take great courage to come out of hiding.

Playful Secrets

The last kind of healthy family secret is the kind we keep for pure fun.

There is a great excitement and secrecy in most families around celebrations involving giving and receiving gifts, like birthdays and religious holidays. Remember how you asked for—or it was hinted you might get—a certain present for Christmas? The excitement built as Christmas drew near. You may remember searching the house from attic to basement looking for hidden presents. You may also remember how exhilarating it was to buy a family member a present that you thought was going to surprise them. Best of all, you may have memories of waking up on Christmas morning to find a present that was a total surprise, something you never dreamt you could get.

Memories like these—and other private family rituals—nurture the sense of identity and belonging in each member of the family.

Families need privacy in order to prosper. Privacy creates natural realms of secrecy, and natural secrecy creates the silence that is worth its weight in gold.

In the next chapter I will look at a whole range of dark secrets, especially various forms of dark secrecy that result when the realms of natural privacy in a family are not honored and protected.

CHAPTER 2

WHEN SECRETS ARE DARK

As children my brother and I were asked to keep a secret and the secret we were asked to keep was that it was not a happy house.

ROBERT BLY

"Why did you marry him?" . . . The question had taken her by surprise and I . . . had asked one of those forbidden questions, one with daunting implications, whose mystery predated our own birth.

PAT CONROY, *The Prince of Tides*

Jane Fonda has publicly confessed that she was bulimic for a number of years. Bulimia is an eating disorder characterized by secret rituals of binge eating and purging by vomiting. The bulimic consciously engages in this behavior in order to maintain a body weight that is dictated by certain cultural norms of thinness. Jane has stated that the onset of her problem coincided with her accidental discovery that her mother, Frances, had committed suicide. Jane had not known this, because her father, Henry, had kept it a secret. When Frances killed herself during a stay in a mental hospital, Henry told Jane and her brother, Peter, who were thirteen and ten at the time, that their mother had died of a heart attack. Henry and his mother-in-law held a private funeral for Frances, to which no one else came. He went onstage the same night.

Frances Fonda was Henry's second wife. He had separated from her two months before she killed herself and had already started an affair with Susan Blanchard, whom he married eight months later. Strangely enough, Henry's first wife, Margaret Sullavan, after divorcing Henry and marrying his agent Leland Hayward, also committed suicide, as did two of Henry's close friends.

During Henry's honeymoon with Susan Blanchard, Peter shot himself in the stomach and nearly died. (Reportedly, Henry did not ask Peter whether this had anything to do with his mother's death.) Ten years later, Peter fell in love with Bridget Hayward, the daughter of Leland Hayward and Margaret Sullavan. During the year of their relationship, she killed herself. Peter also had a friend who committed suicide.

This startling pattern of suicide, attempted suicide, and friendships with people who committed suicide is reported by Monica McGoldrick and Randy Gerson in *Genograms in Family Assessment,* an important source that I will return to several times in this book. It is a dramatic example of the incredible power of dark secrets to impact a family's life.

Why did Henry Fonda keep his wife's suicide a secret? Why did he refuse to talk about it to his children? We can only speculate about his motives, and about the toxic mix of grief, guilt, and avoidance he may have felt. I do know that suicide falls into the category of human experience that is extraordinarily perplexing and shocking. Suicide has a long cultural history of toxic shame and silence. In the past Jews who committed suicide were buried outside the walls of the cemetery. Until recently, the Catholic Church refused burial services to members who committed suicide. Suicide was considered by many religions the unpardonable sin and those doing it were considered unforgivable. A suicide brought great moral shame and humiliation to the suicide's family. Perhaps this collective tradition was the background for Henry Fonda's decision.

Few people today believe that suicide should be looked at moralistically. It is related more to deep depression (often chemical) and to a sense of shame and loss of meaning. Yet suicide itself involves a dark secret. Suicide is a death shrouded in mystery.

Henry Fonda may have believed that he needed to protect his children from the truth of their mother's suicide. Protection is a common motivation for secret-keeping. Yet there is no real protection to be had from the profound impact of a mother's suicide. And, however painful it might be, the children had a right to know the truth about their mother's death. Precisely because suicide itself involves some dark secret that eludes and cuts off the other family members, it needs to be *talked* about by the survivors. Not talking about it constitutes another dark secret. In the aftermath of suicide, much needs to be expressed and grieved, and each person has their own unique feelings in relation to it. When a father or mother refuses to express their own feelings of guilt over a family member's suicide, they set the children up in a bond of loyalty to preserve the secret itself. This is also true of other types of shameful deaths that are not talked about, such as murder and mutilation, or death by torture, or the humiliating deaths that Jews suffered in the Nazi concentration camps.

When such traumatic events are denied and made into dark secrets, a family's loyalty to the secret may appear in subsequent generations as reclusiveness, morbid fear, obsession with death, bizarre and unexplainable death-defying crazy behavior, and suicide attempts on an anniversary or at the same age as the first death.

Suicide and bulimia touch upon death and eating, two of the areas of natural concealment that I have described as belonging to the realm of the private. It is my contention that when the inner sanctum of modesty is perverted or violated, toxic shame takes its place, and toxic shame is a major source of dark secrecy.

TOXIC SHAME

Our innate healthy shame or modesty, nurtured by privacy, is the foundation upon which we develop good flexible boundaries. Without boundaries, we have no limits.

When our natural shame, which guards our privacy and the unique dignity of our self, is violated, we take on a false, pretend self that is shameless. Shamelessness takes two forms: We act shameless by attempting to transcend our limits as human beings; we try to be *more than human*—we act perfect (we never make mistakes), we act needless (we need no help from anyone), we act righteous (we are saved and others are not), we act authoritarian (we have the right to violate others' space), we act patronizing (we know it all).

At the other extreme we can act shameless by acting *less than human*. We let others violate us or we violate ourselves. We become shameful failures, victims, addicts—the dregs of society. We are so hopeless, we lose all sense of limits. We believe that everything about us is flawed and defective.

Because the English language has only one word for shame, I called both of these forms of shamelessness *toxic shame* in my book *Healing the Shame That Binds You.* Whether it is righteous or depraved, shamelessness is toxic. Toxic shame does not protect our wholeness and selfhood—it tears them down.

Once we've become shame-based, we believe that we are a mistake. We feel that our very *being* is flawed and defective and that we must be secretive about everything in our lives that is authentic.

Toxic Shame and Dark Secrets

Toxic shame, whether righteous or depraved, is at the root of many dark secrets. Toxic shame forces us to literally lose face and then to try and save face. In order to save face, we go into hiding and isolation. We seek ways to always be in control. We guard lest we ever be caught off guard. We live covering up our pain. This requires an arsenal of secrets. We have secrets to cover secrets, lies to cover other lies.

Toxic shame affects not just our *doing* but our very *being.* Deep down we feel like something is very wrong with us. Toxic shame demands that I wear a mask, put on a disguise, develop a false self. If I were to let you see me as I really am, you would see that I am flawed and defective and reject me. I must therefore remain silent.

Once we put on the mask of hiding, it becomes second nature and unconscious. The person wearing the mask doesn't know that it is a mask. This delusional state of total secrecy I call the state of *mystification.*

Toxic shame secrets tend to cluster around the violations of those areas of privacy that we looked at in Chapter 1. Chart 2–1, while not intended to be exhaustive, gives you an extensive look at the many species of dark secrets. Since they are grouped according to their content, you will note that the general categories (birth-related, death-related, and so on) follow the outline in Chart 1–1, which contains the natural behaviors of privacy.

With that in mind, it is well to be as clear as possible about the scope of destructive secrets and how they cause family dysfunction, diminish awareness, impede our freedom, and block the full actualization of our individuality.

It would take too much space to give an example of *every* category on our list of dark secrets on Chart 2–1. I have chosen certain examples from my own twenty-five-year counseling files and from my research for this book.

CHART 2-1

DARK SECRETS, GROUPED BY CONTENT

RELATED TO THE SACRED

Whatever is judged to be sinful
Whatever profanes or defaces the holy
Phariseeism
Hypocrisy
Using a religious facade for sex, money, or
power
Religious addiction
Cults (secret rites), Ku Klux Klan
Being the "wrong" religion
Satanic cults
Spiritual abuse

BIRTH-RELATED

Pregnant when married
Adoption
Deceitful parentage
Foster care
Orphanhood
Illegitimacy
Unknown siblings
Infertility
Test-tube baby
Ethnic shame
Racial shame

DEATH-RELATED

Suicide
Violent death
Murder
Mutilation
Missing (disappeared)
Concentration camp
Ethnic cleansing
Tortured to death
Depersonalized hospital death
Process of dying
Terminal illness

SUFFERING-RELATED

Mental illness
Emotional illness
Disabled, chronic pain
Institutionalized for mental illness

Retardation
Going to psychiatrist
Genetic illness
Alcoholism, drug abuse
Substance abuse (any)
Venereal disease
All forms of abuse
Cutting (self-mutilation)
Münchausen by proxy syndrome

BODY-RELATED

Eating

Anorexia
Bulimia
Binge eating
Obesity
Thin/fat obsession

Elimination

Shame concerning elimination
Sexual perversion with elimination

SELF-RELATED

Good name

False self
Self-esteem issues
Perfectionism
Criticalness
Judgmentalness
Righteousness
Racial supremacy
Self-punishment
Self-contempt
Self-blame
Masochism

Face

Freckles, birthmarks
Beauty/ugliness
Slapping the face

Body

Physical defects
Deformities
Genital measurements
Awkwardness, gangliness
Too fat, too skinny
Exercise addiction
Physical abuse
Battering

RELATED TO SUCCESS/ FAILURE	Money addiction Work addiction Poverty Joblessness Firing, demotion Unwillingness to work Living off parents Living off wife Loss of family/spouse's money "Wrong" class Immigrant shame Loss of good name
RELATED TO POSSESSIONS Tangible	Cheating Shoplifting Embezzlement Stealing business secrets Scam, con artist Theft Burglary Murder Hit man Drug dealer Imprisonment Mafia/crime ring membership White-collar crime Tax evasion
Intangible	Repression of emotions Ego defenses—automatic and unconscious Secret negative thoughts and resentments Stealing ideas, intellectual property, plagiarism Shame over failure to achieve one's dreams or to live up to one's ideals Violations of one's own moral values
INTIMACY-RELATED	Marital discord (chronic fighting) Multiple marriages Bigamy Betrayal (affairs) Gay or lesbian married to heterosexual Betrayal of friends Cross-generational bonding with children

Abandonment fears
Engulfment fears
Commitment phobia
Spousal abuse
Battering
Stalking
Spousal murder

SEX-RELATED
Sexual preference
Cross-dressing
Transvestism
Sex-role secrets
  Women (anger)
  Men (fear)
Sex addiction
  Sexual anorexia/nonintegrated celibacy
  Multiple affairs
  Chronic masturbation
  Chronic masturbation with pornography
  Sex with animal
  Fetish
  Voyeurism, exhibitionism
  Indecent liberties
  Phone sex
  Massage parlor sex
  Prostitution
  Sex cults
  Wife-swapping group
  Sadomasochistic sex
  Autoerotic strangulation
  Child pornography
  Child prostitution ring
Sexual harassment
Satanic cult with sexual perversion
Incest
Molestation
Rape
Date/marital rape
Sexual dysfunction
Disorder of desire

SEXUAL SECRETS

Germaine speaks in anxious tones as she begins her first session of counseling. She tells of the dark secret in her marriage. Her husband has had numerous affairs, the most recent with her best friend at work. She feels ashamed of herself for tolerating his behavior. She says she vowed she would never tolerate even *one* affair—and yet this was her husband's fifth affair in three years of marriage.

After several fact-finding sessions, the counselor asks Germaine if her father ever had an affair. "Oh, gosh no. He's a wonderful man," she instantly replies. "He's an elder at our church and rigid in his beliefs about sexual fidelity. He made a lot of money and retired early. He has a soft spot in his heart for women who are in trouble. He financed a halfway house to help troubled women. He was interested in helping prostitutes. He would visit them and even bring them presents."

The counselor asks if Germaine can get her mother and father to come to the next therapy session. "What on earth for?" she asks. "Trust me, it will help you," the counselor replies.

The parents come willingly, saying they would do anything to help their daughter's marriage. Germaine's father is very handsome and charismatic, while her mother is overweight and obeisant and defers all questions to her husband. But when the counselor asks her husband if he has ever had an affair, she painfully answers yes for him. "It's time we got this out in the open," she says. Germaine almost falls off her chair. Her father begins to weep.

It turns out that Germaine's father has had numerous affairs. Germaine's mother simply suffered in silence. Again and again the father has vowed repentance, only to fall again. His wife has endured all of this for the sake of her daughter and to keep the family image intact.

Germaine's family is entangled in a sexual secret. The father is sexually compulsive and addicted to sexual affairs. His wife is his enabler. She fosters his addiction by covering up for him and by not insisting that he get some kind of treatment for his problem. She is addicted to her husband's sexual addiction, and she is the collusive partner in this dysfunctional marriage.

Acting Out

Germaine has not been consciously aware of what's been going on. However, she actually does know about the secret—at an unconscious level. And at an unconscious level, she is motivated to make what is covert overt. She makes the dark family secret overt by finding and marrying Jim, who is even more blatantly addicted than her father. In a very short time, he has an affair. Amid pain and sorrow he vows never to do it again. Within three months he has another affair, and then another, and another. There is nothing covert about Jim's problem. He is out of control in a big way.

Jim has his own history. His father was also sexually compulsive, and he saw his father run around on his mother. Not only did his father violate Jim by his bad example, but he also bonded with him in a conspiracy to keep the secret from his mother. This unholy alliance forced his son to break the lines of privacy between generations, and it put him in a double bind: In order not to betray his father, Jim had to betray his mother. The father abused him by *using* him to hide his own shameful behavior. And as James Baldwin has said, "Children have never been very good at listening to their elders, but they never fail to imitate them." Jim, much to his own chagrin, imitates his father's behavior.

Jim and Germaine thus serve as a metaphor of the dysfunctional marriage relationship that both of them grew up in. Germaine and Jim have both made overt the covert secrets of their families of origin. They are saying to all the world, "Look—here is the dark secret we both grew up with."

Counseling for the whole family brings the covert dark secret into the open and allows the family trance to be broken. Germaine and Jim *no longer have to act out their parents' dark secrets.* Breaking the trance gives them the opportunity to own their own lives, eliminating the dark secret that has literally ensconced their freedom.

There is also a price that the secret-keeper must pay: Germaine's father lived a life of hypocrisy. He maintained his dark secret of sexual addiction by means of his own deep denial. As the problems caused by his affairs intensified, so too did his mental obsession intensify. He thought about sex all the time. Sometimes he thought about it by fighting the urge to flirt and be seductive. Sometimes he thought about it by obsessing on an individual woman. And sometimes he compulsively thought about what he had done in the past or was doing now. Such obsessional thinking causes a kind of narrow-mindedness or cognitive closure.

While he was having an affair, he would expend an enormous amount of mental and physical energy planning his rendezvous, covering his tracks, and guarding his every word, lest he accidentally let slip some piece of information that would make his wife and daughter suspicious.

Like all addicts, Germaine's father felt more and more isolated, alone, ashamed, and hopeless as his addiction progressed. Even though he tried to maintain the image of a model family, he had no real intimacy in his life. Germaine's father was living a lie. He pretended to be loving and honest to the world, while he practiced unloving and dishonest behavior toward his family. As he lost more and more of his self-respect, he tried to enhance his phony false self with his charitable grandiosity.

Acting In

Germaine and Jim "acted out" their family secret for all to see. My client Sereva responded in a different way—by "acting in."

Sereva's father was an alcoholic and a womanizer. Her mother was a devout Catholic and believed that a good and holy wife should suffer her husband's abuse in silence. The husband's affairs were never talked about. On one occasion Sereva went with her mother to pick her father up at another woman's apartment. He came out with lipstick all over his shirt. Riding in the car, her mother and father talked about the weather. Later, when Sereva asked her mother about the incident, she refused to talk about it. Sereva developed a deep disgust for her father, which extended to all men and to anything having to do with sexuality.

During her senior year of high school, Sereva decided she had a "vocation" and entered a Catholic convent to become a nun. By going to the convent, she was "acting in" her disdain for sexuality. As she entered into the disciplines of celibacy and asceticism, she was attracted to a form of self-flagellation that she read about in a book about the life of a female saint. Fasting and beating herself with a leather whip gave her a certain sensation of warmth and pleasure.

I counseled her some years later. She had left the convent but was still using the leather whip. In counseling she came to see that she had internalized her mother's behavior. Her mother modeled the belief that women are inferior to men and that a good woman's lot is to suffer. Punishing herself with flagellation was Sereva's way to feel good about herself as a woman.

In Sereva's family everyone knew what was going on, but out of loyalty to the devout Catholic family image, no one spoke about the secret. This misguided loyalty cut Sereva off from any healthy information about love, marriage, intimacy, and sex. The secret kept her enmeshed in her dysfunctional family. Like her mother, she became a co-addict, obsessing on her father's drinking and womanizing. And like her mother she also became severely codependent. *Codependency* is a disease of the developing self, whereby a person loses contact with their own internal experience. Because a codependent person does not know what they feel, need, or want, they do not know who they are. Their developing sense of self is frozen, and a false self must be chosen. The false self is constituted by those behaviors, feelings, needs, and wants that the family authorizes as lovable. Sereva's model was her mother. She learned that the way to be lovable was to be *needless* and *wantless* and to suffer in silence. The cost to Sereva because of her family's dark secret was psychological death. What she learned was that her authentic self must die in order for her to be loved and valued.

SEXUAL ABUSE AND SILENCE

In our sexist patriarchal society, sexual harassment and the sexual abuse of women and children (including a large percentage of boy children) has been and is still a dark secret. It has existed in every social institution, including religion and government. Both the offenders and victims have kept their dark secrets. The offenders' reasons for doing so are obvious. But except for the obvious reason that most often no one would listen to them, the victims' silence has been perplexing and mysterious.

Victims of sexual abuse often believe that they are responsible for what happened to them. Older children often believe that somehow they "came on" to their offender. They feel confusion and responsibility if the act was pleasurable in any way to them. In the past no one understood that victims of severe abuse become identified with their offenders, that they either dissociate from their own *selves* or repress the memory in order to defend against the pain they experienced. Because the victim so often identifies with their offender, and because the offender is shameless and devoid of guilt at the moment of the violation, the victim feels and carries the offender's shame and guilt. The victim feels soiled and dirty and believes that they are unclean. This feeling is intensified if the offender is the victim's parent or caretaker. When it is the very one who is their model and protector who is violating them, the child believes it must be their fault.

In families where incest is happening, the violated child often will not risk telling the nonviolating parent, for fear of breaking up the family. If the child does tell, often the nonviolating parent does not believe the child, sometimes because of their own denial, sometimes because of ignorance, sometimes because they are being victimized themselves. Incest is far more widespread than anyone had ever guessed. As our knowledge about incest changes, many survivors of sexual abuse are coming forth and telling their secrets.

Rape, molestation, sexual liberties, and sexual harassment have also been repressed and hushed up for generations. Women have been routinely violated sexually for generations.

Our male-dominated society protects the patriarchal definitions of male/female relationships and the inequality of the male power structure. Victims, most often women and children, have been battered sexually, physically, and emotionally into self-desecration.

Victims have maintained the silence in other ways besides simply not telling. Physical pain, torture, and severe emotional abuse not only resist being expressed in language but actually destroy language, causing the victim to regress to a state sometimes referred to as *preverbal powerlessness*. A victim of torturous sexual abuse and physical violence resorts to sounds and cries that one uses before language is learned. The violence becomes truly *unspeakable*.

Battered wives and children help maintain the silence out of fear, shame, and learned helplessness. When people are chronically abused and powerless, they learn how to be abused. In the face of abuse they feel helpless. Abuse feels normal. Abused women are often afraid their families will deteriorate because they have been taught to be reliant on men. Many are already poor and are burdened with children for whom they will be responsible. So these victims learn to deny their own experiences. With extreme wife-battering and early and prolonged child sexual abuse, the pain a woman feels may be so unspeakable that it can be expressed only through extreme dissociation, amnesia, or self-effacement.

In the past our culture supported this silence. The battering of women was commonplace and acceptable. The phrase a "rule of thumb" originally referred to the width of the rod a man could legally use to beat his wife. There was not even a word like *battering* in the language. For the victim, "the lack of language becomes a lack of consciousness," as social worker Joan Laird puts it. Once the physical abuse of women was named *battering,* a new awareness was created. This new awareness led to the formation of crisis hotlines and women's shelters, and the wall of silence surrounding generations of abuse finally cracked.

BIRTH SECRETS

Mary Sue had been going steady with Joe since their freshman year of college. Joe wanted to get married, but Mary Sue had concerns over their sex life and Joe's financial situation. Mary Sue liked sex and had experienced a torrid sex life with her high school sweetheart until they broke up. She loved Joe, but she missed the sex life she had known before. One day, out of the blue, the high school boyfriend appeared on campus. What started out as a chat about old times ended up as two hours of sex at a nearby motel.

Mary Sue felt terrible and vowed never to tell Joe. Within a few weeks she discovered she was pregnant. She decided to urge Joe to get married immediately without telling him about her condition. Later, when a boy was born, Joe thought the child was his son.

Mary Sue and Joe had two more children, both girls. The son was very different in temperament from his half-sisters. He was boisterous and energetic, while they were both quiet and shy. Mary Sue overprotected her son, a telling consequence of her dark secret. She refused to see how physically abusive he was with both of his sisters. When the girls tried to enlist their father's protection and help, he believed Mary Sue's claim that "the girls were making it up to win his favor." As the years went on, the boy out and out tortured and tormented his sisters.

Mary Sue's overprotection began to cause serious arguments between her and Joe. Joe had secretly felt that it was strange that his son did not resemble him physically, but he never voiced his feelings on the matter. Mary Sue had been constantly on guard lest she say something spontaneously that would let the secret out. This anxiety caused her to distance herself from Joe, creating a wedge that blocked any real intimacy between them.

By keeping her dark secret, Mary Sue seriously damaged her family's ability to function properly. Her dark secret created a toxic cross-generational alliance between mother and son, as well as emotional cut-offs between the son and his father and sisters. As a result, the son never felt close to his father or sisters, but instead felt isolated and had an unexplainable sense of shame. He repeated his mother's secret by having an affair with a married woman and getting her pregnant. She stayed with her husband and had his child, which he grieved about for years.

Mary Sue revealed the secret to her son after Joe died. Her son was furious at her and cut her off emotionally, refusing to speak to her. He ended his life two years later in a drunk-driving car accident, without ever reconciling with his mother or sisters.

Mary Sue's shame thus engendered more shame and isolation. By keeping her dark secret, she could never *heal* her own guilt over her dishonesty or repair the damaged loyalty between herself, her husband, and her children. The secret prevented her from the possibility of ever receiving forgiveness and reconciliation with her family.

Adoption and Other Birth Issues

Adoption has long been a huge area of secrecy around birth. Many families are still grappling with the legacy of adoption secrets. Others are confronting the new dilemmas resulting from the recent movement toward open adoption and unsealed records.

The central premise upon which traditional adoption rested was that the adopting parents and the adoptee should resemble a biological family. In order to support this view, the system tried to deny anything that made adoption different from biological parenting. And since the child's biological parents were the greatest threat to this denial of difference, the connection with the biological parents was totally broken.

Once the biological mother gave her child up for adoption, she ceased to exist. As Ann Hartman, of the Smith College School for Social Work, puts it, "She not only carried a secret, but she *was* a secret." Until relatively recently, birth fathers had no rights at all in determining their child's future. Like the birth mothers, they were supposed to disappear, carrying with them their unresolved pain and loss. And adoption records were sealed so that adopted children could not trace their parentage.

Those who defend secrecy and closed records do so on the grounds that they protect the child from the stigma of illegitimacy, protect the adoptive parents from intrusion by the birth parent, and protect the birth parents from further intrusion by the adopted child.

Those who argue for opening the records do so on the grounds that every human being has the right to know his or her biological relatives.

Adoptive parents seem to be mixed in their opinions on opening the records. Some are fearful that the biological family will disrupt the security of their family. Others have found that sharing in their adopted children's search has brought them closer together.

In my counseling experience, the most important factor is the pain adoptees feel about their situation. They seem to have an innate need to know their biological parents, and no matter why their parents gave them up, they feel a deep sense of rejection.

Children are egocentric in their mode of knowing. That means that they personalize things. Children believe that if they're not allowed to know something about themselves and their past, then it must be bad. This is a powerful argument against preserving adoption secrets— even when the truth to be uncovered is distressing or disruptive.

A still uncharted area of secrecy has developed around infertility and the new reproductive technologies that are being used to treat it.

Underlying this whole advancing field is the question of genetic lineage, which seems to be a major issue for our society, especially for men. Infertility itself is often kept secret. It is clear that many men and women feel grief, shame, and social stigma over being unable to achieve pregnancy.

Given surrogacy, artificial insemination, and in vitro fertilization, it is now technically possible for a child to have a total of five "parents": three types of mothers (genetic, gestational, and rearing) and two types of fathers (genetic and rearing). This possibility raises huge moral, ethical, and psychological issues. Only after the child is born are its full implications and its impact on the child's self-concept and identity formation seen.

Most of the major religions strongly oppose noncoital methods of reproduction, and surrogacy and sperm donation are still widely subject to legal and moral challenges. This stigma has led to massive secrecy among couples who have used these fertility technologies to have babies.

As with all secrets, we have to question the impact of the secret on the one from whom it is withheld, namely the child. The religious and moral condemnation, along with the couple's own sense of shame over not being able to reproduce like everyone else, means that the child will probably carry a heavy burden of dark secrecy. In the case of surrogacy or donor conception, there is a third "parent" whose absence represents some vital loss to each member of the family.

DEATH IS THE MOST COMMON DARK SECRET

Freud believed that psychologically we *must* deny the reality of death, that no one can really grasp their own death. Most of us live as if death were not a part of living. But keeping death a secret keeps the fear of death active, even if guarded and unconscious.

The secret of death is the controlling factor in a family's ability to face up to the threatened loss of a family member. Once the family can stand up to the secret of death, they can deal with the loss and grieve it. Each person's anticipation of loss will be unique, and each person's grieving will be unique.

Parents often keep secrets about terminal illness from their children because they think children cannot handle death and dying. Keeping these secrets, however, can have dire consequences.

Jamie's father had terminal cancer when he was eight years old. No one told him that his father's illness was serious and that he would probably die within six months. His mother, older brother, and older sister believed he was too young to know and kept him ignorant to protect him. This is a good example of a dark secret of ignorance.

When his father died, Jamie was totally unprepared. He told me in a counseling session thirty years later that he had never fully gotten over being left out of his father's terminal illness. "I always knew something was going on," he told me, "but I always felt there was something wrong with me. I was too unimportant and too insignificant to be a part of what was going on. I hated them for leaving me out. I never really got to say good-bye to my dad."

I had another client who was kept away from his mother's funeral. He had never really grieved his mother's death, and as the years went by, he felt a sense of outrage. A person's mother's death is one of life's most sacred moments. To be deprived of participating in it is a loss that can never be overcome.

The Brontës

In *Genograms in Family Assessment,* McGoldrick and Gerson present another incredible example of the impact of a dark secret related to an ungrieved death: the family of Charlotte and Emily Brontë, the sisters who wrote respectively the novels *Jane Eyre* and *Wuthering Heights.* There were six Brontë children, all born in a seven-year period. The mother died shortly after the birth of the youngest.

After the mother died, the house was frozen for the next thirty years—nothing was changed or painted. The children were raised in almost total isolation, not being allowed to socialize or play with other children. Whenever any of the Brontë children tried to leave home, they suffered a variety of symptoms and returned before long. All died before the age of forty. The two youngest daughters developed fatal illnesses the first time they left home and died within a short time of each other. Branwell, Emily, and Anne died within nine months of each other, suggesting that they were so fused that it was impossible for them to live without each other. Only Charlotte was able to leave home for brief periods of time. She married at age thirty-eight but died nine months later—just after her childhood nurse died. She was the same age her mother was when she died. The strange secret in this family seems to have been the father's refusal to accept his wife's death. The children were never allowed to develop enough of a sense of separate selfhood to go out on their own.

SECRET SUFFERING

By far the most startling and frightening examples of "acting in" that I have encountered are the people known as *cutters.* My first experience with a case of this kind was in the late 1970s. A fine intelligent young woman came to see me for counseling. I'll call her Lorna. She came from a wealthy family and had been given every advantage. She dressed very modestly and always wore long-sleeved blouses. One day when she reached up to catch a comb that was falling out of her hair, the sleeve on her right arm pulled back and I saw several scars on her wrist. They were cut in three rows of X's. I asked her about them, and she started to weep as she answered. She mumbled, "I cut myself in order to hurt so that I can feel better." I looked at her blankly, not knowing how to respond. She broke eye contact and looked down. "When I say those words aloud, I know it sounds really crazy. But it feels like a normal way to deal with pain to me."

Lorna had been incested for over a year by her grandfather. Her family was very proper and image-conscious and shut down emotionally. She had "tried" to tell her father, but he had refused to talk about it because of the shame it would bring to the family. He forbade her to bring it up again. She had dissociated from the pain and was almost completely numbed out emotionally. Inflicting pain through self-mutilation allowed her to *actually feel*. In fact, it was the way she felt sane. When she looked at the scars, they were verification and validation that she was not crazy. The scars were the visible proof of the inner scar she carried in silence. Her grandfather had died suddenly of a heart attack about a year after the incest began. She was totally confused about his death. She felt dirty and ashamed and thought that her disgust for her grandfather might have contributed to his death.

Self-mutilation is a dark secret in our society, but some clinicians estimate that there are nearly two million people in the United States alone who repeatedly bite, scratch, cut, burn, and brand their skin, bang their heads and body parts against walls, pull their hair out, and break their own bones. Some victims swallow sharp objects, such as nails, or beat themselves with hammers. In the most psychotic cases the self-mutilation can be as extreme as gouging out eyes or amputating genitalia.

One of the most famous self-mutilators was Charles Manson. He is covered with scars on his arms, neck, and wrist. Manson, repeatedly beaten and sexually abused as a child, is reported to have set himself on fire at age five and choked himself until his windpipe collapsed at age eight.

Cutting, bleeding, and scarification recall primitive Stone Age initiation rites. The ritual intent of such rites was to let evil spirits and poisons out of the body. My client Lorna was quite literally trying to let her demon dark secret out. The X's reassured her momentarily that it was gone. They also symbolized a cry for help.

SECRETS ABOUT EATING

When a person is hurt and angry or when their modesty has been violated, they may ritualize a behavior that is inherently private as a way of expressing what they are afraid to speak about. One of the most common symptoms of dark secrets is an eating disorder.

Jane Fonda's eating disorder, bulimia, seems to be a modern cultural phenomenon. Although there are records of it dating from the 1600s, there is no information suggesting that bulimia was a common disorder in the past. It is predominantly found today in young upper-middle-class females. Women feel immense pressure from our culture to measure up to certain norms of thinness and beauty. Image-conscious young upper-middle-class girls gain social status by living up to this ideal.

This striving alone would not explain the secret rituals of bingeing and vomiting, however. There must also be emotional pain for bulimia to become an addictive activity. We don't have to guess what was eating away at Jane Fonda. The loss of her mother, with the accompanying unresolved grief and anger over her father's betrayal, set her up for some kind of addictive acting out. Jane's beauty and her life as a glamorous actress made bulimia an easy choice.

Women's Dark Cultural Secret

Bulimia is only one eating disorder common to women. Women are more burdened than men by obesity, anorexia, and the mood-altering obsession with food and diet called the *fat/thin disorder*.

Although men also have these eating disorders, women seem to struggle with eating far more than men. Some people have argued convincingly that this difference is due to cultural sex role expectations for women, not only regarding thinness but regarding the unrealistic expectations that women must act as the primary family mediators and nurturers.

Laura Gait Robert, a psychologist at Eastern Virginia Medical School, believes that eating disorders are the mood-altering mechanisms of choice that women use most often to distract themselves from their dislike of the roles they have inherited from our culture. Women use overeating and its related disorders as a way to avoid the anxiety and anger they feel over this fact.

All eating disorders are forms of addiction. They are all pathological relationships with a mood-altering substance or activity that has life-damaging consequences. All are secretive. All hide feelings. Binge eaters who eat themselves into a stupor can temporarily shut out their sadness and deep sense of emptiness. Anorexics use starvation to bring on mood-alteration and body numbing. In my limited work with anorexics, the hidden feeling I found most often was anger. Starvation also retards sexual development, so that young anorexics often do not reach menarche. This suggests a revolt against becoming a woman. Consider the case of Juliette's daughter.

Juliette's Daughter

When Juliette first came to see me, she was fifty pounds overweight. She was married to a wealthy man, but she spoke of her disdain for his tyrannical ways and her disgust at having to have sex with him. She was polite and people-pleasing to a fault, and she spoke in a Pollyanna good-girl manner. Juliette claimed she was afraid to express her discomfort because her husband was irrational and verbally rageful. I worked with her for a few months, supporting her need to have more power in her life, but I felt we made little progress.

Five years later Juliette returned to tell me that her husband had caught her in an affair and that her oldest daughter was getting thinner by the day. Her middle child, a boy, was excelling in school but failing as an athlete, and her youngest was quite depressed. This time I saw the whole family in therapy. The oldest daughter, a fourteen-year-old girl, weighed seventy-eight pounds. The father, alarmed, had been weighing the daughter and coercing her to eat, offering her money and other bribes. After getting the anorectic daughter to a doctor, I worked mostly with Juliette and her husband.

Juliette remained overtly polite and obeisant to her husband, but it was clear that she was furious at him. He was rigidly controlling and demanded that everyone conform to the game of happy family. The secrets in this family were threefold: the father's almost paranoid fear of everything and everyone (the reason for his rigid control); Juliette's rage at her own mother and at her husband and at the rigid expectations demanded of her as a woman; and Juliette's acting out sexually in her affair.

Anorexia is a disorder that disturbs the onset of menarche. It was clear that Juliette's daughter did not want to be a woman like her mom, or to feel the rage and fear that permeated her family. She wanted her own individuality. She was totally aware of how unhappy her mother was and how discontented her family really was in spite of their image as The All-American Family. Her anorexia was a mystifying double bind for the family. Her emaciated body said, "Look, I'm dying," while her straight-A report cards and extraordinary athletic achievements said, "I know better than anyone what is going on here. Leave me alone and give me some privacy, and I'll be in control."

Her illness thus symbolized:

- the rage she carried from her mother
- her disdain for the role of women
- her need for real relational nourishment
- her refusal to conform
- her taking control of the family from her father
- her effort to distract the family from its real pain—lack of intimacy
- her need to mood-alter her own loneliness, fear, and anger

SECRET THOUGHTS AND FEELINGS

People often think of secrets primarily in terms of the concealment of events and facts. But in my experience the withholding and concealment of thoughts and feelings are among the darkest family secrets. It can be crazy-making for family members when other members, especially Mom and Dad, act as if they are not feeling what they are really feeling. Many of you *knew* when your mother was angry even though she pretended she wasn't. You may have known your dad had negative thoughts about your grandmother, even though he didn't express them.

These psychic secrets are often extremely destructive to the open communication a family needs for intimacy. There is nothing more powerful in forming healthy intimate bonding than being vulnerable about our feelings. When I am in my feelings, I am authentic and unguarded. This allows others to see me as I am in all vulnerability. Others can get close to me because I have taken down my walls of defense.

In addition, when parents withhold and repress their thoughts and feelings, the children have to carry them and act them out or in.

"Children tend to inherit," writes Harriet Goldhor Lerner, "whatever psychological issues parents choose not to attend to."

Secret Anger

Perhaps no feeling is more hidden in families than anger. I have shown you the part that secret anger plays in eating disorders. It is also a

major block to intimacy in marriage and to building solid selfhood and
individuality in families. When we can't express our anger, we have to
go underground with it. It comes out as an eating disorder, or it comes
out as a sexual disorder. Unexpressed anger can be the cause of the
inability to have an erection, premature ejaculation, and vaginismus.
Unexpressed anger is often a root cause of severe headaches and back-
aches and a host of psychosomatic disorders. Families with dark secrets often have a covert "don't feel" rule and an overt "don't feel
anger" rule. When anger is repressed, joy and the full expression of all
the other emotions is also repressed.

When parents keep their feelings a secret, their children often become confused and anxious. In an attempt to explain to themselves
what is going on, the children will often create private beliefs or fantasies about themselves and later act out these beliefs and myths in
symptomatic behavior.

Depression and anxiety often persist across generations. Genetic
predispositions often coincide with family dynamics, and a child may
take on unresolved feelings of sadness that have come from previous
generations. This phenomenon has been referred to as the *felt sense*
of the family. I can attest that it is a reality. Sometimes I feel overwhelmed with sadness for no apparent reason. I've learned that I'm
experiencing my family's unresolved grief.

Ambiguous Loss

Shirley's father was always a mystery to her. She never knew what
he thought about things, and she always had the feeling that he was
preoccupied with something other than what was going on in the
family.

After he died, she opened his safe and found a number of pictures
of a woman whom no one in the family knew. When she showed them
to her brother, he said he had seen the woman at their father's funeral.
After some investigation, it turned out that Shirley's father had actually
lived with the woman in the picture when he traveled to Dallas on
business two days each week. He was a pharmaceutical salesman, and
Dallas was part of his territory. He had made it a hard and fast family
rule that he was not to be called when he was working on the road. It
was his custom to call home on the second day of a trip to be sure
everything was okay. Shirley's father had a live-in girlfriend in Dallas

for twenty years! This revelation helped explain Shirley's feeling that her father was physically present but emotionally absent.

This type of feeling is described by therapist Pauline Boss as *ambiguous loss*. It is one of the general effects that a dark secret has on the other family members. Keeping a dark secret requires chronic deception and a certain amount of defensive evasion. Such an energetic facade creates emotional distance and inhibits spontaneous communication. The dark-secret-keeper is experienced by the outsiders as never being fully present. Something is missing, but it is hard to say exactly what it is.

THE SECRET OF CROSS-GENERATIONAL BONDING

In Chapter 1, I spoke of the importance of good generational boundaries and the value of a "generation gap" within the family. When generational boundaries are blurred or violated, children become enmeshed in their parents' marriage. This is sometimes called *spousification*. Spousification is an unconscious dark secret with long-term consequences. It can happen in two basic ways.

A child can be used to keep the marriage together, in any of a variety of ways. The child can be the scapegoat who behaves in ways that worry his mom and dad so much that they get closer together. This was the case with Juliette's daughter. Or a child can be the "pretty one" or the "talented one" or the "athletic one," whose accomplishments absorb the parents' attention. In both cases the focus on the child distracts the parents from their own problems. The child is *used* to keep the marriage together, but the child cannot know he or she is being used. How do you feel when you know you're being used in a relationship? Generally angry and resentful. Children can't know they are being used at a conscious level, but they know it at an unconscious level. Their anger and resentment are "hot" issues that will be dumped on their lovers, spouses, or children.

The second way a child is spousified is by taking care of one parent's emptiness, pain, and disappointment. The marriage is too conflict-ridden or dead to provide for the parents' intimacy needs. So the child becomes one parent's "special one."

Pat Conroy describes this powerfully in *The Prince of Tides*. Tom Wingo's mother pulls him to her:

"No," she said harshly, pulling me close to her again . . . "You're
the only one I care for. That'll be our secret." . . . I left her room
less of a child. I walked toward the rest of my family with my heart
troubled with adult terror.

Some parents are not as explicit in their demands as Tom Wingo's
mother, but the child always feels this adult terror. It's too overstimu-
lating to be intimate with Mom or Dad. Children need their own peers.
When they are used to take care of Mom or Dad's emptiness in the
marriage, they lose the innocence of childhood.

Chart 2–2 offers a comparison of constructive and destructive family
secrets. It is based on my belief that constructive secrets are the natural behaviors of concealment guarded by modesty. When these behaviors are thwarted and violated, we must use destructive secrets to
protect ourselves. We also use them to violate others' privacy. We
choose privacy; secrets are a *necessity* precisely because we no longer
have our privacy. Destructive secrets are used to have power over
others. They diminish our life and cause us confusion and mystification. They force us to spend all our energy guarding our selfhood.
They isolate and destroy trust, honesty, and mutuality.

SUMMARY: THE IMPACT OF DARK SECRETS

Dark secrets cause varying degrees of family dysfunction:

- *They organize the way the family perceives things.* Certain topics
  become taboo, and unspoken rules spring up around forbidden
  areas that are considered off limits. Myths are often created to distract family members from looking at what is really going on.
- *They create and maintain chronic levels of intense anxiety.* There
  is an intensity of feeling surrounding a secret that is difficult to disguise.

  The very act of keeping a secret generates anxiety in the person,
  who must be constantly on guard against disclosure, avoiding particular subjects and distorting information. The secret-keeper must be
  careful to avoid peripheral subjects that would expose the secret.
- *They keep members bonded to the family.* They make it difficult to
  separate.

CHART 2-2

COMPARISON OF CONSTRUCTIVE AND DESTRUCTIVE FAMILY SECRETS

CONSTRUCTIVE	DESTRUCTIVE
Shared power	Abuse of power
Natural shame	Toxic shame
Functional—Secrets are rooted in modesty and protect privacy. This sets up good boundaries and allows family to cope well.	*Dysfunctional*—Secrets are rooted in necessity. These secrets are used to replace the boundaries of privacy. They create rigid or enmeshed boundaries. They make it hard to cope.
Protective—Secrets protect basic rights.	*Disruptive*—Secrets disrupt basic rights.
Generative—Secrets enhance individuality, awareness, and freedom; expand life.	*Degenerative*—Secrets diminish or destroy individuality, awareness, and freedom; deadly secrets destroy life.
Generational—Secrets that keep boundaries intact. 　Marriage secrets 　Father's secrets 　Mother's secrets 　Siblings' secrets	*Cross-Generational Bonding* 　Parent/child triangles 　Spousification of children 　Enmeshment into family pain or 　　marital pain, or enmeshment 　　with either parent's pain
Enhance trust	Create distrust
Build community	Destroy community
Open communication	Close communication
Aid in the formation of strong self-identity	Confuse, mystify, and cause false self or loss of self
Aid in a high level of intimacy	Cause intimacy dysfunction
Benign—Allow fun, play, creativity, dreams.	*Distressful*—Cause tension, isolation, loss of spontaneity. Destroy creativity

- *They isolate the secret-keeper.* Secrets cut the keeper off from forgiveness and reconciliation and mutuality.
- *They keep the family from resolving the past.* They thereby maintain multigenerational dysfunction.
- *They damage trust and reliability.* They often must be maintained through lying and deceit: "One secret buries another."
- *They lead to confusion and mystification.* This causes us to create false selves as protective strategies, which prohibit intimacy and set up pseudobonds and enmeshment.
- *They support dysfunctional family processes.* They do this by creating coalitions and cross-generational alliances and by stabilizing triangles.
- *They limit the range of thinking and imagining.* Therefore they severely limit freedom of choice.
- *They create unhealthy family loyalty to a group trance.*
- *They create a sense of ambiguous loss.*
- *They are the core of obsessive and compulsive behaviors.*
- *They rigidify family rules and roles.*
- *They divide the family.* Those on the "in" can communicate with each other better on any issue than they can with anyone who is "out."

In the case of severe abuse, dark secrets cause further dysfunction:

- *They set up a whole gamut of autohypnotic ego defenses.* These include repression, denial, and sensory numbing, to avoid the hurt and pain that come with the violation.
- *They cause the victims to turn their hurt and anger toward themselves or project it onto others.*
- *They create the compulsion to protect our parents.*
- *They keep us from knowing ourselves and the "truth" of our childhood.*
- *They are "acted out" or "acted in" in present or future generations.*

Acting out and acting in behaviors are especially paradoxical symptoms of the mysterious power of dark family secrets to destroy an individual's freedom and right to selfhood. *The paradox is that at some mysterious level of consciousness, the secrets are not really secrets.* Many family therapists believe that *everyone* in the family knows the secret at some level of awareness and that the more the secrets are denied, the more they get acted in or out. In the next chapter we will probe how it is possible both to know the secret and to not know that we know it.

CHAPTER 3

HOW IS IT POSSIBLE NOT TO KNOW WHAT YOU KNOW?

The range of what we think and do is limited by what we fail to notice and because we fail to notice *that* we fail to notice there is little we can do to change until we notice how failing to notice shapes our thoughts and desires.

R. D. LAING

There probably exists in the mental life of the individual not only what he has experienced himself, but . . . an archaic heritage. . . . The archaic heritage includes not only dispositions, but also ideational contents, memory traces of the experience of former generations.

SIGMUND FREUD, *Moses and Monotheism*

One March more than twenty years ago, a mother and father brought their oldest child to see me. Seven-year-old Beverly Sue Smith kept running away from school. She refused to talk about what was bothering her and was hostile to her parents. This was a radical departure from her normal responsible behavior. It had begun in late October shortly after the school year began. Both the school authorities and her parents were at their wit's end. They brought her to me for counseling. She was sullen and absolutely refused to talk. I tried all the techniques that were usually successful with children—painting, drawing, imagery, sand sculpting, play figures—but nothing worked. So I referred Beverly Sue to a friend of mine who was a family therapist. He was using a relatively new approach called family systems theory, based on the work of Dr. Murray Bowen, a psychiatrist at Georgetown University.

Over the next five months, I forgot all about Beverly Sue. Then one Sunday her parents came to my adult theology lecture at Palmer Church. After the lecture they thanked me for the referral and asked me to say hello to Beverly Sue, who was coming from the children's Sunday school. When she arrived, she was animated, shook my hand, and seemed like a normal seven-year-old. The contrast was remarkable. I was too proud to ask the parents what the other therapist had done, but I called him as soon as possible. We had lunch, and he told me the problem was that Beverly Sue's parents had been in a rather destructive conflict for some time. Beverly Sue's grandfather was dying of cancer, and her father had shut down emotionally and refused to talk about it. He was sullen and withdrawn around the house. Beverly Sue's mother was a Southern Belle type who had been brought up to take care of everybody's feelings and fix everybody's problems. At first the mother had tried to cheer her husband up with special dinners and overly solicitous gestures. But the more she tried to cheer him up, the more he withdrew and refused to talk. After a few months Beverly Sue's mother started getting angry. Like many overfunctioning caretakers, rather than expressing the anger, she cut her husband off emotionally and would hardly speak to him. By the time they brought Beverly Sue to see me, they were sleeping apart and living like ships passing in the night.

My therapist friend told me that, as the oldest child, Beverly Sue would tend to be especially responsive to her father's emotional issues. First children often either protect and promote or else challenge their father's values, he said, more than children in any other birth-order position. Beverly Sue was very close to her father and very possessive of him, especially since the birth of her two sisters. According to my therapist friend, she had taken on his pain, acting out his depression, apathy, and refusal to speak. She was also attempting to fix her parents' marriage. By behaving in such a dramatic way, she forced her parents to pay attention to her and eased their accelerating hostility toward each other. From a traditional psychotherapeutic viewpoint, she looked like the "problem," but she was in reality the "symptom-bearer" who was trying to find a solution to the problem. *The real problem* was her father's deep anxiety over his own father's terminal illness and his inability to talk about it to anyone. In addition to his unresolved conflicts with his dying father, he had some real intimacy problems in his marriage. Quite unconsciously, Beverly Sue was bringing these dark secrets into the open.

From this experience, I began to understand a whole new way of viewing families and their problems. I came to understand what is now simply called the Bowen Theory.

THE BOWEN THEORY

Over the last forty-five years there has been a growing awareness that families are social systems bound by precise and predictable dynamics, or what I will loosely call laws. These laws operate throughout entire kinship networks for at least three generations, which interact as a functional whole. In the social system mode, a family is more than the sum of its parts; it is the interrelationship of its parts.

To make this idea clearer, I like to use the analogy of myself as a human person. I am composed of several *systems*—nervous, endocrine, circulatory, immune, and so on—as well as of the organs—brain, lungs, heart—that make up these systems. And yet I am more than any one of these systems or parts alone. All my systems and parts interact to make one unique reality, myself, as a human person.

Any disturbance, however, in one of my systems has an impact on my life. A change in any one part impacts all the other parts. In the relationship between the parts, their vital balance is the measure of my health.

To continue the analogy, sickness occurs when one of my systems malfunctions. When I am sick, the symptoms of my disease are a reflection of the system that is out of harmony.

To complete the analogy, my total reality is also influenced by my family and its past. My inherited genes predispose me to repeat certain patterns of sickness and health. My genetic inheritance also allows me to make predictions about my future. When I get a medical check-up, I receive an evaluation of how all my systemic functions are working.

In Beverly Sue's family, her dad was thrown off balance by *his* father's terminal illness. This caused her mom distress, and soon the marriage was in conflict.

When their parents' marriage is out of whack, children are pushed by the energy of the system as well as by their own need for self-preservation to try to restore family harmony. They will go so far as to sacrifice their own psychological or physical health to preserve family harmony. What looks like an emotionally disturbed child—Beverly Sue, for example—is really a child sounding the alarm about the parents' marriage. Children will choose to be sick if it means that their parents will work together to make their marriage better. Children intuitively know that if the marriage breaks down, they will be left out in the cold. Family therapists call a child who becomes the symptom-bearer the *scapegoat child.* When there are siblings, it is not always clear why one child will take on this role rather than another. Some of the answer may lie in birth position. This was certainly true in Beverly Sue's case.

From the parents' point of view, if they focus their attention on their "problem child" rather than on their marriage, *a burden* is lifted from them. If their child is the "problem," they can avoid looking at their own issues. In fact the parents may come to have an *investment* in the preservation of the child's sickness.

There are other multigenerational issues in the Smith family that impact Beverly Sue. I will come back to them to illustrate the use of the three-generational family map in Chapter 5.

Murray Bowen was one of the pioneers of this systems approach to the family. For over forty years he amassed an amazing body of research and clinical experience demonstrating in detail how families function. Every person working in this field today draws on his descriptions of healthy and unhealthy families.

The essence of Bowen's theory is that a mature family allows each member to separate and develop a solid sense of self-identity. When anxiety is present for any reason, the family moves toward stuck-togetherness and rigidity. The stronger the sense of solid self in individual family members, *the less the family stays stuck together.* Functional families resolve the problems that are causing anxiety, while dysfunctional families repress the problems or choose ineffective ways to resolve them.

The Bowen Theory is composed of eight interlocking concepts. I will discuss each of these briefly, because they are key to understanding how everyone in the family knows the secrets.

1. Self-Differentiation

The first concept is *self-differentiation.* I have been describing how families with dark secrets retard their members' ability to separate and develop a strong sense of self. The goal of a family is to provide an environment where each person can get their basic needs met and grow as a unique individual. A person with a strong sense of self has values and priorities and acts according to them. Such persons can state their differences with the family and act according to them *without leaving the family*. They can be separate and together at the same time.

Ideally a husband and wife can rework their own unfinished childhood developmental dependency needs by committing to love each other and by doing what love requires: working on those family-of-origin issues and being willing to learn the skills necessary for mutuality and intimacy. Thus the marriage itself is a way of continuing self-differentiation. All couples have wounds and unfinished business from the past. Marital love is a way of continuing to stretch and grow.

As the marital partners get their needs met through mutuality and their own resources, the children are free to get their needs met through parental protection, teaching, and good modeling of boundaries and privacy. Above all, the children do not have to please their parents or fill up their parents' emptiness and unfulfilled needs. Parents who achieve high levels of self-differentiation are also able to attain high levels of intimacy. This safeguards the children from the kind of spousification I described in Chapter 2.

However, if a parent remains at a lower level of self-differentiation and is unfulfilled in the marriage, they may turn to one of the children to get their needs met. A mother who never felt loved and valued by her own mother may try unconsciously to keep her own child dependent on her. A father who was toxically shamed by his father may toxically shame his own children and keep them from developing any self-confidence, causing them to depend on him for advice in decision making. This dependency is referred to as *bond permanence* or *enmeshment*.

By keeping the child dependent, the mother or father can feel loved and valued and complete. The child's natural urge to grow initiates a desire for separation and autonomy. Since separation and autonomy threaten the insecure parent with rejection and withdrawal of love, the child cannot separate. This means that the child never truly connects with his own feelings, thoughts, and desires. This lack of connection with his own experience blocks the child from developing a strong self and differentiating from the family.

2. The Nuclear Family as an Emotional System

In Bowen's theory the marital union is the chief component of the family, and its maturity is key to the health of the entire system.

During courtship, Mom may have seen Dad as the strong nurturing father she never had. She may connect with him to fill up the emptiness she feels as a needy little girl. When she "falls in love," the power of that feeling is the oceanic sense of wholeness it brings to her. For Dad, Mom may represent the vulnerable femininity that he feels deep down but was prohibited from expressing. Her swooning over him allows him to connect with a missing part of himself. He too feels whole and fulfilled by being "in love" with her. But there is a trap here for both of them. In order to keep Mom's swooning obeisance, macho Dad *must* continue to look and act strong and powerful. He must keep his vulnerable and fearful part a secret. And Mom must conceal—even from herself—her own adult strength.

If Mom's and Dad's love is to truly grow, they must slowly express their full nature to each other. This will involve giving up their romantic dreams and grieving the disappointment that comes from realizing that the beloved cannot fill up the void left from childhood deficits. If Mom and Dad are not willing to grow, or if they are too deeply wounded, they will push their energy in the direction of their false selves and toward pseudo-intimacy. Then they may act out their unresolved childhood deficits in several ways.

In the case of Germaine (whom we met in Chapter 2), her father filled his unmet needs by having mood-altering sex; his wife filled hers with mood-altering obsessing on her husband and his addiction. Their marriage was mostly pretense and phoniness. Germaine was bonded to her mother and mood-altered by taking care of her mother's emptiness. The whole family structure was constituted around the dark secret of her parents' pseudo-intimacy. Germaine was caught in what Murray Bowen called the nuclear family's emotional field or the "undifferentiated family ego mass," a kind of *group think trance* that the whole family lives in.

I remember working with a family in which each member took turns being depressed. Over the course of two years, the father, mother, and four children, two of them in their early twenties, each went through a distinct period of apathy and passivity characterized by a negative outlook on life.

Being depressed was the way this family maintained a kind of rigid stuck-togetherness. No one had left the family's emotional system. Both of the older children left, only to return (remember the Brontë family in Chapter 2). The parents were bonded codependently, each representing the primary source figure from the other's family of origin. They bartered selves like dealers at a swap meet. Each was literally terrified of going it alone. The children were also bound to the parents by secrets. The oldest son and father conspired against the mother; the mother and second daughter had secrets pertaining to the father; and so on.

This family was frozen. When I asked each of them to draw a picture of the family, the oldest three siblings drew the seventeen-year-old daughter as a child of about six. She was nicknamed Baby and was the most depressed of all. In fact, this family *needed* to be depressed, because being depressed was familiar and kept them together.

Thinking Versus Feeling

In looking at the nuclear family's emotional system, Bowen viewed the level of family members' self-differentiation primarily in terms of the separation of thinking and feeling.

A person who has a strong self, with good ego boundaries, can think about their feelings without being dominated by them.

A person who can't do this believes that if they feel something, it must be true.

A person who has a strong sense of self-differentiation can also set good boundaries with other family members. Good interpersonal boundaries allow us to think about an interaction with another family member without overreacting or becoming emotionally overwhelmed. When we are in the throes of reactivity, we do not think. We are "carried away" by old familiar family processes and submerged in the family's emotional field.

Because this kind of family-feeling enmeshment is so common, people have enormous reservoirs of what I have called *original pain*. Original pain contains the feelings that we were not allowed to express in childhood and that were repressed. We learned to feel only the feelings that were family-authorized. The reservoir of original pain is part of the emotional pain of the nuclear family. As long as we keep these feelings repressed, we stay bound to the family's emotional system.

Working through original pain is described in my book *Homecoming*. By reconnecting with unresolved grief, and by expressing hurt, sadness, and anger, we can gain freedom from the nuclear family's emotional system. The more we work through these feelings, the more we can stop and "think" rather than having a "no choice reaction" to our emotions. When we are not capable of thinking about our feelings, their source is truly a *secret* we keep from ourselves.

3. Parents' Projection Process

Through what Bowen calls the *parents' projection process,* one or more children are either chosen by their parents or pushed by the internal laws of the family system to be the recipient of the parents' or the family's unresolved issues (dark secrets). Beverly Sue, Germaine, Sereva, Lorna, and Juliette's daughter are all examples of this projection process.

To help you understand how this happens, let me describe the natural psychological process called *identification* and how identification can become a defense mechanism.

Identification is particularly significant in early life. The earliest identification, often called *primary identification,* is that between infant and mother. There is good evidence that during this earliest stage of development, infants literally cannot distinguish between themselves and their mothers.

Identification also refers to the unconscious tendency of all human beings to internalize parts of their environment. We internalize others as mental representations in memory. In a sense they are psychologically "swallowed" and digested, becoming part of our personality.

When healthy identification takes place, a child internalizes aspects of his parents' thoughts, feelings, or behaviors. If all goes well, this internalization is temporary, supporting the child while he gradually becomes more autonomous.

But when the parent with whom the child identifies feels empty and is troubled with unresolved issues from childhood, the parent often uses identification as a defense mechanism.

Projective Identification

If a mother disdains her own dependency needs, she projects her feeling of dependency onto her child, rewarding the child for being dependent and helpless and withdrawing her love when the child shows signs of autonomy and independence.

The mother needs the child to stay dependent in order to avoid having to accept and deal with her own morbid dependency needs. Projecting her neediness onto the child by rewarding only dependent behavior sets the child up to identify himself as lovable only when he is dependent. The mother may even verbally exhort the child to be more autonomous, but she may still actually reward only dependent behavior. This process is called *projective identification.*

Germaine was quite clearly identified with her mother. She eventually did exactly as her mother had done—she found a man who ran around on her. Germaine and her mother even had the same mannerisms and body posture.

Germaine's mother, like all co-addicted people, was filled with loneliness, fear, and anxiety. She had excessive dependency needs. As she mothered Germaine, she used her to fill this emptiness and avoid facing up to it.

In the Bowen Theory the secret-bearing parent passes on the secret through projective identification.

4. Multigenerational Transmission Process

Bowen noticed that families repeat themselves. Similar issues are often played out from one generation to the next. He referred to this as *the multigenerational transmission of family patterns.* Dark secrets, more than any other single factor, keep the process going. Secrets are not talked about, so there is no way for them to be resolved.

A therapist friend told me an extraordinary story about multigenerational transmission. Every year on or around February 14, a patient of his named Roberto developed a red rash on his neck. The rash lasted about ten days and then went away. The rash had first appeared when Roberto was eight years old. There was no medical explanation for the outbreak of the rash.

Roberto was eighteen when his father died. Shortly before he died, he told Roberto a shocking secret: Roberto's maternal grandmother and his mother had both committed suicide. His grandmother had slit her own throat, and his mother had hung herself. His grandmother's death took place on Valentine's Day. His mother had died on February 16 when she was twenty-six years old—six years after Roberto was born.

Roberto's mother knew about her own mother's suicide and killed herself just two days after an anniversary of her mother's death. Here the generational pattern is clear.

Somehow Roberto already "knew" about his grandmother's and his mother's suicide. But until his father's deathbed confession, no one had told him. So how did he know? How did Germaine know about her father's sexual affairs? After all, no one told her. How is it possible to know a secret and not know that you know it? The secrets must be known, or they cannot be reenacted. In the Bowen Theory the secrets are part of the family's emotional system. When the secrets gets acted out or in, these reenactments are symbolic attempts to bring the dark secrets out of hiding.

5. Triangles

In the Bowen Theory the triangle, a three-person emotional configuration, is the molecule or basic building block of any emotional system. A two-person system may be stable as long as it is calm, but when anxiety increases—for instance, when a marriage has an intimacy conflict—it immediately involves the most vulnerable other person to form a triangle. This is what happened to Beverly Sue. When tension in the triangle is too great for the threesome, it involves still others and forms a series of interlocking triangles. When tensions become very high in families and available family triangles are exhausted, the family system triangulates with people from outside the family, such as therapists, police, and social agencies.

Triangulated relationships are also part of normal development and are an essential part of socialization. A healthy child breaks the primary bond with his mother by entering into a triadic relationship with both Mom and Dad. If a mother blocks this crucial expansion to father because of her own wounds, she makes it difficult for the child to bond with anyone else.

Parents who are unable to deal in triads do not want to grow. Those parents have probably been put into *bondage* by their own parents, who could only deal in dyads. Such parents were often narcissistically deprived. They failed to get the proper mirroring they needed as children. They live their lives in an insatiable quest, looking for themselves in substitute mirrors. They cannot imagine sharing their life with more than one person.

Adults who are afraid to get married, or couples who are isolated and live only for each other, may reflect this narcissistic disturbance.

6. Sibling Position Profiles

Bowen was fascinated by the work on sibling positions done by a Viennese-born professor of psychology, Dr. Walter Toman. Toman's book *Family Constellation* (1962) presented detailed descriptions of how each sibling position affects personality and social behavior. He wrote about the personality characteristics of the oldest brother of brothers, the oldest brother of sisters, the male and female only child, the oldest sister of sisters, the youngest sister of sisters, and so on. He based his descriptions on extensive interviews and clinical observation. He then worked out every possible combination of sibling position in marriage, offering some highly useful predictions about the compatibility of each combination.

During the past thirty years, Toman's work has been questioned, debated, corrected, and even rejected. Part of the problem is that his work was not based on a coherent theory of the family system.

It was the work of Jerome Bach and Alan Anderson, two psychologists working at the Bach Institute in Minneapolis, Minnesota, in the 1970s, that offered a coherent theory of four basic sibling positions based on the dynamic needs of the family understood as a social system. Bach and Anderson based this theory on hundreds of hours of discussion, clinical observation, interventions in therapy, and consultation with many schoolteachers.

I will summarize some of their conclusions in this section. Knowing your own, your relatives', and your parents' birth positions may offer you clues to sorting out the secrets in your family's underground.

You must keep in mind that there are many factors in addition to birth position that affect family systems. The traits presented here are typical of the role a child in each birth-order position plays. The manner in which the role is played out is determined largely by the rules that govern the family system in general, as well as the idiosyncratic factors in each individual family, like individual uniqueness, ethnicity, and circumstances. But ideas on birth position provide a new way to understand how a particular child is chosen as the object of the parents' projection process. Sibling positions also affect how each sibling reacts to the disclosure of a family secret. Bach's and Anderson's profiles also enable us to make reliable presumptions about the personality of people in past generations for whom verifiable facts are missing.

First Birth-Order Position

The Bach-Anderson theory views the whole family as an individual entity with very definite needs. The first need is for productivity: taking care of the physical security of the family. When the first child is born, that child bears the family's projected hopes for continuity and survival. The first child's performance is a major issue because of the issue of productivity. The first child feels the pressure of the parents' rules and expectations. If parents' expectations are unrealistic, a first child may give up and fail to achieve.

"Firsts" bear a special relation to the father. If the father is not fulfilling his role, first siblings often assume responsibility for his inadequacies. First siblings may fight for their father or with their father to try and make him be more responsible. They may become overly responsible toward their mother to compensate for their father's lack of responsibility, or they may protect their father from their mother's attacks on him.

First siblings will act out their father's secrets more than any other sibling position. Whatever unresolved emotional baggage the father is carrying, whatever the father is not dealing with openly, the first sibling will often take it on. Beverly Sue's father was actually angry at his own father for rejecting him. With his father terminally ill, he felt caught up in ambiguity and guilt. Beverly Sue acted out her father's anger by running away from school.

Second Birth-Order Position

Second-position siblings respond to the emotional maintenance needs of the family system. They try to see to it that each family member's emotional needs are met, and they feel especially responsible for the mother. Second siblings are especially aware of the elements implicit in family rules and relationships. *They will probably pick up the family secrets faster than their siblings, especially the mother's secrets.* Their identity is involved with being in touch with the underlying situation and with making the implicit explicit. Second siblings focus on feelings and symbolic meanings. They tend to get confused when there are incongruities between overt and covert rules, between values and expectations. Second siblings absorb other people's feelings as if they were their own. They often perceive issues in polarized terms and have trouble with ambiguity. Second children need acceptance as people and need to establish clear boundaries.

Third Birth-Order Position

Third-position children feel responsible for maintaining the quality of the marital relationship. Their self-esteem is connected to the stability of the marriage. They need to be connected to both Mom and Dad. *"Thirds" will probably be enmeshed in the secrets of the marriage more than their siblings.* And they are more likely to act out the marital secrets. If Mom and Dad have lots of anger that is not being dealt with, the third child might act it out by getting into trouble at school. I know of several third children who have done this, but there are also many other ways they might act out their parents' unresolved issues.

Third-position children often feel responsible for all the dyadic relationships in the family. They tend to think in terms of connections. "Thirds" can look unfeeling, but they feel deeply.

Third children are threatened by a lack of choices and by interpersonal conflict. In the face of conflict, third children may disappear into introspection and appear apathetic. They need others to appreciate them for what they do. When they are stuck, they need help in creating choices.

Fourth Birth-Order Position

Fourth-position children take on the family's need for unity. If there are only three children, the third child will take on the traits that I'm describing for "fourths." "Fourths" feel responsible for harmony in the family. They focus on the goals of the family as a whole. They look at wholes first and then at the parts. Their self-esteem is very wrapped up in the family's happiness. *They are most prone to be enmeshed in the secrets shared by the whole family, and they feel a sense of loyalty to keep secrets known by the whole family.* They can be easily overwhelmed by the amount of conflict in the family.

Fourth siblings often feel responsible for disruption and pain in the family. They need help in delimiting their part of the family burden so that they don't take on too much of it. They need lots of approval, and they need to be told that they are not to blame for the pain and tension in the family.

Beyond the Fourth Position

Siblings after the fourth position repeat the cycle. "Fifths" are like "firsts," "sixths" are like "seconds," and so on.

Blended Families and Other Complexities

Birth-order issues become very confusing in step- or blended families. Generally speaking, siblings who have the same birth order in the blended family that they had in their original family will have certain issues to work through.

Two first children will vie for leadership. Two "fourths" may feel a lot of responsibility for working things out in the blended family, or they may want to keep their original family unified. Each family of origin will have a propensity to form alliances and keep secrets from the family they are blended with.

It is impossible to predict exactly how siblings will resolve birth-order issues in blended families. I've never known of a first child who adopted the traits of a second-position child after moving into a blended family where there was an older first child. I have seen two first children unite in their blended family and play out their roles more or less together. I once worked with a blended family where the parents were both alcoholics. Each parent had three children. The two first children, both girls, literally divided the parenting chores in raising the other four children.

In the case of twins, the firstborn will take on more of the first-sibling issues. In the case of a child born with much older siblings, the birth order remains unchanged. A third child born when his brother and sister are in their teens is still in the third position. But such a child may also have certain characteristics of only children. If a child dies, the birth order remains the same for those who survive.

Only Children

Only children may take on all the birth-order roles. If their parents are immature and unfulfilled, they are sure to be projected on. If their parents are mature, they usually fare well. Only children often act more adult than their peer group, and they often want things their own way.

Any in-depth discussion of other sibling constellations would take us too far afield, but I urge those of you who want to delve deeper to read Margaret Hoopes and James Harper's book *Birth Order Roles and Sibling Patterns in Individual Family Therapy*. Bach and Anderson have endorsed this book.

7. Emotional Cutoff

In my family anger was prohibited. As in many good religious families, anger was considered one of the deadly sins. When I was angry, I didn't know what to do, so I withdrew, often hardly speaking to the person I was angry at. In later years I cut off communication with people I was angry at for longer periods of time, sometimes completely. I always got back together with family members, but sometimes only after a long hiatus. In the Bowen Theory this withdrawing without resolution is called emotional cutoff.

Emotional cutoff is a strategy that family members use when they are unable to resolve conflict. It normally means that a relationship is very intense, and the family members do not know how to resolve it. It often means that the persons involved really care a lot about each other but don't know how to deal with their love.

Cutoff patterns in adulthood are determined by the way people handle their unresolved emotional attachments to their parents and siblings. The lower the level of differentiation, the more intense the unresolved attachment and the more prone a person is either to severe enmeshment or to severe cutoff.

Emotional cutoff patterns can help you fill in data about people in your family who seem secretive and strange—the black sheep, the "weird" ones, the ones that left the family. The more intense the cutoff, the more likely it is that the individual will have an exaggerated version of his parental family problem in his own marriage, and the more likely it is that his own children will have an even more intense cutoff with him in the next generation. The person who runs away from the family of origin is as emotionally dependent as the one who never leaves home. This concept can help to understand some seemingly bizarre family behaviors.

8. Societal Regression

Societal regression refers to the way that emotional problems in society are similar to emotional problems in a family.

Just as chronically sustained anxiety in a family leads to repetitive cycles of emotionally distorted thinking and reactivity, the same pattern applies in society. Increased chronic societal anxiety leads to emotionally contaminated decisions to allay the anxiety, and these decisions in turn result in greater symptoms of dysfunction. Our so-called "correctional institutions" re-create the exact conditions of privacy violation and shaming humiliation that produced the criminals in their dysfunctional, shaming, privacy-violating families. Many soul-murdered criminals violate the innocent just as they were once violated as children.

BEYOND BOWEN

The Bowen Theory gives us a rich framework for understanding how we can know the dark secrets of our families but not consciously know that we know them. Lack of strong selfhood, enmeshment in the family's undifferentiated ego mass, enmeshment in projective identification with one or both of our parents, bond permanence—all describe why we carry the secrets. But these concepts do not tell us *precisely how the secrets are transmitted, how they are communicated to the next generation, and how they sometimes even skip generations.*

At least four other sources throw some light on these more mysterious and puzzling processes:

The science of kinesics, which studies, among other things, nonverbal communication in families.

The phenomena of unconscious knowing and choosing.

The psychology of group cognition, which studies group consciousness and group avoidances or blind spots.

Rupert Sheldrake's hypothesis of formative causation, a biological theory that studies how forms of things and forms of behavior are passed down from former generations.

Nonverbal Communication

The science of kinesics studies holistic human communication. Dr. Ray Birdwhistell, a professor of communication at the Annenberg School of Communication at the University of Pennsylvania, and others have amassed an enormous amount of evidence on the use of *all the senses* in human communication. Birdwhistell began his career in anthropology, which led him to study how the information conveyed by human gestures and movements is coded and patterned differently in different cultures. These codes and patterns can be discovered by skilled scrutiny of particular sequences of movement within a social unit like the family. There are many things children must learn in their family in order to express the gestures and movements prescribed by their sex and culture. Foreigners and immigrants often experience shame and humiliation simply because they are not aware of the nonverbal levels of expected behavior. A child can learn these behavior expectations because they are patterned.

Birdwhistell and others have done extensive filming of different families at mealtime. All families, both functional and dysfunctional, have very patterned rituals, although no one in the family calls what they are doing a ritual or recognizes that the orderly nature of their verbal interactions is regulated by nonverbal unconscious rules.

Birdwhistell's tapes of highly vocal dysfunctional families show completely predictable patterns of dinnertime quarrels. He writes: "It sounds almost as though each member of the family had learned his lines, knows his cues and synchronizes in the family drama."

He concludes that the verbal rituals in these families were a kind of subterfuge that carried the *official* version of the family and served as a screen "behind which the family members covertly went about the remainder of their communication." These covert communications—including secrets—were going on nonverbally.

Birdwhistell describes his own mother as an "expert in *untalk*":

She could emit a silence so loud as to drown out the scuffle of feet . . . and even the grind of my father's power machinery, to which he retreated when, as he said, "Your mother's getting uneasy."

He goes on to say that she was the epitome of the gracious hostess and would often say, "No matter how much I disagree with a guest, I never allow an un-Christian word to cross my lips. I just smile." But as Birdwhistell tells it, his mother's thin-lipped smile was accompanied by an audible intake of air through her tightened nostrils, which "required no words—Christian or otherwise—to reveal her attitude."

Think about the nonverbal clues in your family. Your brother's sullen look, your sister's thrust lower lip or nostril flare, your dad's tight-ened jaw, and your mother's obsessive talking are the undeniable marks of a family code. No one ever taught you this message system, but within your family it often speaks louder than words.

Unconscious Knowing and Choosing

There is a rather extraordinary feat that certain blind people are able to perform. If asked to reach for an object placed in front of them, they can find it without hesitation. This unique ability is called *blindsight.* It is explained by the fact that in these people blindness came about through brain injury or stroke. The part of their brain that is damaged governs, not seeing itself, but *awareness* of what is seen. Their visual capacity is intact.

Anthony Marcel, a psychologist at Cambridge University who has done a lot of research on blindsight, has come to the conclusion that even in normal people the mind has the capacity to know without awareness of what is known.

In one experiment Marcel showed that most people can read un-consciously. He flashed words on a screen for a few thousandths of a second—much too fast for them to register consciously. Then he asked his subjects which word in a subsequent pair of words meant or looked the same as the one he had just flashed. The subjects were right in guessing the related word ninety percent of the time.

This kind of study, along with other research, has led modern cogni-tive psychologists to the rather startling conclusion that much of the activity in the mind goes on *outside of awareness.*

Our conscious minds have a very limited capacity.

Harriet Lerner, in her superb book *The Dance of Intimacy,* makes it very clear that at one point in her teenaged life she made the "un-conscious choice" to remain a behavioral problem. As she puts it, she chose "not to change" even though her family had sent her to get psychological help.

Harriet's mother had cancer, and there was a strong chance she would die. At some unconscious level Harriet chose to keep on being a problem in order to keep her mother alive. Years later she checked this out with her mother, who had indeed survived the cancer. Her mother verified that she had been quite obsessed with what would happen to Harriet if she died. Who can say whether Harriet's choice really saved her mother's life!

What is relevant here is that Harriet made a profound choice that was totally unconscious.

Mate Selection

One of the most striking examples of unconscious choice that we make is mate selection. Relationships are a major arena where we resurrect our first attachment feelings. We also choose mates in an attempt to resolve old frustrations and unmet developmental dependency needs.

How do we know that the person we choose has the exact issues we need to work out with our parents? In the year after I left my seminary studies, I dated four older women who had my mother's exact unresolved emotional issues. We may come up with all kinds of conscious reasons for choosing that particular mate, but we make the real choice outside our own awareness. Jane Middelton Moz, a psychotherapist who specializes in the treatment of individuals who suffered childhood trauma, suggests that we choose what is familiar, "in much the same way that someone from another country might seek out others with the same customs, language, and values. We feel 'at home' with them. They embody defenses, nonverbal communications, emblems, mannerisms and cues that are similar to our own. They speak our language."

Almost all couple therapists have found that there are two levels to every relationship commitment, and that a couple's unconscious agreements may contradict their conscious ones. When troublesome behaviors go on for many years in a marriage, it's very clear that the couple have secretly agreed to them. Each unconscious agreement has certain payoffs that keep the couple comfortable at an unconscious level. A typical unconscious contract might be, "I'll be the distancer and you be the pursuer"; or "Whenever we get too close, I'll start a fight"; or "I'll be the underfunctioner and you be the overfunctioner"; or "I'll put up walls, and you try to tear them down."

I remember, for example, a couple who were magna cum laude graduates from a major eastern college. They had been married for eighteen years and had been fighting over *laundry* for most of that time! One of the therapeutic tasks I gave them was to monitor their laundry fights. Every time they fought over laundry, they were to write a description of what had taken place the day before the fight. The descriptions were inevitably about times of closeness. It became clear that their laundry fights were a way to adjust and get more distance whenever they got too close. Agreeing not to get too close was their *secret* contract. Their laundry fights were a feedback loop—a convenient way to honor their contract even while they kept it secret.

The Mutual Pact About What Not to Notice

Both partners in a marriage learn that certain areas are very touchy, and they unconsciously agree to steer attention away from these trouble spots, so they can get along better and insure themselves against abandonment. When both partners agree to a such a selected avoidance, they create a shared secret or a joint delusion, which becomes part of an unconscious agreement.

Erving Goffman, in his book *The Presentation of Self in Everyday Life,* presents the rather unsettling belief that relationships can be strengthened by such secrets. He notes:

> In well-adjusted marriages we expect that each partner may keep secrets having to do with financial matters, past experience, current flirtations, indulgences in bad or expensive habits, . . . true opinions held about relatives or mutual friends.

According to Goffman, these secrets make it possible to maintain a desired status quo.

What is certain is that all couples have an unconscious agreement about certain areas that says, "If you don't tell, I won't ask." Over the first years of a relationship, these forbidden areas are chosen from troubled experiences, and the agreement is made unconsciously. The areas that are out of bounds are protected by an unconscious mutual pact that delineates what should not be noticed or talked about.

If the veils of these unconscious agreements are pulled away—say, in a divorce—things can get real ugly. As Daniel Goleman says, "Beneath the surface of this uneasy alliance of inattention there may be a cesspool of anger, resentment, hurt—all unspoken, if not unnoticed." When the couple separates, the unconscious collusion to preserve the status quo at the expense of openness evaporates. Everything comes spilling out, and the "civilized" couple can suddenly turn into savages.

Many of these unconscious mutual contracts of inattention between a husband and wife are extended to the children. All the members of the family unconsciously agree to a number of shared blind spots or secrets that govern what can be noticed and talked about and what is not to be noticed or spoken about. The saying "What you don't know won't hurt you" is a conscious statement that supports the unconscious dynamics of these shared alliances of inattention.

Perception as Selection

As we are indoctrinated into our family's secrets, we enter into unconscious processing of its selections and agreements. The member who is a secret-keeper intentionally wants to conceal certain information. Children learn to perceive the family situation in the way that pleases their parents. Children want to matter to their parents, and they want their parents to be okay. As you have noticed in the case of Beverly Sue, a child will even become emotionally disturbed in order to care for their parents.

Children learn not to notice the things that are painful, unpleasant, and cause anxiety to their parents. And as Goleman has convincingly shown, in order to deal with anxiety, all human beings alter attention and perception. There is always a trade-off between anxiety and attention. We learn to select what we perceive, and we select those parts of our environment that bring pleasure rather than pain. Hiding your eyes or looking away from a horror film is the simplest example I can give of this.

What is pleasant and rewarding is habit-forming, and we learn to see, hear, touch, taste, and smell what brings us the most comfort.

Trading off awareness for security is the mechanism of defense that our mind uses to survive. Denial and repression are the most extreme examples. If I don't see the horror scene, I don't get scared. If I deny that my father is mean and cruel, I don't have to feel the wrenching pain of his rejection. If I make up the fantasy of a loving nurturing mother, I can believe that she will protect me. If I completely dissociate from the sexual violation that is happening to me, I will not experience the pain associated with it or remember it. All the human psychological defenses are autohypnotic survival mechanisms. We trade off perceptions (actually feeling the pain of what is happening) for the security of being numbed out or being somewhere else in fantasy. Our defense mechanisms allow us to survive, but we pay the price of diminished awareness.

The Psychology of Group Cognition

Gregory Bateson pointed out that human learning is patterned, that we learn how to learn, and we learn how *not to learn*.

We perceive in patterns, and we remember in patterns. Cognitive psychologists call these patterns *schemas*. A schema is a private, unarticulated theory about all the experiences, people, and events we interact with in our lives. The sum total of our schema is our private theory of the nature of reality. Schemas are the building blocks of knowing.

Schemas change as we grow, and mental development is cumulative; our understanding builds on what we have learned before. And like theories, our schemas are subject to revision. We even develop metaschemas—schemas that dictate the operations of other schemas.

Our schemas determine what we will notice; we also have schemas that determine what we will *not* notice.

If you think about it, there is always more to see than we can actually see. We look at this rather than that, but why? And do we really see what we look *at*? The evidence seems to say that we see what we look *for*.

One cognitive psychologist, Ulric Neisser, made a one-minute videotape of four guys playing basketball. About thirty seconds into the tape a beautiful woman dressed in white and carrying an umbrella saunters through the game. She is on the screen for four full seconds. Neisser would show the tape to visitors at his lab, who were instructed to press a button whenever one player passed the ball. When Neisser asked the viewers if they had seen anything unusual, not one mentioned the women. They hadn't seen her. Neisser's instruction to watch the ball created a schema that excluded her.

If we apply this idea of schemas to family secrets, it is certain that the secret-keeping parent or parents guide their children's perceptions. In short, *children learn what the parents want them to see and what they do not want them to see.* Consciously or unconsciously, the secret-keeper selects a "safe" focus of attention as a way to divert attention from the "dangerous" secret. We know well what subjects are permissible and what are not.

The Family Personality

We could go so far as to say that a family has a personality and that the family personality has needs just as an individual personality does. The family personality is guided by a conglomerate mind, which is a unique creation of the sum total of shared schemas of its members. This conglomerate mind resides not only in the mind of each member but also between them. And the family personality, which is created by the group mind, has its conscious and unconscious aspects.

The family's codes, its regular and recurring patterns, serve as a kind of group memory. Some recurring events, such as holidays, arguments, and various outings, are the key repositories of the family mind.

All families draw the line somewhere between what can be said and what cannot be said. They have their shared focus and their shared denials. Families often have one member who sanitizes the information flow so that it conforms to the family's basic doctrine. In rigid fundamentalist-religious families, all new information is monitored as to its truth or falsity. Mother or Father is the mind guard. They ask, "What does the Bible say about it?" If it is not in the Bible or if it violates *their interpretation* of the Bible, then it is rejected.

Most families have a mind guard, someone who says, "Where did you get such a *crazy* idea?" This question means that the idea does not fit into the family's group belief. A powerful mind guard is the statement, "What you don't know won't hurt you."

"The first victim of group think," writes Daniel Goleman, "is critical thought." Children growing up in patriarchal or matriarchal families are not allowed to question. The main rule is never to question the rules. This creates a hopeless kind of cognitive closure. Germaine's perception was so fashioned that the obvious *could not occur to her.* She could not ask herself, "Is it possible that my father is taking in all those troubled women to have sex with them?" The more secretive a family, the more their perceptions are shaped, and true alternatives are ignored, no matter what advantages they might offer. Facts that challenge the official doctrine or threaten the family's personality are simply brushed aside.

The darker the secrets, the more likely the family will resort to a pretense of stability.

Families with dark secrets create blind spots. There are rules saying what family members are not to notice, and another rule that says, "Do not notice the rules for what you cannot notice." Children cannot see these rules that limit awareness and experience because they operate outside of consciousness. In addition, children have genuinely limited cognitive experience. They cannot be aware of any alternative explanations, even if it is safe to have them. The rules for what not to notice, and the metarule of not noticing the rules for what not to notice, are to the family's group mind what the individual's ego defenses are to the individual's mind.

The Theory of Formative Causation

None of these theories satisfies me completely. Lately, I've been attracted to another way of looking at the transmission of secrets.

It comes from the Cambridge biologist Rupert Sheldrake, who has spent his life trying to understand how the forms of living things are passed on from generation to generation. For example, how does an acorn become a mighty oak tree? Sheldrake is also interested in whether newly learned behavior can be passed on without being taught. His answers might help us to understand how the very problem that is hidden in one generation—say, sexual addiction manifesting as multiple affairs—is acted out by succeeding generations, even when they have no knowledge of the past. Basically, Sheldrake has arrived at the belief that when newly learned patterns of behavior within a given species reach a certain behavioral threshold, the behavior is passed on to all the offspring of that species. The following generations will already know the behavior without going through the learning process of the past generation.

The new behavior can be either something creative or something destructive. In either case, when a certain threshold is reached, all new generations will receive the newly acquired behavior as their natural inheritance.

Sheldrake's theory of formative causation is based on modern research into energy fields. It states that certain thresholds of new behavior create an energy field that, along with DNA, conditions the next generation's inherited traits. The forms of new behavior are passed on through this energy field. A simple analogy helps me to grasp this theory.

Look at a TV screen, and ask yourself: How does the picture get on the screen? In other words, how are the forms produced? We could imagine there are little people in the set. (Actually, the explanation of how an acorn becomes an oak was this simplistic until recently.) If we look behind the screen, however, we don't find little people—we find wires and conductors. Wires and conductors are analogous to the DNA that we all inherit genetically. They are like the piles of lumber and bricks at a construction site, the building blocks for a house. But the building blocks alone do not give the house or the TV picture its *form*. For the TV screen to have form—that is, to show a picture—we have to tune into a channel. The channel is an energy field that exists outside the set.

Sheldrake calls the fields that transmit behavior *morphogenetic fields*, literally "fields of energy that give form." If we applied his theory to the family as a social system, we could say that a family with its special personality operates like a species, and that when a threshold of new behavior or habits is reached in a family, everyone in the succeeding generations will know them. They may be good behaviors or virtues or bad habits or vices. Once the threshold is reached, the behavior is passed into the group mind or family energy field. Each descendant knows the new behavior, although not everyone will necessarily act it out. It may even skip generations.

This may sound somewhat mysterious, but its mystery is surpassed by the mystery and power of the family. Nothing I've written about can fully explain how family secrets shape our lives.

YOU AND YOUR FAMILY

By now, you may be clearer about some healthy secrets in your family of origin and in your present life, family or otherwise. You may also know or suspect that the family you came from had some dark secrets, and you may have discovered a dark secret or two of your own.

What I most hope is that you have become aware of the powerful impact that your family has had on your freedom of choice.

You may have come from an open and expressive family and have an unquestioned and unqualified commitment to privacy. If so, you were free to become yourself and make your own individual choices.

Unfortunately, such ideal families are rare. Most people I know fall somewhere on a continuum closer to the families with dark secrets that I've described. All of my experience points to a rather disappointing conclusion about human freedom: Most of us are a lot less free than we think we are! We've looked at the lives of a number of people who thought they were their own masters, making their own choices. They subsequently learned that they were acting out their family secrets. In my own life it took me forty years to realize that I was acting out permanent bonding with my mother's dark secret wound. I can honestly say that her dark secret has cost both my mother and myself decades of intimacy dysfunction. And even with that realization, I still struggle in my efforts to be close to the ones I love.

If you have some suspicions about dark secrets in your family system, Part Two will help you uncover them. I want you to see how certain patterns based on dark secrets may have impaired your freedom and shaped your identity in ways you may now want to change. *I want you to see that what you don't know* can *hurt you.* But Part Two will also deepen your awareness of the rich depth and mysterious power of your family. You may also discover great strengths that you developed in order to deal with the anxiety brought on by the dark secrets. And one of the best things you may discover is how you have embodied your mother's or father's or even an ancestor's noblest dreams.

PART TWO

TRAVERSING THE HAUNTED FOREST

Who knows what all of us have in us not just of our parents but of their parents before them and so on back beyond any names we know or any face we would recognize if we came upon their portraits hanging on an antique shop wall?

FREDERICK BUECHNER, *Telling Secrets*

CHAPTER 4

BEGINNER'S MIND
Re-imagining Your
Family

This is what makes me crazy in this family, Dad. . . . I
can't stand it when I state a simple fact about this family's
history, and I'm told by you or Mom that it didn't
happen.

PAT CONROY, *The Prince of Tides*

To do your best work in deciphering dark family secrets, take the attitude that anything and everything could be a clue. Deciphering dark family secrets is like a psychic archaeological expedition. It's impossible to be totally unbiased because you already know the secrets on an unconscious level. But it is best to have as few preconceptions as possible. As crazy as it may sound, it's best not to know what you're looking for. There's no such thing as raw objective data. Every idea or concept is made out of the perceptions we have chosen from the ocean of sensory experiences that are bombarding our senses at any given moment. We have already discussed how the defensive anxiety of dark secrets can shape our perception. So we have our work cut out for us. As Rachel V. points out in her book *Family Secrets,* we have to "take apart a defense system, a rationale, a worldview."

Buddhist philosophers talk about putting on "beginner's mind" as an essential step in gaining awareness. To convey the idea of beginner's mind, I will retell Hans Christian Andersen's story "The Emperor's New Clothes." As you may recall, the emperor was so fond of new clothes that everything in his life centered around showing them off.

One day two con men arrived in the large town where the emperor had his palace. They claimed to be weavers of the most marvelous and extraordinarily beautiful cloth, which had the strange quality of being invisible to anyone who was stupid or unfit for office. The emperor immediately ordered some clothes made from the cloth.

The con men set up their loom and demanded fine silk and gold thread from the emperor (which they kept for themselves). As the expenses mounted, the emperor (fearing that he himself might not be able to see the clothes) sent his prime minister to inspect the work. When the prime minister, who was acknowledged to be the most virtuous and honest man in the kingdom, stepped into the room, he could not see a thing, but he was too afraid to say anything out loud. The con men said that they were not quite finished and needed more silk, gold thread, and money. The prime minister assured the emperor the clothes were worth it.

When the con men finally announced that the clothes were finished, the emperor had to look for himself. Of course, he could not see a thing, and he felt inwardly ashamed that he must be stupid and unfit to rule. But he pretended that the new clothes were magnificent and announced that he would wear them in a great ceremonial procession the next day.

And so the emperor walked stark naked in the procession under his crimson canopy. And all the townspeople who lined the roads and hung out of windows exclaimed, "What a magnificent robe!" The emperor's clothes had never been such a smashing success.

All of a sudden a little child cried out, "But he doesn't have anything on!" The child's father, realizing the honesty of the statement, cried out, "Listen to the innocent one." Soon other people whispered among themselves and repeated what the child had said. "He has nothing on!" shouted all the people at last.

The child in this story has beginner's mind. "From the mouths of babes" the truth often flows more poignantly. "A little child shall lead them," Scripture tells us. A child is not yet contaminated by the secrets and vital lies that maintain the family's balance. A child has not yet been set up to be loyal to the covert family rules of exclusion and has not yet been taught what not to see. Beginners know nothing; experts think they know everything.

All of us need to reclaim our eyes and ears if we wish to achieve freedom. I'm going to ask you to start with the assumption that nothing in your family is as it seems. Part of the role of human creativity and critical reflection is to challenge the status quo. Creators see that which is obvious but which no one else seems to see. It takes great courage to be the only one who stands up and says, "But he doesn't have anything on!" And most security-seeking, role-playing, numbed-out, culturally conditioned adults won't do it.

WAYS TO PUT ON BEGINNER'S MIND

There are a number of things you can do to help yourself create beginner's mind. In my book *Healing the Shame That Binds You,* I suggested a technique for dealing with criticism that I called *Columboing.* Named after the brilliantly awkward TV detective, played by Peter Falk, Columboing consists of playing dumb and asking lots of questions when someone criticizes you. Putting on beginner's mind is not about responding to criticism, but Columboing is a good model for how to proceed. Starting with the assumption that everything in your family could be other than what it seems, you need to ask yourself and others lots of questions. Columbo's genius lies in his attention to detail. His perception is not selective.

The Role of Memory

Before we begin, I'm going to ask you to keep an open mind even about your own memories. Memory is one of our most precious human assets, but it shares in our human imperfection. It is subject to distortions, forgetting, and lapses.

It is perfectly normal to have only very scanty memories from the first seven years of your life. Later memories from childhood are often blurred and fragmented. And even if you do have clear memories, *your initial perceptions may have been quite distorted.* As a child, at least prior to age seven, you thought in a way that is best described as emotional and magical. Thinking emotionally means confusing emotion with fact. Thinking magically means projecting your own subjective experience onto everything, so that the line between imagination and reality is still unclear.

As a child, your perceptions, emotions, and reasoning may have been discounted. The discounting of experience is a common practice by parents who have had their own experience discounted. Children often vividly see or hear what is going on. Mom and Dad are loudly fighting in their bedroom—the child becomes frightened and ventures in to see what is the matter. He is told to go back to bed, that *nothing* is going on! When this happens, a child stops trusting his own senses.

Discounting also extends to feelings, needs, desires, and thoughts, which lead to a state I described in my book *Creating Love* as *mystification.*

A mystified person is not present in their own experience. Their false defensive self has taken over and is totally absorbed in the details of behaving in the guarded ways that once brought love and security. This defensive living distorts their memory of the past.

Your memory can also become biased by your current concerns and passions. It is possible to manipulate memory to fit whatever you need to verify.

If you're a person who loves to please other people, you may even try to remember things just to please me and satisfy the thesis of my book. Let me assure you unequivocally that I have no need for you to remember dark family secrets. I would much prefer that you uncover long-forgotten memories of a pleasant kind: a joyous family outing, a special birthday party, the day your dad read you a story or your mom rocked you to sleep.

As I mentioned the phrase "long-forgotten memories of a pleasant kind," you may have *actually remembered* a long-forgotten pleasant experience! Words are powerfully suggestive and persuasive, and speech alone can have a hypnotic effect. As someone speaks to us, we go to our long-term memory of sensory experience to make some meaning out of what they are saying. One major problem with memory is that it can be contaminated by suggestibility. All of us are vulnerable to the persuasion of a book because we tend to overvalue books and give enormous authority to authors. I think we like to make people authorities because we so desperately want clear and distinct answers to our questions. And no questions are more important than questions about love, marriage, family, and children.

The issues of false memory and repressed memory have recently become the focus of heated debates, professional confusion, and even lawsuits. I discuss this controversy in the Appendix. For now, your understanding that not every memory should be taken at face value will help you be more responsible in Columboing.

The exercises I will offer you as aids for creating beginner's mind are not foolproof ways to recover memories. They may nudge your process of recollection, but they may also result in fictions. I encourage you to be cautious and to pay attention to the *feelings* that come with recollections. Strong feelings about something you have remembered are often a signal that you need to delve deeper. The feeling accompanying a memory is often (not always) more important than the factual data recalled. And sometimes the feeling is about some other unconscious matter.

Imagining "What If"

Your imagination can be a powerful tool in developing beginner's mind. For example, in Chapters 7 and 8, I'll ask you to think of five things your dad or mom would never do, and then imagine them doing these things.

See if anything clicks when you do that. Remember that when someone is covering up a secret, they tend to go to extremes to be sure they are hiding it well. If I must be sure no one knows about my private sexual behavior or my affairs, I might present an image of myself as just the opposite—prudish or uninterested in sex.

What if your puritanical father or mother were actually highly sexual? If nothing clicks, move on and let that go.

I remember a woman who came to me for counseling. She was dressed in the most provocative way you can imagine: a tight-knit miniskirt and almost-see-through blouse over large buttocks and bulging breasts. She told me she was having trouble with her Bible study! She asked me if I believed in the Second Coming, a reference to the promise of Christ to return again after His death and resurrection. I humbly admit that I was not thinking of anything biblical when she asked this question.

It turned out that this woman was completely split sexually. While she was avidly involved in biblical study, she was also the mistress of a man who was embezzling money from his firm. She was later indicted as an accomplice to his crimes and sent to prison.

The darker the secrets a family harbors, the more likely they will resort to a stratagem like the one R. D. Laing called "The Game of Happy Family." This game is constituted by rules like "If you can't say anything nice, don't say anything at all," where Mother and Father reward only smiles and obedient conformity. The image of normalcy is created to distract the outside world from what is happening.

There is evidence that a high incidence of incest families are involved in strict religious practices, especially those that isolate them from the rest of society. Daniel Goleman notes that "it is well known in the literature that incest families often seem *too* happy."

Here are some other "what if" questions—all drawn from true examples. What if your anti-Semitic stepfather actually came from a Jewish family? What if your white supremacist grandfather was partially black? What if the man you called Uncle Joe was actually your father? What if your moralistic mother was having an affair with your best friend's father next door?

No matter how someone's image in the family appears, use beginner's mind to challenge your familiar way of viewing it!

The more *extreme* that image or role is, the more I would question it. Toxic shame manifests itself in the polarizations of either shameless inhuman perfectionism and moral righteousness or shameless dehumanized promiscuity and failure. Extremes are a red flag for the cover-up of dark secrets.

Interviewing Relatives and Friends

Detective work involves asking lots of questions. I have found that older relatives like the attention of being interviewed. Often great-aunts and -uncles or grandparents have information that no one has ever asked them about because of the "no talk" rule in the family or because of the way the family stories and myths have been structured. Wait for a time when the conversation is pleasant and casual to ask your questions. Overt detective work usually meets with lots of resistance. Each relative carries a different view of the family story, and you need as many perspectives as possible.

Siblings can be a gold mine in deciphering family secrets. As my brother and sister and I have shared our awareness in recovery, we have spoken about many things that I either did not remember or that have given me a whole new perspective about certain family matters. Our siblings are the inheritors of the same multigenerational family legacy but with a different view of the story.

Don't overlook people outside the immediate family. Columbo's great skill includes questioning those whom no one else seems interested in or who seem to be irrelevant to the case. He also looks for trivial and seemingly unrelated details. Your grandparents and parents may have had friends or business acquaintances that can give you some clue about a dark secret. Question those who seem to be out of the question. Look at details you've never looked at before.

Decoding Family Myths and Stories

Family stories are often told and retold until they become like polished stones. They are part of the family folklore and need to be challenged. Family stories form the family mythology. They are often distractions aimed (consciously or unconsciously) at focusing your perception on something that covers up the secrets. That often-told story about your grandfather's standing up in church to challenge the minister may have been an act of drunken defiance rather than an assertive questioning of dogma. Your grandmother's dizzy spells may have been more about pill addiction than about the malaria she had as a child. Your dad's business trips and his heroic work habits to support the family may have been about his long-standing girlfriend in another city.

Ask yourself, too, who appears most often in the family stories. In what other ways did they dominate the family? And who is missing? Sometimes one entire side of the family is a blank, while the other is represented by vivid events and characters. You need to know what is behind that silence.

Mining the Family Photo Album

If I asked you what happened and how you felt when you were eight years old, you might draw a blank. But if I showed you some photographs of yourself and your family—at your eighth birthday party, for instance—you would probably start to remember bits and pieces, and then more and more.

Any family photos you have access to can be a mine of information and memory triggers. Who is pictured most often? Is anyone missing? What do the people's expressions and body language tell you about their relationships? Where was that backyard or summer cottage you were in? If most of the pictures show a carefully posed, "perfect" family, can you recall how you were feeling behind your smile? What else was going on?

TOOLS FOR REMEMBERING

There are several other tools that can help you remember, get you in touch with your feelings, and stimulate your insight. I will outline the main techniques here, and then suggest specific exercise topics in the remaining chapters of Part Two.

If you are working with a therapist and this work appeals to you, talk it over with your therapist. Be sure that these exercises are consistent with what you are doing in therapy. In many cases it may be an added benefit to the work you are already doing, and this work can be integrated into your therapeutic process.

Writing

More than any other technique I know of, writing has been clinically proven to help us clarify our feelings and thoughts. Writing involves all our senses. It is a physical behavior. When you hold a writing instrument in your hand, it is connected to your entire body, which holds the record of your senses.

When writing, it is important to record as much detail as possible. Detail gets you into sensory-based experience—what you saw, heard, tasted, touched, smelled. It also evokes feeling. In the next three chapters, I will ask you to write out scenes from your past, like your "best day" and "worst day" with your grandfather, grandmother, father, mother. Writing about these scenes with as much sensory-based detail as possible helps you reexperience them; and as you reexperience your childhood feelings, you bring your new adult experience and awareness to that scene.

Writing about painful scenes is also an accepted way to help heal traumatic memories. Carolyn Foster, in *The Family Patterns Workbook*, writes:

> As you bring the memory back through writing you will be better equipped to heal it of some of its sting. Though bringing back the details may be hard, you get the experience out of your body and onto the paper and that eases the burden.

Spontaneous Writing

Another way of writing, especially when you feel stuck in a narrowly focused perspective of a family member, is *spontaneous* writing.

Take a ten-minute time space, and write anything related to your family or to the member of your family you have chosen to focus on. Let your mind go wherever it needs to go, writing whatever comes to it.

Associative Clustering

This is a brainstorming technique that was pioneered by Gabriele Rico in her book *Writing the Natural Way*. It is designed to stimulate your intuition and generate new ideas about a subject. To use this technique, you pick a topic—say, "sadness in my family"—that you are trying to make more conscious. You turn the phrase into one word—*sadness*—put it in the center of a blank sheet of paper, and circle it.

This becomes the nucleus. You link your first association to it with a connecting line. You can take that association and branch out to other associations. When each new idea is exhausted, you return to your nucleus word and branch out in a different direction. Each branch from the nucleus becomes a work sketch that adds some substance to the original word.

When I say "sadness" in relation to my grandfather, I think of his rigidity. Then I think of his "being in a rut" with very "limited knowledge" and his being "biased and bigoted." I would draw it like this:

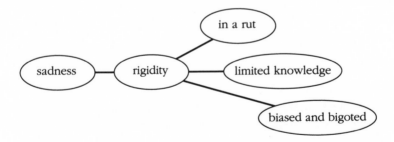

I feel sadness that his life was stifled by his rigidity.

I would also use associative clusters to focus on wonderful memories about someone from the past. If I wrote about good times with my grandfather, it would look like this:

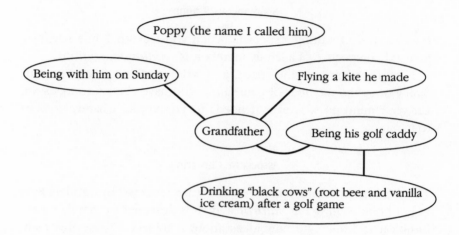

Sentence Completions

Completing unfinished sentences is a way to tap your deep unconscious. For example, you might write:

I am angry because my dad _____ .

You put down the first word or phrase that comes to mind. In the next three chapters, I will suggest some other techniques that may help in making unconscious secrets conscious. They may also help you make clear the significance of existing memories.

Lists

Writing out lists can be a useful way of triggering facts about your family. For example:

- My father's favorite sayings were:
- My father's favorite amusements were:
- The things that annoyed my mother most were:
- The family members I feel most comfortable with are:

Dialogues

Dialogues with ancestors can produce very interesting and unexpected responses. You can write dialogues between your ancestors, your mom and dad, your siblings, or a parent and yourself. You can also write dialogues with different parts of yourself. In one exercise I will ask the part of you that is blind to a secret to dialogue with the part of you that knows it.

I will also ask you to dialogue with yourself as a child. I will suggest that you write to the child part of you (your inner child) with your dominant hand and answer as the child with your nondominant hand. Writing with the nondominant hand feels like writing did when we were still struggling to learn. It can stimulate deep awareness from childhood.

Visualizations and Drawings

Dialogue can also be done through mental imagery. You can close your eyes and imagine yourself talking to your deceased grandfather or any other relative. You can imagine talking to your unconscious self. We will expand on this in Chapters 7 and 8.

I'll also ask you to draw your image of the relationships between the members of your family. You might draw a picture of your family as you remember it in your childhood. You can even be more specific and draw a picture of your family at dinnertime. Sometimes drawing a detailed floor plan of a house or houses that were significant to you can bring back specific memories.

Drawing a three- or four-generational family map, or genogram, will give you the most help in discovering family secrets. I will introduce this technique in Chapter 5. The family map is a structured technique used by family therapists to see a person's symptomatic behavior in a broader frame of reference. It will help you see your family's dark secrets in a less blaming way. It will draw out more knowledge of your family than you ever knew you had.

Working with a Group

You can do all the exercises in this book alone or with another person, but the most useful way to do them is with a small group of three to eight persons.

The group can offer you four kinds of feedback:

- Helping to clarify a memory
- Checking the congruity of a memory

- Validating the feelings associated with a memory
- Offering empathic feelings in response to a shared memory

Helping to Clarify a Memory

Members of your group can help enrich or flesh out your memory. They can do this by asking you questions about the memory. Group members' questions should be gentle rather than grueling. Suppose I'm writing about my childhood, and I start remembering being shamed for wanting to sleep with a teddy bear. I remember hiding the teddy bear and sneaking it out at night.

When I share this with my small group, someone might ask, "How specifically do you know you were shamed for wanting to sleep with your teddy bear?" Asking someone "how specifically" helps them elicit sensory-based information. Sensory-based information is the highest-quality information.

I would answer by saying, "I can vividly remember the teddy bear. It was brown, one eye was missing, and patches of hair were missing. I don't remember having the bear when we lived on Louisiana Street when I was four or five years old, or on McDuffie Street when I was six and seven years old. I remember getting scolded for wanting to sleep with the bear when I was eight years old and we were living in Harlingen, Texas. I can also remember hiding the bear when we lived at 2617 Westgate and I was nine and ten years old. I used to hide it at the bottom of my toybox, and when I went to bed, I had to quietly take all my toys out to get the bear and then carefully put them back in the morning."

There is a lot of concrete specific information in my answer.

Sensory-based information is concrete and specific. It involves visual ("I saw"), auditory ("I heard"), kinesthetic ("I felt"), gustatory ("I tasted"), olfactory ("I smelled") data. It also involves time (dates) and space (places).

My memory associated with the teddy bear has a lot of validity because it is supported by many concrete specific details.

Checking the Congruity of a Memory

Group members are not there to judge whether the memory is true or false, but they can give feedback about the congruity or incongruity of your sharing. *Congruity* refers to the match between what you say and how you say it. Saying, "It doesn't bother me that my lover left me," with your voice cracking is incongruent. Your words and feelings simply don't match. I pointed out how the feelings that come with retrieved memories are significant. It is also significant when someone is reporting something very painful and sad with no emotions at all.

Group members can help you in your discovery process by giving you feedback about congruity and incongruity. If they say, "You spoke about how your brother hurt you, but you spoke quickly and had a smile on your face. You seemed to feel nothing," you may begin to be aware of the secret pain you are keeping from yourself.

Validating the Feelings Associated with a Memory

Group members help you by giving sensory-based feedback about your feelings. After you've shared a memory, a member might say: "I saw your lips trembling. I heard your voice rising. You hunched your shoulders, lowered your head, and clenched your hands. You sort of looked like a child. It was clear to me how afraid and sad you were and how painful that experience was for you." By validating the experience, group members help the person own it. By owning it, the person can internalize it rather than reject it or listen to the internal voices that shame him for being vulnerable and weak. The internal voices were originally the parental voices. When our parents wouldn't accept their vulnerability, they projected that onto us and rejected our vulnerability. Validation helps us to be present in our own experience. It allows us to accept the previously rejected and secret parts of ourselves.

Offering Empathic Feelings in Response to a Shared Memory

Group members can offer empathic feelings to the person who is sharing. In order to do this, they simply reflect their own feeling response (not their thoughts) during the time the person was speaking. This form of feedback is used best when a person is sharing a painful scene.

During painful or traumatic experiences, our brains use defenses to block out the pain. Consequently we do not feel the feelings that are appropriately triggered by the trauma.

These feelings smolder in the secret recesses of our unconscious. They often come out in very inappropriate ways called *overreactions.* Since we are out of touch with the feelings, we can't express them and allow them to dissipate. Having a group of people give you accurate empathy when you read or tell them a painful traumatic scene can help you own and reconnect with your own feelings. As you feel your own feelings, you can discharge them and respond more appropriately to what is happening to you.

SOME FAREWELL WORDS BEFORE YOUR JOURNEY

Before going any farther, I want to underscore the human tendency to make relative matters into absolutes, to make parts into wholes. Finding dark family secrets is not a way to salvation. I have often been guilty of salvational thinking myself, and I see carloads of books and TV infomercials that promise salvation in one form or another. The message is, "If you just get this book or set of tapes, you'll be rich, be happy, have hair, or a perfect golf swing!"

Finding dark family secrets will not cure all your problems or make you successful, happy, and free. It certainly won't do anything for your golf swing.

Remember also that searching for dark family secrets may not be what you need to do *now*. You may need to get your addiction under control or do something about your marital problems or deal with your teenager's acting out first. Follow your own impulses and intuition. The older I get, the more I'm attracted to the anonymous aphorism that says, "No one can give you better advice than yourself."

If you discover some troublesome information about your family and decide to leave things just as they are, that's also your choice. I believe that the most damaging secrets need to be dealt with. (In Chapter 10, I will identify these as first- and second-degree secrets.) But I also believe, with the great therapist Milton Erickson, that the unconscious mind knows a lot more than the conscious mind and that you may have good reason not to do what I suggest in Chapter 10. Your unconscious mind is also very wise. You will retain the information in this book for a long time. If this is not the time to use it, your unconscious will let you know when and if another time is better.

Finally be aware that by doing the work in this section, you do *run some risks*. You may discover something that is very upsetting to you or something that would upset the family status quo. If you have repressed memories of traumatic abuse, the material that follows may stir them up. If that is the case, you will need a competent mental health professional to work with you. If you are seeing a therapist now, be sure to get their permission before doing the work that follows.

I can honestly say that you run a risk in not knowing about the depths of your family. For me, the risk is greater in not knowing than in knowing. In cases of first- and second-degree secrets, there is a risk in disclosing them. But to do nothing is also to take a risk.

CHAPTER 5

DRAWING YOUR FAMILY MAP
The Genogram as Rosetta Stone

The past is the present, isn't it? It's the future too. We all
try to lie out of that, but life won't let us.
EUGENE O'NEILL, *Long Day's Journey Into Night*

Those who cannot remember the past are condemned
to repeat it.

GEORGE SANTAYANA

If you have ever been lost in a shopping mall, you know there are
maps posted in strategic places that say, "You are here." They are very
helpful. We need to know where we are now. And in order to know
where we are now, we need to know where we have come from. Our
personal history has shaped our core beliefs, and we must know that
history if we want to change.

In this chapter I will guide you in drawing a three-generational family map that family systems therapists call a genogram. You will need a
family map to uncover and decipher dark family secrets.

THE GENOGRAM

The genogram evolved from the work of Dr. Murray Bowen. It has
been refined and polished by the contributions of many other family
systems therapists.

The genogram is a visual map of your family tree, but it includes more than your factual genealogy. It is used to gather information about family relationships over several generations. It offers a broad frame of reference within which symptoms and problematic behavior can be understood in a new light.

A genogram can give you a more expansive view of your place in your family history. It can offer you a new way to view yourself, as the patterns that recur across generations become visible. These repetitive patterns can help clarify unresolved emotional issues and suggest areas where toxic shame and dark secrets are being concealed. This broadened frame of reference helps to deintensify the family's narrow focus on a current problem or on a single family member who is viewed as the "problem." By looking at the multigenerational context within which they are experiencing difficulties, members can come to see their dark secrets from a less blaming and less pathological perspective.

A genogram also allows you to freeze-frame your family at any given moment in time. This is especially valuable for exploring family dynamics at a particular point in the past—for example, at the time of your birth.

The larger picture can also point out positive dynamics and hidden strengths in your family. This can be very helpful in revealing your own potential and pointing out directions for change.

The Genogram as Rosetta Stone

For me, learning how to use the genogram was like finding the Rosetta stone. The Rosetta stone is the stone slab found in Egypt in 1799 that bears parallel inscriptions in Greek and in ancient Egyptian hieroglyphics. No one had been able to understand hieroglyphics up till that time, but the Rosetta stone unlocked the secret to deciphering them.

I had no idea of the family issues that shaped my life until I learned how to draw and use a genogram. It helped me to understand myself much better. I saw immediately that my life *up to that point* was much more about my family history with its unconscious influences than it was about me. Things that I had always considered to be my own idiosyncrasies—my emptiness and recurring sense of meaninglessness, my fears about life, my limited hope of earning money, my life choices, even some troubling sexual fantasies—appeared in an entirely new light. The genogram helped me realize that many aspects of my life were part of my multigenerational history rather than decisions based on my own thoughtful choices.

When I drew my own genogram, I was surprised to find some startling similarities over the three generations. I found several early marriages due to pregnancy. I found recurring sexual dysfunction and impaired intimacy. I found cross-generational bonding that involved the spousification of a child by a parent. And I found some dark secrets that had directly impacted my life and impaired my freedom. I had been acting out things that were never talked about. The genogram was for me the primary tool in deciphering my family secrets.

As you draw your genogram, I will offer suggestions for collecting information about your family and give you guidelines for interpreting your family map based on the Bowen Theory of family systems that I outlined in Chapter 3. Bear in mind that my suggestions are based on my own interpretations of Bowen, for which I take full responsibility. In several places I have changed the terminology to help the ordinary reader who is unfamiliar with clinical language. Changing carefully thought-out designations runs the risk of losing the precise thought that the creator of a theory was trying to convey. But I feel that it is worth it, because technical terms can be a true stumbling block.

Genogram Symbols

The genogram has evolved over the last thirty-five years, and there is no unanimous agreement on its *proper* use. However, a task force of family systems researchers, led by Monica McGoldrick, has collaborated to standardize the symbols and procedures for drawing the genogram. You can find the standard format in the book *Genograms in Family Assessment* (1985) by Monica McGoldrick and Randy Gerson. I recommend it as a resource if you want to dig deeper than we can here. Some of my symbols are borrowed from McGoldrick and Gerson. Others are my own and help me to see my family history more clearly. The most important thing is to decide on one set of symbols and be consistent.

I also highly recommend a videotape produced at the Menninger Clinic in Topeka, Kansas. It is called *Constructing the Multigenerational Family Genogram: Exploring a Problem in Context.* I like the simplicity of the Menninger approach, and I will use their focus questions in what follows.

CHART 5-1

BASIC GENOGRAM STRUCTURE

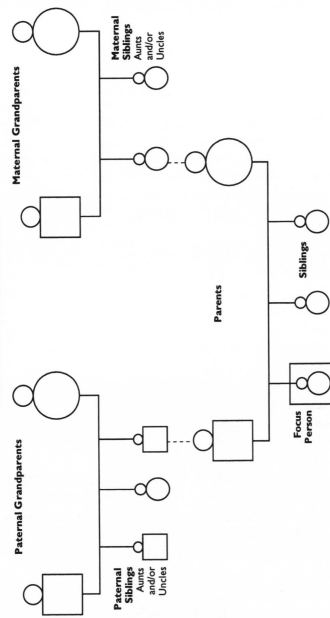

Beside each person, put their full name, date of birth, level of education, date and cause of death, and any physical and emotional difficulties. Put their current age inside the square or circle that represents them. On the horizontal line between grandparents and parents, put dates of marriage and/or divorce.

Chart 5–1 shows you the overall structure of the basic genogram. The *focus person* is the one whose genogram is being drawn. You are the focus person for your own genogram:

As you can see, both sets of grandparents are on top. Beneath them are your parents, together with their siblings, your aunts, and your uncles. In order to highlight your parents and provide more space, their figures are repeated in a third line underneath the line containing them and their siblings. You are at the bottom, set off by a box, with your siblings in their proper birth order.

On this genogram males are drawn as ☐ and females as ○.

Put each person's current age into the square or circle that stands for them. Beside each figure write in as much of the following data as possible:

- full name
- date of birth
- highest level of education
- date and cause of death
- serious physical and emotional difficulties

Next, you will begin to indicate the nature of the relationships among the various family members. If you don't know what kind of relationship two family members have, you can put a question mark in between their figures.

A good relationship is represented by three parallel lines with lines one and three entering the partner's inner space:

Lines one and three signify that the partners allow each other inside their psychic space. For example, I might tell my wife that I'm afraid about investing money. Disclosing that fear allows my wife to come into my inner emotional space. Line two in the three parallel lines means that intimate partners also have boundaries. Each has some private space that is their own safety zone. That space may be physical, sexual, emotional, intellectual, or spiritual.

Healthy relationships have flexible boundaries; the partners can let each other in but can also stand on their own. Unhealthy relationships have either enmeshed or walled boundaries.

Enmeshed boundaries are represented by figures that overlap:

A distant relationship, with walled boundaries, is represented by a dotted line:

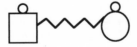

These relationship symbols are generally not applied to siblings, but this is primarily due to lack of space. Sibling relationships are quite important in discovering the health of a family's boundaries. Parent/ child coalitions often seriously disturb the sibling system in a family, causing conflict and emotional cutoff. Older siblings often abuse and traumatize younger siblings.

I know of several people whose older siblings tortured, abused, and tormented them throughout their childhood. I know of others whose emotional bond with a sibling conditioned their life. I know of still others whose sibling relationship was the healthiest and most significant relationship in their life. If your sibling relationship was significant, either positively or negatively, you can indicate this on your family map with the same symbols I've used above.

When a relationship is in conflict, I indicate it as follows:

A marriage is represented like this:

Note that the husband in a current marriage is always on the left. Put the date of the marriage on the horizontal line. To represent separations, draw a single line across the horizontal line and give the date and the letter *s* for separation.

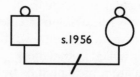

The same symbols can be used for a gay or lesbian primary relationship.

To represent a divorce, draw two lines across the horizontal line, with a *d* signifying divorce, and note the date:

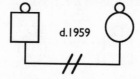

If a couple is unmarried but living together in a significant relationship, use this figure:

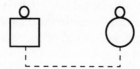

Children are shown by vertical lines extending down from the horizontal marriage line. You'll notice that I draw children smaller than the parents. Draw them according to their birth order, the oldest on the left and the youngest on the right. Place their ages within the square or circle. Also write the date of birth (and death, if it has occurred).

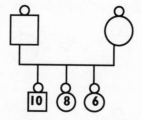

If the marriage is conflictual, I like to add a figure that represents an intimacy vacuum. It looks like this:

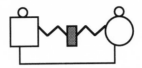

As long as it remains unresolved, such a relationship always creates some intimacy vacuum. This intimacy vacuum is important in understanding family systems. The balancing principle operating in families means that wherever a vacuum or void appears, one member will try to fill it. If Mom and Dad have an intimacy void in their marriage, one of the children will automatically move to fill it. If the child is very talented, Mom and Dad can avoid their loneliness and lack of intimacy by focusing on the child's performance. An especially handsome or beautiful child may also be the focus. If Dad is a work addict and spends no time with Mom, one of the children could take care of Mom's loneliness. A girl could play the role of Mom's Sorority Sister; a boy could play the role of Mom's Caretaker. In each of these cases, the child *triangulates* the parents' marriage. I represent marriage triangles with a child as follows:

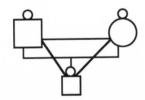

Marriage partners can also triangulate an in-law:

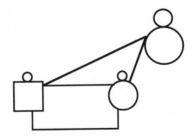

Or they can triangulate an outsider in an affair.

If there is space, you may want to show interlocking triangles:

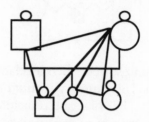

In this diagram the parents' marriage is triangulated by the first child; the other two siblings are in chronic conflict and have triangulated their mother in order to ease the tension.

When a parent uses a child to relieve the tensions in the marriage, the relationship between them is often referred to as *vertical* or *cross-generational bonding.* Cross-generational bonding may be part of a triangle. I like the circling because it is more explicit in representing the primary bond involved:

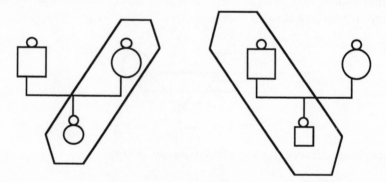

This symbol is especially useful when parents are divorced or the parent is widowed, or it is clear to everyone that the parent cares more for their child than they do for their spouse. A parent of either sex could turn to a child of either sex. In my examples, a mother is bonding with her daughter and a father with his son.

Some relationships are emotionally cut off. A mother may not talk to her daughter for years after the daughter marries someone of another faith or race. Brothers may argue over family property and never see each other again. I represent an emotional cutoff as follows:

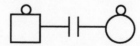

The examples here show cutoffs between two siblings and between a father and son.

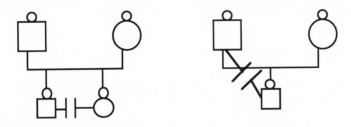

For a pregnancy use this figure:

For a spontaneous abortion use:

For an induced abortion use:

For a stillbirth use:

For fraternal twins use:

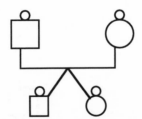

For identical twins use:

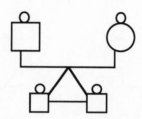

If the person is dead, I draw an *X* on their chest with their age at death:

If they committed suicide, I put an *S* on their face:

If they were murdered, I put an *M* on their face:

If the person was killed in an accident, I put an *Ac* on their face.

A man with several marriages is pictured with his previous wives on the left, with the most recent of his earlier marriages last. His current wife is on the right.

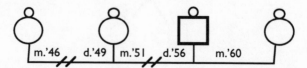

A woman with several marriages is pictured with her previous husbands on the right, with the most recent previous marriage first. Her current husband is on the left.

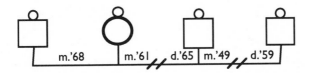

When a man and woman who have had previous marriages get married, things get very complicated. The standard solution is to place the most recent relationship in the center and put the previous spouses on each side:

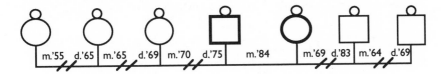

The situation gets even more complex if previous spouses have been previously married:

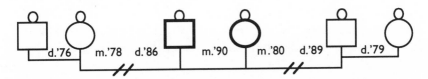

Finally, to really complicate things, we can look at blended families. Take Joe and Sue, who have each been married twice before. Each has a child from a previous marriage. They have two children from their own marriage. Relations in such blended families get very complex, and the secrets in such families become extremely complicated. I follow the usual practice of circling the members of the immediate household with a dotted line. This is valuable for representing blended families where children from previous marriages spend time in the household.

Sue's son lives with Joe and Sue and his two half-siblings, but Joe's son lives with his mother.

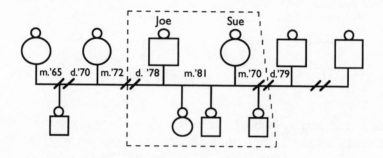

An adopted child has an *A* on their face. Biological parents are indicated by a dotted line. Give birth date and adoption date.

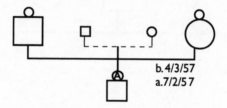

A child born out of wedlock has an *OW* written on the face. If the father is unknown, indicate him with a question mark:

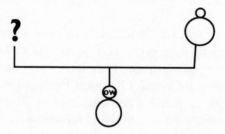

When a child is placed in a foster care institution, give birth date and placement date. Draw a dotted box around the entire figure.

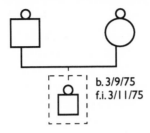

b. 3/9/75
f.i. 3/11/75

In Chapter 6 you will start drawing your own family map. I'll take you through it step-by-step, beginning with your grandparents (or your great-grandparents, if you know about them). But to put some flesh on these bones right away, let me use Beverly Sue's family, the Smiths, whom you met in Chapter 3, to illustrate some facets of genogram usage. I cut my family systems teeth on Beverly Sue's therapy, and I'm grateful to the Smiths for allowing me to use them as an example.

BEVERLY SUE'S GENOGRAM

The genogram can help you discover predisposing factors that have set you up to become a dark-secret-keeper or to be the prime subject for the projection of family secrets. It can also help you to see why you may be the most likely one in your family to act out the secrets. We can see these predisposing factors clearly in Beverly Sue's genogram.

Family therapists often look at four basic questions when they make use of the genogram. I suggest you do this with each person you focus on.

1. What is the presenting problem?

You may recall that Beverly Sue began to act in a very strange and atypical way in October 1971. She had previously been a cheery, curious little girl, seven years old, who made straight A's in school and was a high achiever in gymnastics. Now she refused to stay in school, and she refused to talk about what was bothering her with the school authorities or her parents. She was very hostile to her parents.

2. What are the facts about the three-generational family that form the context of the presenting problem?

In addition to the family dynamics I discussed in Chapter 3, here is what my therapist friend found about the Smith family in 1971. Beverly Sue's dad, Sidney Smith, is very depressed over his father's terminal illness. He is quite withdrawn and noncommunicative. If you look at Chart 5–2, you can see that Sidney is the third child of Harold Smith, who was, prior to the onset of his cancer, a hard-driving self-made man.

Sidney's older brother, Sam, was killed by a drunk driver in a tragic car accident when he was a freshman in college. Harold, their father, has never gotten over his death. Sam had shown real interest in running the successful grocery business his father had created. He was his dad's hope for keeping the business in the family. Sidney is not interested in his dad's business. This has been a constant source of conflict, especially since Sam's death. Sidney's sister, Shirley, is happily married and does all the accounting for the grocery store. She is her mother's confidante. Sidney has been completely left out. He feels like a lost child.

Jane Eller Smith, Sidney's wife and Beverly Sue's mother, was described by Sidney as the perfect woman. Her mother, Judy Eller, brought her up in her own fire-and-brimstone Bible-based religious tradition, "where women know their place." Jane was her mom's favorite child. Jane's mom had a stroke in 1962 and died of complications in 1963. Jane's dad is a good honest man who still teaches high school chemistry. He is church-going, but not a fanatic like his wife. Always somber, he's become clearly depressed since his wife's death. Jane's older sister, Doris, is the rebel in the family. Both her mother and father cut her off emotionally when she ran off and got married at sixteen. Divorced three years later, she remarried and divorced again and is now living with a man her father despises. She bore his child, Pat, in 1969. Betsy, the third daughter, is five years younger than Jane and is deeply enmeshed with her father. She is very depressed. She is in a graduate nursing program, lives at home, and has hardly ever dated.

Jane had a secret affair about two years after she married Sidney. This affair took place shortly after her mother's stroke. Jane says that she does not know why she had an affair. It was a guy at church, and it just happened! She has terrible guilt feelings over it and has tried to

CHART 5-2

THE SMITH FAMILY IN 1971

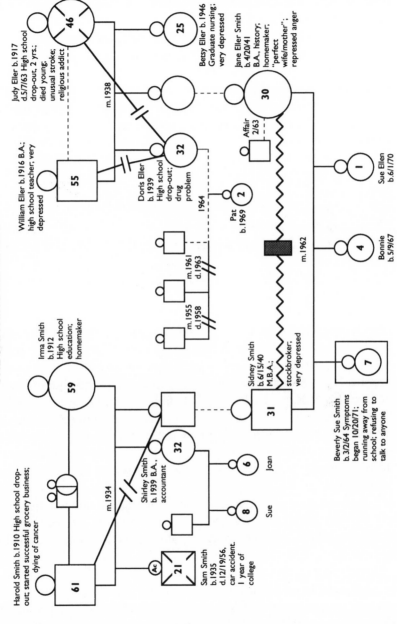

make it up by being a perfect wife to Sidney and a perfect mother to her daughters. Her daughters are her pride and joy. She is specially bonded to Bonnie, her second daughter, who was premature and almost died at birth.

From this information we can see Beverly Sue's behavior in a larger context. We can ask to what extent Beverly Sue is caught up in the chronic unresolved anxiety and emotional secrets that this family maintains. In addition to what I've said about Beverly Sue taking the heat off her parents' marriage, we cannot help but wonder whether Beverly Sue's hostility is a metaphor for the unexpressed anger in this whole family system.

3. What was the emotional climate when the subject of the genogram was born?

Knowing this will help us to see if the focus person is likely to become symptomatic of the family secrets at stressful periods in the family's life.

In Chart 5–3 I have freeze-framed the moment in this family's history when Beverly Sue was born.

At the time of her birth on March 2, 1964, Beverly Sue's mother, Jane, is carrying the grief over her mother's untimely death a year ago. She had an affair in February 1963, just a little over a year before Beverly Sue's birth. Beverly Sue's grandfather Harold is still in deep grief over his favorite son's untimely death fifteen years ago. Sidney has just finished his M.B.A. and has told his father he will not take over the family grocery store. His father is furious and cuts him off emotionally. Beverly Sue's Aunt Doris, the family rebel, has just been through her second divorce and has started living with the man her father bitterly dislikes. Beverly Sue's maternal grandfather is also in deep grief over his wife's death. We can suppose that Jane's grief over her own mother's death triggered feelings of love/hate ambiguity. She was her mother's special child and was set up to take care of her mother's emptiness. She was also emotionally abused by her mother's religious addiction.

Beverly Sue is born into a world of tension and unresolved conflict. It is reasonable to predict that she will be the child chosen for her parents' projection process. She is their first child—the child Jane had desperately wanted in order to please her mother, and the child who might relieve her guilt feelings over her affair. She is the child Sidney

CHART 5-3

EMOTIONAL CLIMATE AT BEVERLY SUE'S BIRTH, 1964

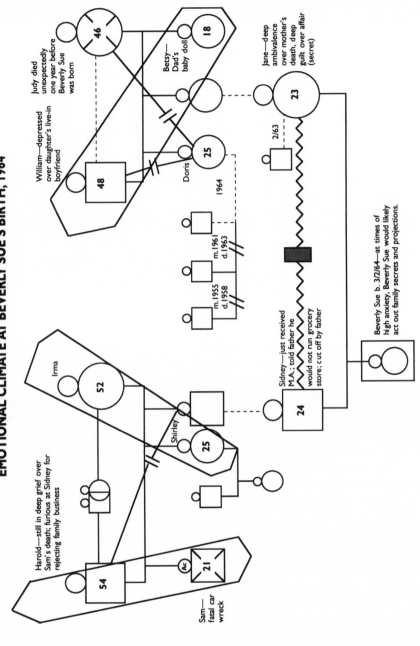

Harold—still in deep grief over Sam's death; furious at Sidney for rejecting family business

Sam—fatal car wreck

Irma

Shirley

Sidney—just received M.A.; told father he would not run grocery store; cut off by father

William—depressed over daughter's live-in boyfriend

Judy died unexpectedly one year before Beverly Sue was born

Betsy—Dad's baby doll

Doris

Jane—deep ambivalence over mother's death, deep guilt over affair (secret)

Beverly Sue b. 3/2/64—at times of high anxiety, Beverly Sue would likely act out family secrets and projections.

m.1955 d.1958

m.1961 d.1963

1964

2/63

might love and be close to as he continues to feel his father's rejection and the pain of being a disappointment to him. The emotional climate of this family would easily lead to overly intense and highly charged parent-child relationships. It is easy to see that at times of high anxiety, like the onset of Harold Smith's cancer, Beverly Sue could take on the role of scapegoat and act out the unresolved secrets her parents and the rest of the family refuse to deal with.

4. What issues arise from the subject's sibling position?

Beverly Sue clearly has some of the ordinary issues of a first child. She is intensely involved with her father, taking on his unexpressed emotional pain. Her need to take care of him frustrates her need, as the first child, to be productive and to achieve. As her parents' antagonism toward each other intensifies, they ignore Beverly Sue. This frustrates her need, as a first child, to be rewarded by her parents for doing well. In addition, as you can see in the three-generational picture in Chart 5–4, each of her parents has unresolved issues around other first-position children in the family. On the one hand, there is Uncle Sam, whose tragic death only enhances his status as the hero who would have dedicated his life to his father's business. On the other hand, there is Aunt Doris, who totally rebels against her controlling and religiously rigid mother and lifeless, depressed father. Beverly Sue may rightly be overwhelmed by the choices presented to her by the polarized examples of the people occupying her birth-order position in the three-generational family system. Her seeming 180-degree turn from cheery superachieving child to irresponsible rebel seems like an accurate acting out of the first-child polarization in this family.

In many ways this little girl carries a lot of the family's hopes and pains. It's easy to see that her parents might have believed she would bring them to greater intimacy. At an unconscious level her birth was the new life that would replace the grandmother who died shortly before her birth. Now another grandparent is about to die. This is a huge unconscious burden for one child to bear. And there can be little doubt that all of these factors predispose Beverly Sue to act out these unexpressed secrets at this particularly stressful time in her family's life.

CHART 5-4

THE SMITH FAMILY: SIBLING POSITION PROFILE

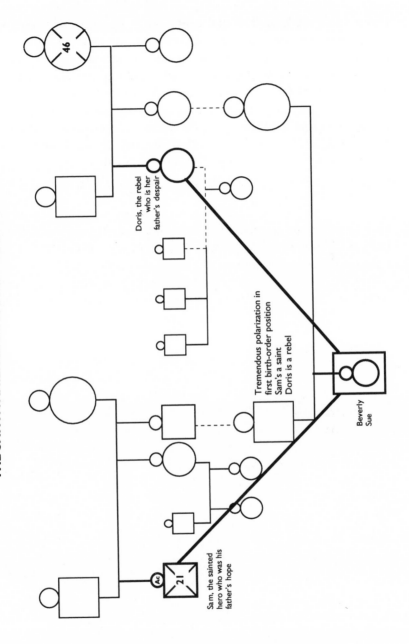

Doris, the rebel who is her father's despair

Sam, the sainted hero who was his father's hope

Tremendous polarization in first birth-order position
Sam's a saint
Doris is a rebel

Beverly Sue

Thinking Versus Reacting

I hope you already see how the genogram can give you a clearer, more objective picture of your family of origin. It forces you to think—and that helps you to get out of your family's emotional field. I have described this emotional field as a kind of trance that is composed of many hypnotic elements. I have also referred to it as group think.

When we are in our family's emotional field, we often become "no choice" reactors. Hidden emotions dictate our response to the family situation at hand; we act without thinking. Beverly Sue knows the family secrets, without knowing that she knows them. As a child with fragile boundaries, she can be easily overrun by the family's secret emotions.

Through the genogram Beverly Sue's behavior, which would once have been looked upon as the antics of a misbehaving and self-willed little girl, can now be seen as a dynamic metaphor for three generations of unresolved emotions.

This may help you to reframe your own idiosyncratic and secretive behavior, placing it in a larger context devoid of judgment and blame.

CHAPTER 6

YOUR ANCESTORS' DARK SECRETS

Neither of my grandparents ever got around to the fundamental business of raising their only child. There was something . . . unreconcilable about my father's quarrel with the world. His children had been a sanctioned debacle of neglect and my grandparents were the pale, unindictable executors of my father's violations against his own children.

PAT CONROY, *The Prince of Tides*

Let's begin our soul-searching journey by looking at your ancestors. I will be giving you a checklist to help guide you in making your family map. I will also be giving you illustrations from a family I'll call the Jeders.

The Jeder family is a composite: A small portion of their history is autobiographical. The rest of the family history is taken from my clinical readings, from accounts by other therapists, from work done at The John Bradshaw Treatment Center at Ingleside Hospital, and from people I have counseled. While the details are factual, anything that might identify actual persons has been changed. My purpose in creating this family, which has a wide range of family dynamics, is to give you an example that might trigger an insight relevant to your family or offer you a clue for your investigations.

A man named James Jeder is my focus person. We will begin by looking at James's great-grandparents, his paternal and maternal grandparents, and his great-aunts and -uncles. As I go through James Jeder's genogram, I will also show you how to make your own.

FOCUS PERSON

You are obviously the focus person for your own family map. The first step is to write out a brief synopsis of your life, including your major problem(s), if any, your relational patterns, your idiosyncrasies, and your own dark secrets. If you like, follow the model of James Jeder's story below.

James Jeder is fifty-four years old. He is a successful English professor at a major university. He has edited an anthology of English poetry and written two books of original poetry.

He has been divorced and remarried and has one son from his first marriage and a daughter from his second. James is a binge drinker and has had many off-and-on bouts with alcohol. He is sexually compulsive and has had affairs during both marriages. He has a secret garage cabinet full of pornography. Several times a year he takes long weekend holidays to an ocean retreat where he views pornographic movies and books and engages in self-sex for hours at a time.

James has attempted to stop drinking on various occasions. His current abstinence has lasted eight months. His affairs created severe problems in his first marriage, and his present wife, Karen, is suspicious of him. This has caused lots of tension, and their sex life has degenerated into a dutiful monthly ritual. James's daughter, Hannah, is the apple of his eye. He gives her the majority of his spare time, often neglecting his wife. James's adult son, Jack, is angry at him and has emotionally cut him off, seeing him occasionally at Christmas.

James's solitary self-sex is his major dark secret. He has never shared it with anyone but his previous therapist. As James has aged, he's felt more and more toxic shame and hopelessness over this compulsive habit. He came to see me after doing ten years of classic psychoanalysis.

James had amassed a lot of information about himself and his family in his ten years of analysis. The genogram labeled Chart 6–1 represents a four-generational picture of James Jeder's family in outline only. We will fill in the details for each generation as we go along.

For your own genogram, chart at least three generations if you can. I will be using a few bits of information from the Jeder family concerning great-grandparents. If you know almost nothing of your great-grandparents, that's okay, but write out whatever you know. For example: Were they immigrants? What was their ethnic and religious background? Are there any family stories about them?

CHART 6-1

FOUR-GENERATIONAL FAMILY MAP OF JAMES JEDER

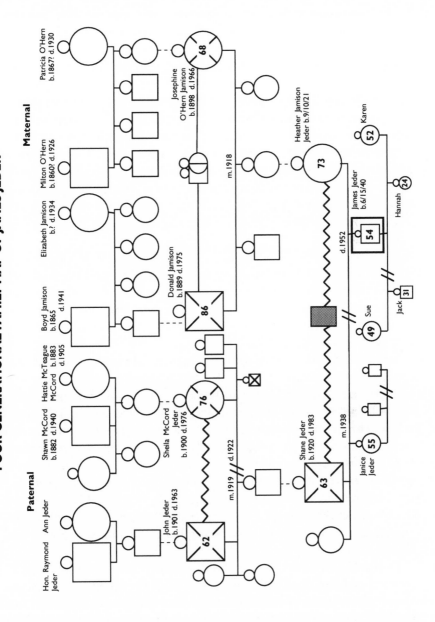

PATERNAL GREAT-GRANDPARENTS

James knows very little about his paternal great-grandparents. What he knows comes from his mother and one great-aunt, Maureen. (See Chart 6–2.)

His mother told him that his grandfather on his father's side, John Jeder, was the only son of the Honorable Raymond Jeder, who had been a distinguished judge in South Carolina. James knows for sure that his grandfather was a member of the Church of England and was highly educated and "refined." He assumes that his paternal great-grandparents were also well-to-do and highly educated. His great-grandfather had to have studied law in order to be a judge. No family stories had come down about Judge Jeder's wife, although it is believed her name was Ann.

Mismatch

It seems clear that John Jeder, James's grandfather, and his family felt that he had made a terrible mistake getting involved with a woman like Sheila McCord, James's grandmother, who was uneducated and far beneath his class. As you will see, John later tried to disavow his actions by disowning his own son, Shane.

The fiery red-headed Irishwoman named Sheila McCord was the offspring of Shawn McCord and Hattie McTeague, born within a year of their elopement in their late teens. Both Shawn and Hattie were alcoholic. When Sheila was five years old, she awakened to her mother's screams as she burned to death in her bedroom. Her mother had passed out drunk with a cigarette in her hand. Sheila was so traumatized by this event that she seems to have rarely spoken about it. Sheila was sent to live with her father's two unmarried sisters. Shawn sobered up, lived respectfully, and remarried, but he would not let Sheila live with him, as his new wife disliked her. He never met Sheila's son, Shane, and he died two months before his great-grandson, James, was born.

Shawn McCord had another child, Maureen, two years after he remarried. Maureen had no contact with Sheila as a child. She secretly connected with her when she was in her early teens. Sheila did not keep up the relationship, but James sought Maureen out later in his life while doing his psychoanalysis.

CHART 6–2

PATERNAL GREAT-GRANDPARENTS

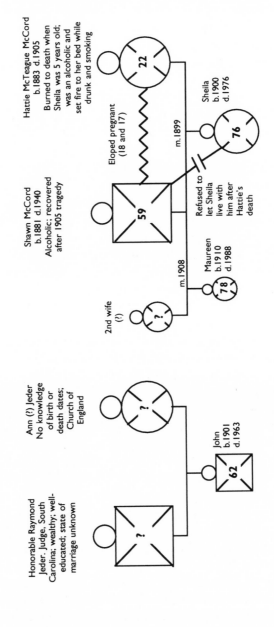

Jeder

Honorable Raymond Jeder, Judge, South Carolina; wealthy; well-educated; state of marriage unknown

Ann (?) Jeder
No knowledge of birth or death dates; Church of England

John
b.1901
d.1963

McCord

Shawn McCord
b.1881 d.1940
Alcoholic; recovered after 1905 tragedy

Hattie McTeague McCord
b.1883 d.1905
Burned to death when Sheila was 5 years old; was an alcoholic and set fire to her bed while drunk and smoking

Eloped pregnant (18 and 17)

m.1899

Refused to let Sheila live with him after Hattie's death

Sheila
b.1900
d.1976

2nd wife (?)

m.1908

Maureen
b.1910
d.1988

MATERNAL GREAT-GRANDPARENTS

James discovered a fair amount about his maternal great-grandparents. (See Chart 6–3.) He also discovered that the most important person in the family, from the point of view of dark secrets, was the person he had never heard anyone talk about: his grandmother's father, Milton O'Hern.

The One Person No One Talked About

James has no recollection of ever hearing his grandmother mention her father's name. It never occurred to him as a child that that was a bit unusual. Yet Josephine O'Hern Jamison was a devout woman who often spoke of the virtue of obedience and of the sacred duty a child had to honor their mother and father!

It is not natural for there to be such an obvious lacuna in a family story. I have often found that the family member that "no one talked about" was the major source of dark family secrets. Watch for such "missing persons" in your own history.

James learned about Milton O'Hern quite accidentally during a confrontation with his mother, Heather. At first she minimized her grandfather's actions, calling him a "character" because he drilled holes in the bathroom wall so that he could spy on the women in the family! Later she revealed that Milton O'Hern had been a rageful and sometimes violent alcoholic. He violated two granddaughters—James Jeder's mother, Heather, and her sister, James's Aunt Virginia. He was physically abusive to his three sons, who grew up to be violent men themselves. The middle son, George, became a severe alcoholic. There is some probability that both Milton and his oldest son Jimmy sexually violated Josephine.

The Saint

Heather told James that his maternal great-grandmother, Patricia O'Hern, was a "saintly" woman who dutifully put up with her husband. Patricia was a devout Irish Catholic who felt that sex was her duty and that a woman's lot is to cater to her husband's every whim. She had a "special" relationship with her only daughter, Josephine. They were devoted to each other. But Patricia was not able to protect

CHART 6-3

MATERNAL GREAT-GRANDPARENTS

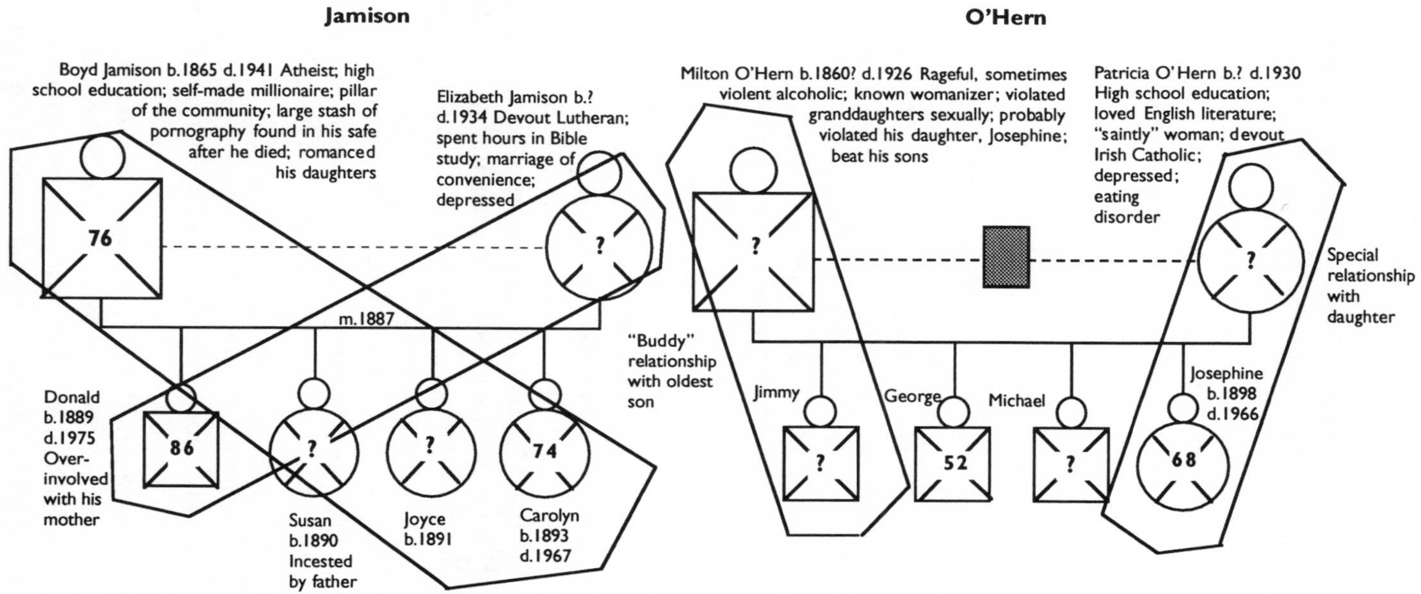

Jamison

O'Hern

Boyd Jamison b.1865 d.1941 Atheist; high school education; self-made millionaire; pillar of the community; large stash of pornography found in his safe after he died; romanced his daughters

Elizabeth Jamison b.? d.1934 Devout Lutheran; spent hours in Bible study; marriage of convenience; depressed

Milton O'Hern b.1860? d.1926 Rageful, sometimes violent alcoholic; known womanizer; violated granddaughters sexually; probably violated his daughter, Josephine; beat his sons

Patricia O'Hern b.? d.1930 High school education; loved English literature; "saintly" woman; devout Irish Catholic; depressed; eating disorder

Special relationship with daughter

Josephine b.1898 d.1966

68

?

Michael

George

52

?

Jimmy

?

"Buddy" relationship with oldest son

m.1887

?

74

Carolyn b.1893 d.1967

Joyce b.1891

?

Susan b.1890 Incested by father

?

Donald b.1889 d.1975 Over-involved with his mother

86

76

Josephine from her three brothers, who teased, tormented, and physically abused her. Milton allowed his sons to run wild, except when they crossed him.

Patricia had a great love for English literature and passed this on to Josephine and Heather. In his childhood, James loved to sit and listen as his grandmother and mother read stories to him. His love of English literature and poetry came from these two women.

Pillars of the Community

James's great-grandparents on his maternal grandfather's side were Boyd and Elizabeth Jamison.

Boyd was a self-made millionaire who was a "pillar of the community," giving generously of his time and money. When the county opened an airport shortly before he died, it was named after him. He claimed to be an atheist. He married Elizabeth Heatherly, a devout Lutheran who spent hours in Bible study and was shut down sexually—although James's grandmother Josephine later claimed that something was "funny" about her husband Donald Jamison's relationship with his mother. She greatly resented her mother-in-law's involvement with Donald and made no bones about it. The only son, Donald had three younger sisters. Boyd was overly involved with his daughters. He romanticized his relationship with them, and Donald often commented that his father was more married to his sisters—especially Susan—than to his mother. In later years it was clear that Boyd and Elizabeth lived a marriage of convenience, and James came to believe that Boyd had incested Susan.

Boyd demanded that the family look good, and they put on a public image as a big happy family. When Boyd died, Donald found a large collection of pornographic books and films in his father's safe.

Although many people cannot trace their great-grandparents, you can see that the more information you have, the better you can grasp your family secrets. James Jeder has a drinking problem and a sexual problem. *Both of these problems were present in his great-grandparents.* One great-grandmother died from her alcoholism, and her husband was also an alcoholic. Another great-grandfather had a stash of pornographic books and films. James's biggest secret is his self-sex with pornography.

GATHERING INFORMATION

Once you have sketched in the basic relationships in your family, take a look at the checklist that follows and do any of the exercises that strike your fancy. They will help you put on beginner's mind. If you already know a lot about your ancestors, these exercises may not be necessary. This basic checklist can also be used to organize information about your parents.

Sometimes gathering information is as easy as asking your grandmother or grandfather, or someone else who might know, about things you have wondered about. Most families that get frozen with dysfunctional patterns develop "no talk" rules. Once these rules are in operation, a "don't ask" rule is also set in motion. Most of us never *thought* of asking for certain information as children. We also got the message "not to ask" about other things. Sometimes the passage of time and changing social attitudes makes old secrets much easier to discuss. Sometimes you will just have to look for hints and clues.

Checklist of Questions for Ancestors

Birth and Upbringing

When were your grandparents born? This knowledge may be easily attained, or you may have to do some work looking up old records. It is also important to note anything unusual about your grandparents' birth. Were their parents married pregnant?

What were the social circumstances surrounding their birth? Were they rich, poor, middle class? What historical circumstances (such as wars, depressions, immigration, racial discrimination) may have had a significant impact on their lives? Were there any traumas in their childhood—a long sickness, hospitalization, a terrible accident, the death of a parent or sibling, the murder or suicide of a relative? What level of education did they reach? This is important because secrets often develop around marriages that cross over class lines, as in the case of John Jeder, James's paternal grandfather.

How were your grandparents raised? Strictly? Permissively? Who raised them? How did they raise your parents?

Anniversaries

Anniversaries are important in looking at a family map. Hot issues from the past are triggered on anniversary dates.

For no apparent reason my client Mildred would go into a deep depression every year around the middle of October. Then I learned that her mother had died very suddenly in early October when Mildred was four years old. She had never grieved her mother's death, and her depression was a reenactment of the unresolved grief.

Anniversary reactions may mark ungrieved family traumas, deaths, life transitions like parents' divorce, family member's institutionalization, job loss, retirement, and/or life cycle changes like children leaving home. They can be important clues to secrets that are causing personal or family dysfunction.

Marriages

Were the marriages in your ancestry strong ones? Chances are they were very distant or very enmeshed. That's the way patriarchal marriages were. The intimacy vacuum in these marriages left an emptiness. The children were often triangulated into their parents' marriages. The children may have been enmeshed into one or the other parent's "unlived life." The cross-generational bonds with parents who had unresolved sexual issues were devastating to the children in the Jeder family.

Did social pressure or religious beliefs demand early marriages due to pregnancy? In past generations, marriage when pregnant, illegitimacy, and adoption were all grounds for dark secrets. Had any of your grandparents had a child out of wedlock or by a previous marriage—perhaps a child that they secretly put up for adoption? I have had several clients who found out that they had a half-brother or -sister after one of their parents died. Some found out while their parents were still alive. They felt angry and betrayed and no longer trusted their parents. "If they could lie about my brother or sister, what else would they lie about?" they thought.

I have also counseled several people who felt that their oldest sibling was unlike the rest of the family. In the privacy of therapy, their mothers revealed that they were pregnant with someone else's child when they married. Such matters are very delicate, and I caution you to move slowly in this area.

Sexuality

Sexuality is far and away the greatest area of dark secrets. We have come out of centuries of hypocrisy and double standards concerning sex. For a long time incest and wife rape have been dark secrets.

Other areas of parental sexual misconduct such as fondling, sexual overstimulation, voyeurism, and sexual harassment, which are now often referred to as *emotional sexual abuse,* were not even considered abusive in the past. *Fondling* refers to icky kissing and touching in a sexual way. *Sexual overstimulation* results from cross-generational bonding with a parent who has unresolved sexual issues. The parent may have poor sexual boundaries and be exhibitionistic or overly romanticize their relationship with their child. *Voyeurism* results from a parent's overinterest in their child's sexual parts and/or violation of a child's sexual modesty.

If this was going on in your family, there may be certain telltale verbal clues. Statements like the following *may* indicate that a relative was sexually immodest or abusive: "He loved women and horses." "He was a philanderer." "He was a dirty old man." "Grandfather was awful about sex." "He set her up in her mother's place." "She made her son promise never to marry so that he could take care of her."

Any polarized extreme may be a red flag for big secrets. Asking what your grandmother or grandfather would *never* have done sexually may be a clue to secret sexual behavior. Asking what horrified them sexually may be a key to their repressed sexual life or fantasies. Secret sexual fantasies can be carried unconsciously by other members of the family. As you explore the dark secrets of your parents' generation, you may actually get a clearer idea of what your grandparents' dark secret may have been.

Religion

What was your grandparents' religious background? Were they true believers or hypocrites? Or were they largely indifferent, just going to church or temple because it was "the thing to do"? Children *know* this very early on. Were they rigid and controlling with religion? Were they lax personally but demanding that their children follow the faith?

Ethnicity

Your grandparents' ethnic background may be a source of pride and strength, but it may also be a factor in understanding your family's underworld. Being a foreigner, espousing a different religion from others in your community, or being of a different color from the majority, can impact the family seriously. In James Jeder's great-grandparents' time, many native-born Americans considered Irish immigrants to be an inferior race. The poor Irish family that Sheila McCord came from had repercussions down into James's generation, as we will see.

Success and Failures

In the Jeder family map there are a number of successes from the point of view of public image. One great-grandfather is a judge and another is a self-made millionaire and philanthropist. Still, there are many dark secrets in this family.

Success often covers a multitude of sins. People often do not believe that someone who is a big success could be immoral or involved in criminal behavior.

On the other hand, failure to live up to a given cultural standard of success may explain why a certain relative was so angry, depressed, or withdrawn. For example, in my parents' generation a family in which the wife had to work was often seen as deviant. Men were supposed to be the breadwinners, and a working wife was a humiliating sign of a man's failure to fully support his family.

Financial Issues

Whether we agree with it or not, financial worth is a factor of success in our culture. Many men harbor deep secret shame over their lack of financial success. Money and success can also bring envy and competition among the members of a family. I know of many families where heirs have fought over an inheritance and cut each other off emotionally.

Saints

Was grandmother or grandfather considered a saint and overly idealized? There is a good possibility that your family saints were very fine people, but only a remote possibility that they will achieve canonization by the Roman Catholic Church! When people are considered "saints," their behavior often goes unquestioned.

Saints usually get their reputation because of what they had to endure. Long-suffering has been a sure mark of sanctity.

Olive's mother had gotten pregnant with her at age sixteen and had married her father (an immature gambling addict) under immense religious pressure from her family. Her mother had a second child fourteen months after the marriage—once again, due to religious prohibitions against birth control. Olive's father left her mother six months after her brother's birth. He paid no child support and disappeared for the next ten years.

Olive remembers her mother being constantly referred to as a saint for raising her two children all alone. Olive also remembers her mother viciously shaming her. She always felt her mother hated her. Olive and her brother did everything they could to take care of their "poor mother's pain."

The fact of the matter is that Olive's mother was no saint. She was, however, bearing the burden of her own sexual exploration, the lack of information she had received about sex from her own mother, and her family's rigid beliefs about sexual morality and birth control.

Sinners, Black Sheep, and Scandals

Was one of your grandparents considered particularly bad? James's paternal grandmother, Sheila McCord Jeder, fits this bill! But as you will see, this woman carried great pain and unresolved grief. She was abandoned and rejected and was never offered an opportunity to be nurtured in her grief.

Often black sheep or "weird ones" carry very tragic dark secrets. Often they are the ones who see how dysfunctional the family has become, and they get out.

Is one or more grandparent never talked about? Remember that no one had spoken of Milton O'Hern during James's entire childhood.

Family scandals may have been carefully hushed up. Check out your grandparents' social standing in the community. Old friends or old business acquaintances may let something slip. I remember a woman who was mortified to find out that her grandmother's "summer retreats" at the family cabin shrouded affairs with locals who hung out at the town pub.

Death

Pay particular attention to deaths you know nothing about. See if you can track down information on mysterious deaths. They may be covering up suicide or other dark secrets.

OTHER SUGGESTIONS

Drawing the House

Sometimes it can help to draw a picture of your grandparents' house and imagine walking through the different rooms. Maybe there was a room you couldn't go into. If so, why not? Who slept where? One client remembered that her maternal grandfather had slept in the attic "because he snored," while her grandmother slept one floor below in an elegant bedroom.

In another instance two brothers came to me for counseling. They were in their early twenties and both had been arrested for indecent exposure. Both remembered engaging in sodomy as early as eleven years of age. Such age-inappropriate sexual behavior is frequently a sign of sexual abuse.

They had spent every summer at their grandparents' farm until they were thirteen. After drawing pictures of the house, the brothers remembered being excluded from mysterious parties down at the barn. Then one of them remembered being fondled by his grandmother. They later discovered that their grandfather had been arrested for indecent exposure.

Exploring Opposites

If you remember your grandparents, list ten phrases that describe each one of them. Then flip each one into its opposite and make as convincing a case as possible that this opposite trait describes your grandmother or grandfather. Do this with any significant relative. This can be especially useful in tracking down secrets, since what persons strive to deny or avoid may be a way to cover up their secrets. As Sam Keen has written, "The fears, forbidden possibilities, and inconceivable alternatives of one generation are passed on in unspoken form to the next."

Here are some additional questions to ask yourself or discuss with your sister or brother or aunts or uncles.

What could never be discussed around grandparents? How do you
   know this?
What horrified your grandmother?
What do you think your grandfather never did? Why?

What do you think your grandparents never did in their marriage? Why?

Sayings, Myths, and Stories

What were your paternal and maternal grandfathers' favorite sayings? Can you put together a list of their favorite sayings? Do the same with your paternal and maternal grandmothers.

Could you write out a list of their Ten Commandments?

What stories do you remember your grandmother or grandfather telling? What covert meaning might those stories have?

For example, I had a client whose grandmother told a story of how her brothers scared her so badly one Halloween night that she went into hysterics and had to be taken to the hospital. Somehow this story always seemed to be incomplete to my client. She did some digging into her grandmother's past. One brother, my client's great-uncle, was still alive, and he welcomed my client's inquiry. He revealed that his father, my client's great-grandfather, was an alcoholic and that he had violated his daughter sexually over a number of years. On one occasion she had to be taken to the hospital because of the physical damage to her vagina and the emotional trauma it caused her.

My client's grandmother believed her own Halloween story. But in fact it was what is called a *screen memory*. Often when an event is severely traumatic, the victim dissociates from the trauma. Dissociation is a defense the person uses in order to get out of their body, away from the event as it is happening. Victims often describe dissociation as a sensation of floating above the scene, watching what is going on as an uninvolved observer. A victim may develop amnesia around some or all aspects of the event. A new memory, more acceptable to the person, may then be used to replace the old memory.

Stories that seem incomplete or that leave you with some lingering doubts may be composed of screen memories. But it's imperative to check for other verification before you come to any conclusions. Several other factors corroborated my client's findings. Her grandmother was agoraphobic and had other symptoms that pointed to incest. Her own mother and three aunts admitted being violated by their mother's father. The living brother verified that his father was an offender.

When stories seem complete, ask yourself what are the *values* in these stories? Why were *these* stories chosen for telling and retelling? Are these stories moralistic—exaggerating and polarizing human life in a more-than-human way? If so, then they may be covering up toxic elements of shame in the family.

Jokes

What jokes do you remember your grandfather or grandmother telling? What was his/her favorite joke? Did they tell "dirty jokes"? If so, what was considered dirty?

One client remembered that the jokes in his family were always bathroom humor about feces or flatulence. This same client remembered being afraid to have a bowel movement for fear of someone violating his privacy. Before going to the bathroom, he would go to every member of his family and ask them not to come into the bathroom while he was using the commode. He also had masochistic fantasies of being defecated on by women. These fantasies were the only way he could become turned on sexually. He came to realize that his grandmother and mother both hated men. He later learned that his grandmother and mother had both been violated sexually by the same man, a great-uncle. Neither had worked through the sexualized rage of their abuse. My client believed they had violated him anally as a toddler. His mother openly admitted to hating to change his diapers and to pushing his face into his soiled diapers to teach him to use the potty! The pattern of jokes revealed some dark secrets in this family.

Writing Scenes

Writing is an important way to get at feelings and painful past truths. Choose five scenes with your paternal grandparents, either singly or together, that were significant to you, and write them out in as much detail as possible. Do you get any new awareness as you write? Do the same with your maternal grandparents.

Wrap-Up Exercise

After you have worked on these exercises for a while, take stock of your reactions:

Did you have any strong physical reaction to the exercises? Did you feel tense, have a pain in your neck or back, have a headache, feel sick to your stomach or light-headed? Physical symptoms may indicate that there is something there worth pursuing. Your body may be telling you something. Trauma is encoded in the body. The body does remember. Also pay attention to any strong feelings you have while doing the exercises or after you are finished with them. You may have been feeling this way as a child but were not allowed to express it.

You may also want to write yourself a note to remember your dreams during and shortly after you do this work. Dream images are another way our psyches express old wounds.

Finally notice any new awareness or insights that come to you. If an idea pops into your mind, write it down and let it simmer for a while. If there is no data to support it, *let it go*.

GRANDPARENTS' GENOGRAM

When you have done these exercises, you are ready to work on your grandparents' genogram. Hopefully you retrieved a lot of material that is relevant for your family map.

Start with your paternal grandparents. On the genogram write out your paternal grandfather's birth date, death date, how he died, his level of education, his occupation, and any known problems. Add any other facts that seem relevant. Then work your way across the genogram through your paternal grandmother, and on to your maternal grandparents.

A Heritage of Abandonment

James Jeder's paternal grandfather, John Jeder, was a highly successful businessman. (See Chart 6–4.) He made a lot of money in the stock market and retired in his middle fifties, only to die of a heart attack at the early age of sixty-two. James never met his grandfather, and in his later years he felt great sorrow that his grandfather had had no desire to see him or have anything to do with him.

When James was in his late thirties, he saw a picture of his grandfather in his father's scrapbook. This was the first time he had ever seen him. James could hardly believe the resemblance—he looked just like his grandfather. According to James's father, Shane, James's grandparents divorced when Shane was two years old. They had married because they were pregnant with Shane. John Jeder felt obliged to marry Sheila McCord in order to honor his religious duty, but both he and his parents felt that he was marrying beneath his dignity.

CHART 6-4
PATERNAL GRANDPARENTS

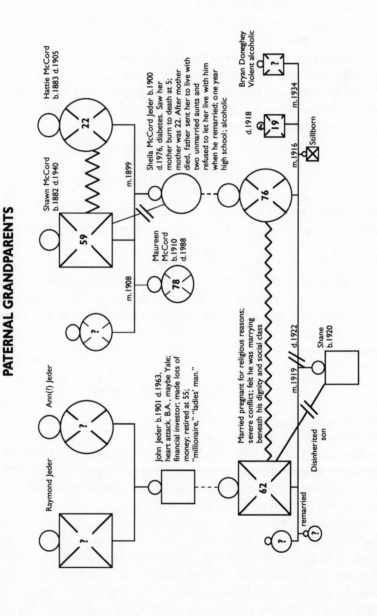

Raymond Jeder

Ann(?) Jeder

Hattie McCord
b.1883 d.1905

Shawn McCord
b.1882 d.1940

22

59

John Jeder b.1901 d.1963, heart attack. B.A., maybe Yale; financial investor; made lots of money; retired at 55; "millionaire," "ladies' man."

Sheila McCord Jeder b.1900 d.1976, diabetes. Saw her mother burn to death at 5; mother was 22. After mother died, father sent her to live with two unmarried aunts and refused to let her live with him when he remarried; one year high school; alcoholic

m.1899

m.1908

Maureen McCord
b.1910 d.1988

78

?

Married pregnant for religious reasons; severe conflict; felt he was marrying beneath his dignity and social class

62

76

d.1918

19

Bryan Doneghey
Violent alcoholic

?

m.1916

m.1934

Stillborn

m.1919 d.1922

Disinherited son

Shane b.1920

remarried

?

?

Shane told James that he had tried to see his father when he was seven years old. He ran away from his mother and rode a bus to the town in Arkansas where his father was living. But John wanted no part of his son and put him back on the bus immediately.

Shane told James that his father had seemed to be embarrassed by his presence. He also told James that when he arrived, his father was having a party with banners from Yale hanging around the room. This made him believe his father was a Yale graduate, but he never checked that out. Shane was rejected again five years later when he called and begged his father to let him see him.

The last act of this tragedy occurred when John Jeder died. Shane told James that he read about his father's death in the newspaper. Shane went to his father's funeral and was told that Mr. Jeder had no son. Shane insisted on staying for the funeral. Later he found that he was completely disowned in his father's will. Shane was already drinking heavily and had low self-esteem. He told James he went out and got drunk, because he felt it was not worth fighting to get his legal inheritance. This was evidently typical of Shane, who was very passive-aggressive.

Marrying Pregnant

James knew a lot more about his paternal grandmother, Sheila McCord Jeder, because she was present during his childhood. What James remembered most about her was her alcoholism. She was an emotionally explosive drunk, either starting fights and raging or going on crying jags. James had absolutely no affection for her.

Sheila had been a rebel and troublemaker from a young age. When she was sixteen, she ran away with a neighbor boy and got married. She was probably pregnant. The baby was stillborn. Her husband died two years later in an electrical accident at his job. Sheila received $60,000 in accidental death benefits. This was a lot of money in 1918. She proceeded to drink and live it up for the next two years. She was quite promiscuous and wanted to break into high society. That's how she met James's grandfather, John Jeder. They had an affair, she got pregnant, they married, and she had Shane. In marrying pregnant she was reenacting her mother's and father's pattern with her. James would later repeat the same pattern with both his wives.

After John Jeder divorced Sheila and abandoned Shane, Sheila moved back into the fast lane. She had spent half of her money before she married John. She continued her wild ways for the next ten years, taking Shane with her to bars and bringing a steady stream of lovers into Shane's life. When Shane was twelve, she finally remarried a violent alcoholic Irishman named Bryan Doneghey. Shane told James stories of coming home at night and finding his stepfather sitting up drunk with a butcher knife, threatening to kill him.

After Doneghey died, Sheila clung to Shane. She called him almost every day with demands and criticisms. She had never really let him separate emotionally from her, and the enmeshment was a severe wound that Shane had to carry.

A Grandmother's Illnesses

James remembered his maternal grandmother, Josephine O'Hern Jamison, as a beautiful but religiously rigid woman who was sick a lot of the time and seldom left the house. Chronic sickness can be a red flag for deciphering your family's dark secrets. (See Chart 6–5.)

Obviously sickness can be real, rooted in virus and biology, but it can also be a symptom of deeper issues. We have seen that victims of severe emotional and sexual abuse often use defenses that numb their feelings as a way to defend against the pain they are experiencing. Numbed-out emotional pain can be expressed in several ways. One way is to convert the emotional pain into somatic disorders, or chronic sickness. The natural state of our bodies is to be healthy, not sick. Someone who is sick a lot of the time without an identifiable disease or organic disability is often converting the painful feelings of sexual or emotional abuse into somatic disorders. James Jeder never knew for sure whether his grandmother Josephine had been violated sexually. He believed that she was, based on what his mother had told him about Milton O'Hern and Josephine's brothers.

James also has memories of his grandmother being very prudish and antisexual. She was a devout Roman Catholic and seemed to distrust men to the point of contempt, often ridiculing them for being led around by their genitals. She often spoke of sex as a woman's burden. But her relationship with her husband, Donald, was very dutiful and obeisant, and she seemed always ready to please him. As her various ailments worsened, she became bedridden. Finally she was diagnosed with cancer of the colon and died a few months later.

CHART 6-5
MATERNAL GRANDPARENTS

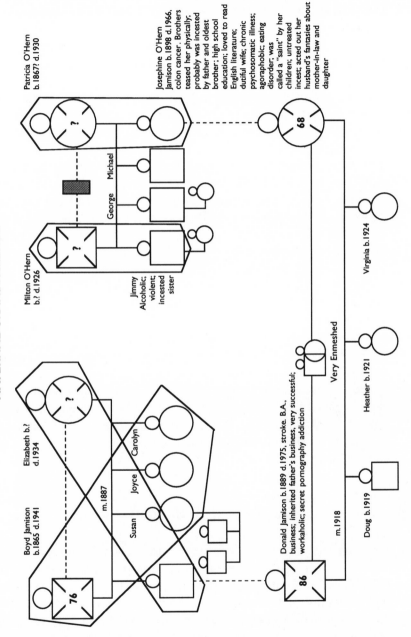

Patricia O'Hern b.1867? d.1930

Milton O'Hern b.? d.1926

George   Michael

Jimmy
Alcoholic;
violent;
incested
sister

Josephine O'Hern Jamison b.1898 d.1966, colon cancer. Brothers teased her physically; probably was incested by father and oldest brother; high school education; loved to read English literature; dutiful wife; chronic psychosomatic illness; agoraphobic; eating disorder; was called a "saint" by her children; untreated incest; acted out her husband's fantasies about mother-in-law and daughter

Elizabeth b.? d.1934

Boyd Jamison b.1865 d.1941

m.1887

Susan   Joyce   Carolyn

76

Donald Jamison b.1889 d.1975, stroke. B.A., business; inherited father's business, very successful; workaholic; secret pornography addiction

86

Very Enmeshed

m.1918

Doug b.1919

Heather b.1921

Virginia b.1924

A Grandfather's Hidden Fantasies

Donald Jamison inherited a fourth of his father's $15 million estate and ran the family business for twenty-five years.

Donald and Josephine bore three children, Doug, Heather (James Jeder's mother), and Virginia. Donald was agnostic and agreed to all three children being raised Catholic.

Doug, the oldest, was gay and was never able to meet his father's expectations of him, although he struggled in the family business for years. His father regularly hired and fired him. He was his father's scapegoat.

James's mother, Heather, was quite beautiful, and she became her father's special child. She was quite reserved and emotionally shut down. Still, she began "acting out" sexually in her middle teens. While Heather seemed repressed and prudish on the surface, it was clear that she was quite seductive. I'll return to this point in Chapter 8, on mothers' dark secrets.

James remembers that Heather used to spend hours with her mother Josephine, to whom she always referred to as a "saint." During her final illness Josephine told Heather that Donald had very aberrant sexual fantasies and that she had complied with them during the first thirty-five years of their marriage.

Recall that Donald Jamison had found a large stash of pornographic films in his father Boyd's safe when he died. He himself became addicted to watching these films and demanded that Josephine perform certain sexual acts he'd seen in them. While some couples enjoy using erotic films as a stimulus, Donald's demands were deeply demeaning to Josephine. He also had some unusual sexual rituals that James discovered later.

GREAT-AUNTS AND GREAT-UNCLES

James was not able to get very much information about other relatives on his mother's side of the family. His mother told him that Jimmy O'Hern had done more than just tease his sister, Josephine, that he had been punished for making her do "funny" sexual things with him. This was a fuzzy remembrance, and he never verified it. But stories like this do not emerge out of thin air. As an adult, Jimmy was alcoholic and violent. Great-Uncle George was a severe alcoholic who died in the VA hospital before his fifty-third birthday. All the O'Hern brothers were dead before they were sixty.

James did find out from his Aunt Virginia that his Great-Aunt Susan was incested by her father, Boyd Jamison. (See Chart 6-5.) She also stated that his Great-Aunt Carolyn talked delusionally about her father's physical affection, adding that she hated his "icky" kisses and felt uncomfortable around him. James's Aunt Virginia had a "nervous breakdown" during the time of his genogram search. This was when she talked about all of this, including Boyd's molestation of her. James's Great-Aunt Maureen, who was Sheila Jeder's half-sister, told James the story of his great-grandmother's traumatic death caused by setting the bed on fire when she was drunk. On one occasion she talked about how she never could understand her father's rejection of Sheila. She told James that she felt he somehow blamed Sheila for his wife's death.

At this point in your own research, you should have a genogram that includes what you know about your ancestors.

You may already have discovered that your own problems and/or secrets have occurred in previous generations. In the next chapter you will be able to fill in the picture in much more detail by focusing on your parents' lives.

CHAPTER 7

YOUR FATHER'S DARK SECRETS

Though I hated my father, I expressed that hatred elo-
quently by imitating his life, by becoming more and more
ineffectual daily, by ratifying all the cheerless prophecies
my mother made for both my father and me.

PAT CONROY, *The Prince of Tides*

I could not point to any need in childhood as strong as
that of a father's protection.

SIGMUND FREUD

Although death ended my father it never ended my relationship with my father—a secret that I had never so
clearly understood before.

FREDERICK BUECHNER, *Telling Secrets*

Richard had suffered deeply from being overweight, having a freckled
face, and being what he describes as "just plain ugly." He felt toxic
shame in every fiber of his being. He defended against his peers' and
family's teasing by isolating himself and focusing all his energy on intellectual achievement. He was quite brilliant and became more so as the
years went on. He handled his own self-contempt by being contemp-
tuous of those who were ignorant. He ridiculed most forms of social
life and friendships, calling them a waste of time. He found a mate in
college who complemented his intellect and who had her own issues
around being overweight and unattractive. They married and had two
children, a boy and a girl.

Although their children were quite attractive, Richard imposed his own defensive intellectualism on them. They grew up believing that intelligence is the only important thing in life. Neither Richard nor his wife ever talked about or expressed their secret grief over their childhood wounds and their own feelings of physical inadequacy.

Their children grew up intellectually sophisticated but socially and relationally isolated. For example, Richard and his wife made no effort to provide them with the clothes that were the norm in their peer group. When his son begged Richard to buy him the brand-name polo shirts and shoes that the other kids wore, Richard just scoffed. "Clothes do not make the man. It's what you know that counts," he told his son. Both children suffered ostracism and secretly came to believe that they were ugly, flawed, and unacceptable. In college Richard's son acted out his family secret with severe drug abuse and later entered a treatment center for drug abuse. The daughter got into a series of sexually exploitative and abusive relationships. Richard and his wife were totally befuddled. "It doesn't seem logical that children with excellent minds and a marvelous education could turn out like this," she told me in our first counseling session. In time the whole family came to see what was going on. The two children—now adults—were able to understand how Richard's dark secret became a force field shaping the entire family. This awareness enabled them to acknowledge their own secrets, change, and move on with their lives.

In counseling them I deliberately used a phrase borrowed from psychologist Alice Miller to describe the process at work in their lives. She calls it the "the logic of absurdity." When Richard grasped the *logical* explanation for his children's seemingly irrational behavior, he broke through his denial and was willing to experience his vulnerability.

Richard's story illustrates how powerful a father's dark secret—even a fairly ordinary one—can be in influencing the life of his children. It also underscores the fact that dark secrets often gather force over generations. Richard's children suffered worse symptoms than he did. Children's need for protection, recognition, and mattering are so great, they cannot help but get involved in their parents' psychological defenses and their parents' unconscious issues.

Absent fathers also exert a major influence over our lives. I had the good fortune to be reconciled with my father in his old age, but he was simply not there for me during my childhood. He was an alcoholic and was rarely home. Yet I obsessed on him all the time, worrying about where he was and wondering when he was coming home. When he had been drinking, I froze with fear. I can never remember a time when I didn't feel afraid and unprotected. When I was twelve years old, he divorced my mother and left for good.

Clinical studies suggest that when no father is present, children often have trouble learning to delay gratification. A father's absence often leads to poverty and scarcity, and children try to get all they can while they can. It has also been shown that the absence of a father often causes his children to feel a deep sense of shame. This was certainly true for me. I was constantly reassured by my mother that my father loved me—a reassurance that never felt right, as there was no behavior to prove it. My father's abandonment will always be a deep wound I have to live with.

REMEMBERING YOUR FATHER

In this chapter I will ask you to work on your biological father's genogram first. Then I will come back to James Jeder and show what he discovered about his father Shane's life. If you never knew your biological father and can't find out anything about him, then focus on your adopted dad or stepdad or whoever comes the closest to being there for you in a fatherly way.

If you have fantasies about your father, they are worth exploring, but be careful about conclusions that are not founded on real data. Your fantasy father may be a powerful part of your inner life. You may be searching for someone—a lover, boss, friend—who fits your fantasy, and if your fantasy is not grounded in reality, your fantasy father may be causing you lots of problems.

Finding out about your real fathering source may also help you discover hidden strengths that you are not aware of.

Be careful of the compulsion to protect your parents and how that can distort your honestly looking at who they really are. It was and is your parents' actual lives that educated you: not what they said, but what they did.

In the exploration that follows, I will be emphasizing your own perception of your father. But it is also important to seek outside verification and different viewpoints.

Interview your aunts and uncles, if there are any, to get information about your dad. Perhaps you know of an old boyhood friend of your dad's. Try calling him and asking him about your father when he was young. Maybe you know some business associates, a former boss, or someone who worked for him. They may be valuable sources for personal as well as work information. If your grandparents are alive, interview them. Ask your mother about your dad. She often knows things that you would have never thought of asking as a child—and that she probably wouldn't have told you when you were younger.

Perhaps your best sources are your siblings. Remember that each sibling position has its own special way of perceiving. Their point of view may be surprisingly different from yours. Add their information to your composite picture of your dad.

Your Image of Your Father

Have someone ask you these questions, or record them on a tape recorder. Pause about one minute between each question.

> **What is your earliest memory of your father? Close your eyes and get into the memory as deeply as you can. What is your earliest memory of a place you lived in with your father? What is your father wearing? What is he doing? What does it feel like to be a small child in your home with your father?**
>
> **Now let other memories come in. How did your father treat you? How did your father discipline you? How did your father show you affection? How soon did you start taking care of your father? What did you like most about your father? What did you dislike most about your father? How did you take care of your father? Now slowly open your eyes.**

Now take a few minutes to notice:

- The state of your inner bodily experience. Do you feel tense, restless, calm, sick at your stomach?
- Any strong emotional reaction—sadness, fear, anger, shame, guilt, and so on.
- Your desires and longings. Did you get in touch with heartache, disappointment, frustration, happiness?
- Any new awareness or thoughts that pertain to secrets. Did you experience something about your dad you've never noticed before?

Each time you do any of the exercises that follow, wrap up with the same questions.

If you have trouble visualizing (which many people do), try writing out answers to the questions about your dad. When you write, stay with sensory-based data. Don't write, "My dad was happy"; write, "I saw a big smile on my dad's face, and he was looking at me and talking in a calm voice."

Remember to ask yourself the wrap-up questions when you write.

Or find as many old photographs of your father as you can. Take the ones that call out to you, and look at them. Spend some time on this (say three to five minutes), then write spontaneously for ten minutes. Write down anything that comes to your mind. Try this with several photographs. Then look over your writing, and see what themes, if any, emerge. Do your wrap-up exercise.

Character Traits

What were your dad's five best character traits? (For example, he was kind, gentle, generous.) Give a specific example for each one. What were your dad's five worst character flaws? (He lied a lot, he was a poor loser.) Give a specific example of each.

Your Father's Rules of Life

What were your dad's Ten Commandments? Take your time and write them out. Try to remember the context for each one—that is, when do you first remember hearing him expounding these rules for life? If they were the original ten in the Bible, what did your dad add to them? For example, "Thou shalt not commit adultery—unless you are discreet about it."

What were your father's covert rules? These rules are not verbal, they are behavioral. For example, your dad may have been the only one who could fart unashamedly. There was no rule stating this, but that's how it was in your family. To be less gross, Dad may have expounded on democracy and the glory of equality, but it was clear from his behavior that he considered your mother inferior to him. He sat down, and she waited on him. You knew from your mother's expression that this service was not voluntary.

Favorite Sayings and Jokes

Make a list of your father's favorite sayings. Do they reveal anything to you about him? Did he abide by those sayings? Imagine him doing just the opposite of each saying, and see whether anything clicks. The saying could be a cover-up. For example, Gary remembers his religiously authoritarian father saying that God intended penises to go into vaginas—that's why gays and lesbians were perverting the laws of nature. When Gary was in his early thirties, a gay friend invited him to go to a gay bar with him. Out of curiosity he went. He was shocked to find his father there.

What were some of your dad's favorite jokes? (Maybe you can remember only one.) Do you see any pattern in his jokes? What does that tell you? For example, if your white Christian father always told jokes about people of color, gays, or Jews, it might tell you not only that he was prejudiced but that he was insecure about his own social standing or sexuality.

Secret Expectations and Disappointments

Your father may have left many things unsaid, such as his secret resentment toward his own parents or his disappointment with your mother. Beneath the disappointments lie his secret expectations, some of which may have been quite unrealistic. Your dad may also feel secretly disappointed in his own life. He may feel that he never lived up to his own potential. His bitterness and cynicism may be symptoms of his frustrated expectations.

Very few people truly find their bliss in life, and very few men live up to our culture's stern measurement of success. Was your father a success in his own eyes? Did he make a lot of money? Did he achieve the goals he set out for himself? What do you know about his dreams and desires? Did he achieve the athletic success he strove for? What about his marriage to your mother? Was he happy and content with her?

How have you taken care of your father's disappointments? Are you an extension of your dad? Did you go to college because he couldn't? Did you become a doctor, lawyer, engineer to fulfill his dreams? How have you taken care of your dad's sadness and disappointment? Think about these questions, and write down whatever comes to you. Try an associative clustering exercise with the phrase "my father's disappoint-ment."

Children know their parents' unconscious wishes and try to please them. Even if your dad never consciously expressed disappointments, you surely picked up on them. You may have spent your life trying to live your father's unlived life for him.

Work and Money

What did your father believe about work and money? Pay specific at-tention to any incongruities between what was said and what was done. Your dad may have said that work and money were a means to an end, but in actuality he may have given them higher value than family or relationships.

Write down your dad's criteria for success. How do you know these were his criteria? Was he successful in his own eyes? Was he successful in *his* father's eyes? Perhaps he acted successful, but you know he was really covering up a secret sense of failure.

What did your father believe about money? Did he put everything else aside to make money? Did he live above his means in order to present an image of having money? Did he secretly feel like a failure because he didn't make a lot of money? Did your dad make the family sacrifice while he indulged himself with sports equipment or other toys (like expensive cars)? Did your father work himself to death for the family or so that you could have nice things?

Religion (Morality)

You may already have touched on some of your dad's moral principles. Think about these questions. What, if any, were your dad's religious beliefs? Did he practice what he believed? Was he balanced, rigid, or lax in his belief? Did his behavior point to other things as his gods, such as money, sex, or sports? Is this where he put most of his time? Did he profess to be an atheist or agnostic? Did he have a well-thought-out position, or was he simply reacting to and rebelling against his rigid, perhaps hypocritical, religious upbringing? All in all, was he an honest believer or nonbeliever?

Sexuality

Sexuality is not something we have, it is something that we are. Your father sexually impacted you for better or worse. Your first beliefs, attitudes, and feelings about sex came from one or both of your parents. They needed to model healthy sexuality for you. They needed to let you know that your sexuality was beautiful, *wonder*ful, and ultimately mysterious and sacred. They also needed to exhibit good boundaries and appropriate modesty around their sexuality. Sex is an area of dark secrecy for many people. Take your time in answering the following questions, and be sure to do your wrap-up questions.

What did you learn about sex from your father? Do you think your father had a fulfilling sex life with your mother? How do you know? What language was used to talk about sex? Did your dad have good boundaries around sexual areas of privacy? Did your father value and respect your sexuality? Did your father have any affairs? How do you know? Do you think your dad had any sexual hang-ups? How do you know? Did you feel sexually uncomfortable around your dad? Why? Did your dad model any kind of disrespect for your mother? Be precise. Was your dad superprotective of your mother in a way that made him superior to her? For example, did he indulge her with lots of sweets, contributing to her obesity? Was this a way to avoid being sexually intimate with her? Did he pamper her sickly psychosomatic behavior and so keep her dependent on him? Was his superprotective behavior a way of saying to her, "Your sex is weak and frail," thus covering up his secret need to be strong and in control and to buffer his fragile male identity?

Friends

Name five friends your father had. Did his friends have anything in common? If your dad had no close friends, what does that tell you about him? Did your dad try to make you his best friend? How do you feel about that?

Hobbies and Recreation

List five things your father did for fun and recreation. Did he seem to enjoy life? Did he neglect you because he was too busy with his hobbies and other activities? Or did your father have no hobbies?

Associative Clusters

Try writing about your dad by using associative clusters. Look at some area in his life—say, his "denial." Put the word *denial* in the center of a piece of paper and circle it. Now let this circle be the center of a wheel, and start making associations with it. Let an association unfold—like lying, for instance—and then continue to add to it.

What comes to me is the phrase "broken promises" and then "cheating on my mom" and then "avoided looking at his drinking" and finally the feeling of being betrayed.

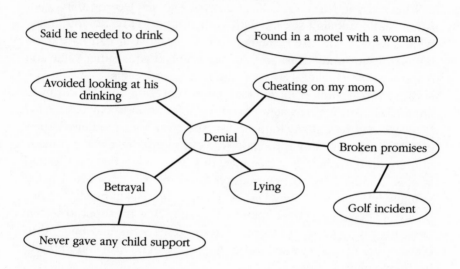

I have strong feelings as I remember the time my dad promised to play golf with me and then left me standing alone and disappointed in front of his office. I cried so hard on the bus, the driver stopped to see what was going on and everyone was looking at me. Pretty painful! My dad lied a lot!

Best Day with Your Dad

If you saw the movie *City Slickers,* you probably remember the scene where Billy Crystal, Daniel Stern, and Bruno Kirby are riding along talking, and each one describes his best day with his father and then his worst day. This is a good exercise to do with a couple of good

friends, or support people, or your spouse—or any partner who will
seriously listen to you. First each of you writes about your best day
with Dad. You can do this without writing, but I have found that writing intensifies the experience. Then take turns reading the scenes
aloud. After each scene ask for feedback from your group or partner.

If you are the listener, pay detailed attention to your own inner
feelings as your partner reads about his or her best day. When the
reading is finished, tell the reader what *you were feeling* during the
reading. Then switch roles. When you are both finished, discuss this
feeling feedback. Often it can help you connect with your own feelings. You may be surprised, especially if you're with a group, and they
all feed back a feeling that you were out of touch with.

Worst Day with Your Dad

*If you know you are a victim of incest, battering, or severe emotional
abuse, please do not do this exercise.* There is too much danger of
your getting back into the hopeless and helpless feelings you had as a
child. There are groups for survivors of incest and other forms of severe abuse in which it is safe to do this kind of work. The group must
be properly facilitated by a group leader who can take care of you if
you should go into an age regression. For someone who has never
experienced another person in an age regression, it can be very frightening. If you've had the kind of severe abuse I've mentioned, you
should not do this exercise without appropriate support.

Write out the scene that corresponds to what you believe to be your
worst day with your dad. Remember to use sensory-based detail. What
did you see? ("I saw my father staggering down the sidewalk." "He
came into my room, he had a drink in his left hand, his right hand was
trembling.")

Take turns reading your scene to your group or partner, and get
their feeling feedback.

Also consider the following questions: What decisions about yourself do you think you made as a result of this experience? Is this decision the source of any pattern in your life right now? That decision
was the best one you had available to you then, but you can change it
now.

If you start working on this exercise and feel frightened or start
having physical symptoms of some kind, stop immediately. Then
check out your response with a competent therapist. You could

possibly be touching on something in your life that has been repressed. I will have more to say about repressed memories in Chapter 9.

Validating Your Feelings

It is important when you have read a scene to be validated by your group or partner. As children our feelings were seldom validated.

We were angry, and instead of someone saying, "I hear or see how angry you are," we were told, "Don't you ever talk back to me again." Our anger was *invalidated*. The same thing may have happened with our sadness, our fear, even our joy, if we expressed it too exuberantly. We can help each other connect with our own experience by saying what we *hear* and *see* the other person saying and doing when they read their scene. (For example, you might say, "I hear how sad you are. Your voice is high-pitched, and it is cracking. I see the tears in your eyes and your lips quivering.")

When our parents could not let us have our own experience, it was because they had a dark secret. They had lots of feelings that their own inner voices criticized. Their parents had not been able to let them have their anger or fear or sadness or desire or joy. When we have our feelings, it triggers their feelings, and since their inner voices say things like "Feelings are weak" or "Real men don't cry" or "Good women are not sexual," they reject their own feelings and project their inner prohibition onto us. The inner voice that says it's not okay to be mad, sad, glad, or afraid was once the voice of the parent. Psychologists call this internalized inner voice an *introject* or *parent tape*. An introject is literally a recording of our father or mother's voice encoded in our nervous system. We also have our parents' good advice recorded and can hear it when it is needed. To the degree that our parents' feelings were shamed and prohibited, to that degree their feelings are split off and unintegrated. It is the split off and unintegrated parts of parents that become the most introjected by the child.

The feelings your father prohibited in you are a clue to his dark secrets. A father who cannot let his children cry (usually his male children) has a secret. He needs to cry, but he condemns that need in himself. A father who ridicules his children's fear is hiding his own secret fear.

Uncontained Feelings

When a father's feelings are uncontained, he may also have a secret. Your father may have raged, expressing his anger in a completely inappropriate way. This may have caused you to repress your own anger because his rage so intimidated you. What you didn't know was that his rage may have been covering up his feelings of fear and impotence.

Uncontained feelings, like repressed feelings, may be polarized clues. Look for the opposite feelings that are being kept secret.

Your mother may have interpreted and tried to rationalize your father's feelings. She may have said something like, "Your father really loves you. He's just under a lot of pressure at the office." That kind of statement usually causes a child to feel confusion and take on guilt. Rather than seeing that Father is out of control, the child feels that it is somehow their fault.

Validation of feelings is a corrective to the toxic shaming most of us experienced as children.

Repression of Feelings as a Dark Secret

I consider repression of feelings a dark secret. Our feelings are part of our natural power. Our anger is our strength, our fear is our prudent discernment of danger, our sadness is the energy that allows us to say good-bye to things, our shame signals and protects our limits, our curiosity and desire gives us the energy to explore, expand, and grow, and our joy allows us to spontaneously celebrate when we are getting all our needs met. When our feelings are working, we *function* as human beings ought to function. When our feelings are repressed by our introjects, we shut down and become *dysfunctional*. The repression of feelings belongs to the realm of dark secrets every bit as much as the covering up of events and behaviors.

Our father's secret shame over his feelings is passed on to us by his shaming of our feelings. His dark secret is dangerous because it makes us dysfunctional. Being numbed out emotionally is the setup for addiction. Those who can't feel, or who want to numb their feelings, use addiction as a way to mood-alter.

Your Dad's Addictions

If your dad was addicted, you saw the outward signs of his dark secret about his feelings. Addictions are ways to hide feelings. Addictions can be about changing the feelings you've got, as in alcohol or cocaine use, or they can be about distracting you from certain feelings you don't want to feel, as with gambling, compulsive work, or sex. The action is the distraction in those addictions.

If your dad was an addict, his dark secret was probably unconscious. The mechanism of repressing feelings starts early in life. More than likely your dad repressed his vulnerable feelings. Men have had stronger taboos against feeling vulnerable than women have.

Carrying Your Father's Feelings

When your father expressed himself without being aware of what he was feeling, it was confounding and confusing to you. You may have experienced him as incongruent as he hit you and told you he was doing that because he loved you. This may have made you feel crazy.

The cruelty of his calm, deliberate punishment and humiliation of you disguised his repressed rage from his own childhood humiliations. You couldn't understand what you had done or why it was so bad. And the fact is that what you did was not that bad, but it reminded your dad of similar deeds in his own childhood that were severely shamed. Because he was a helpless child, whose self-protective anger was condemned with the threat of more shaming and humiliation, he had no way of expressing his anger over what had been done to him. You *now* are the recipient of an anger that has festered secretly for all these years.

As Jane Middelton Moz writes, "The taboos against our feeling and expressing anger are so powerful that even knowing when we are angry is not a simple matter." Once your dad has passed his secret anger on to you, you may repress it so deeply that you lose contact with it. You no longer know when you are feeling it, because you develop a large array of alternative ways to express your anger—sickness, back pain, headaches, passivity, numbness, intellectual criticism, hurtful passive-aggressive behavior, or dumping your anger onto your children. The passage of anger from one generation to the next is one of the darkest secrets of patriarchal/matriarchal childrearing. Children are the receptacles and carriers of their parents' unexpressed emotions. You can know one of your father's dark secrets quite well by being aware of what emotions appropriate to the situation he was *not* expressing, or by becoming aware of his incongruent communications.

Dialogue: Your Father's Worst Fear

Either have someone read this to you, or put it on a tape recorder. You can do this dialogue even if your father has already died or if you haven't seen him for years.

> Close your eyes, and imagine your dad sitting across from you. If he's alive, see him at his present age. If he's dead, see him at the age he was when he died. Imagine he has come to you because he wants to make amends for the ways that his secrets have hurt you. He doesn't have very long to live, and he wants to answer any questions you have for him. Ask him, "What is your greatest fear?" Really let the image of your father answer you. Do not try to control what he says. Let his response be as spontaneous as possible. (*Pause for about five minutes to listen to his answer.*) Now ask your father, "What must you be sure of?" Once again let the image of your father answer the question. (*Five-minute pause.*) Now ask any other question you want to ask. (*Pause.*)
>
> Now imagine your father leaving, and ask yourself, "What would my father never have done?" Let your imagination run freely until something clicks and your response feels right for you. Now ask yourself, "What ways of life were out of the question for my father?" Let your imagination run freely. When you have finished, open your eyes.

Remember to do your wrap-up exercise. Your father's worst fear, the thing(s) he must be sure of, what he would never do, ways of life that are out of the question for him, are all ways to see what he secretly was afraid of. These fears were all passed on to you.

Probing Your Father's Shadow

Carl Jung described the repressed and rejected parts of ourselves as the *shadow*. Our shadow self is the part of us that harbors our secrets. We are often so afraid of these parts of ourselves that we go to the opposite extreme to cover them up. A person who feels a deep sense of toxic shame might cover this up by striving to be perfect or by doing only those things that they have mastery over, thus never risking failure.

Enemies

Make a list of all the people or kinds of people your father hated. Then star the ones he hated with a passion. The more energy he expended putting them down, the more important they are.

Imagine that all those enemies represent parts of your father's self that he did not want to look at, parts that he rejected in himself. He may have loudly bashed gay men. Is it possible he feared the part of himself that was effeminate or vulnerable? Did he fear his own masculinity?

People who feel deeply flawed and defective often join sects or cults or rigid religious communities that tell them with absolute certainty that they are saved. This gives them a sense of righteousness. Perfectionism and righteousness become an obsessive and mood-altering way of life. The person loses touch with their own humanness, and the part of self that is frail and imperfect becomes their shadow.

Embracing Opposites

What characteristics would your dad strongly deny if you ascribed them to him? What are five ways you described your dad earlier? Now imagine that he is just the opposite of those five descriptions. Pretend that you are a lawyer arguing that he is just the opposite of the way everyone perceives him.

What could you never talk about with your dad? How did you know that you couldn't *talk* about it? Write down all the elements that composed your father's shadow.

YOUR FATHER'S WOUND

What do you know of your father's childhood? For example, were your grandparents rigid? Or did they spoil your father? Was your father abandoned by either of his parents? Was he neglected? Was he physically, sexually, or emotionally abused? Was he traumatized in any other ways? Trauma, whether from abuse, abandonment, neglect, sickness, disaster, or accident, has powerful consequences that we are slowly coming to understand.

Post-Traumatic Stress Disorder

Some of our new understanding about the effects of trauma have come from working with soldiers returning from war. Many have been diagnosed with a condition called *post-traumatic stress disorder* (PTSD). PTSD is viewed as a set of clearly defined symptoms brought about because the horrific trauma of war cannot be fully integrated when it is happening. In order to survive, soldiers need to stay focused on the threats that are all around them. They need all their energy and vital attention in order to keep from being killed. They cannot stop and grieve the violence and horror they are experiencing.

They carry their unresolved trauma and frozen grief home with them. Later their traumatic stress disorder manifests itself in symptoms like an obsessive need to control, nightmares, flashbacks, being easily startled, and hypervigilance, as well as other symptoms of traumatic memory.

Your father didn't have to be a soldier to have signs of PTSD. Abandonment, neglect, physical, emotional, intellectual, and sexual abuse can be just as traumatic for a child as being under fire.

In a study reported in *The New York Times* in June 1990, the National Center for the Study of Post-Traumatic Stress Disorder concluded that one catastrophic experience, when a person is powerless, is enough to permanently change brain chemistry. How is that possible? Such an experience creates a kind of indelible learning. During trauma there is a tremendous surge of adrenaline, a hormone that alerts the brain to the presence of threat. There is also an increase in endorphin, a hormone that eases pain and helps the brain to remember. The message is imprinted in the cells: "This is a life-threatening situation. Don't ever forget it." In this way the brain prepares itself so that it will not be caught off guard again. It is as if an on-button designed only for brief periods of crisis gets stuck and remains on all the time. A state of extreme alert or hypervigilance remains that may trigger panic or anxiety attacks, mood irritability, fright, and insomnia.

When trauma is chronic, avoidant symptoms often develop: loss of motivation, withdrawal, dissociation, amnesia, isolation, and depression. In extreme cases the victim may be in a constant state of "feeling helpless" and even "hopeless."

Kindling

The most common single symptom of PTSD is called *kindling*. Kindling is a phenomenon in which little events that a normal person would shrug off as minor stress suddenly produce a full-blown case of "frayed nerves." You left your skate on the floor, or played your radio too loud, or bumped your bicycle against Dad's car—all seemingly inconsequential events—and Dad erupted into full-scale rage. It's as if Dad could never relax. He was always on edge or in a state of overarousal. Raymond B. Flannery, Jr., in his book *Post-Traumatic Stress Disorder,* states that "for the victim with kindling, both negative and positive events of life may produce the small increments of norepinephrine that bring about the unpleasant arousal and vigilance." What that means is that if Dad is a PTSD victim, no matter what is going on, if it produces any excitement, he's going to be upset. Things like arguments, traffic, and long lines at the store produce the hypervigilant response. And so do pleasant events with high energy, like parties, having company over, sporting events, and dramatic or sad movies.

According to Flannery, it is also common for such people to dampen their chronically aroused feeling state by avoiding people and places as much as possible. He says, "This can include solutions like driving in non-peak hours, going to the supermarket late in the evening when the crowd is gone, or going on vacation in the fall to secluded beaches when most people have returned to work."

If you identify several of these symptomatic behaviors in your father, there is a chance that he may have been traumatized during his childhood or adolescence. He may also be a war veteran. Your dad may have been not the weird, worried, antisocial stick-in-the-mud you thought him to be, but the victim of childhood abuse or terrible wartime experiences.

Addiction and PTSD

Your dad's addiction may also be rooted in PTSD. When a traumatic crisis has passed, victims enter into hormonal withdrawal. This leads to symptoms like restlessness, agitation, some minor trembling in the body, and other flulike symptoms. This withdrawal takes place each time an episode of kindling occurs. Paradoxically the victim often becomes frightened when withdrawal takes place. This results in another hormonal surge, and kindling occurs again. It becomes a vicious cycle.

The most common strategy for the victim is to self-medicate the unpleasant withdrawal symptoms by engaging in some form of addictive behavior. Sexual addiction, binge eating, self-mutilation, cocaine, alcohol, and reckless driving all produce a short, intense endorphin release. Since the release only lasts a short time, the person must use it over and over.

This rather long explanation of PTSD symptoms and behavior may not be relevant to your father. Knowing that childhood abuse is part of normal patriarchal/matriarchal parenting suggests to me that some of our parents' behavior may be rooted in this secret. I hope my children read this because much of my parenting was rooted in PTSD.

TAPPING YOUR UNCONSCIOUS KNOWLEDGE

We almost always know more about our parents than we allow ourselves to know. The following three exercises are designed to give permission for this knowledge to emerge.

Drawing the House

Draw a picture of the earliest house you can remember where you lived with your dad. Draw a floor plan with every room as you remember it. Imagine all the details in each room. Then locate the space your father most often occupied. Imagine you are walking into that room, and you see your father hiding something. Ask him what he is hiding. Then see him showing something to you that explains his secret.

Letter from Dad

Imagine that you receive a letter from your dad. It is a letter asking your forgiveness and telling you how much he loves you. You read along until you come to a line that says, "Now I want to tell you my darkest secrets. . . ." You must finish writing the letter. Write it boldly and without hesitation. Remember that unconsciously you already know all the secrets.

Dialogue with Your Unconscious

Record this exercise, or have someone read it to you.

Close your eyes and take about five minutes to relax. Focus on your breathing. . . . Just notice the air as you breathe it in and out. Relax your muscles. . . . As you breathe in, say, "I'm getting," and as you breathe out, say, "Calm." Now imagine that you see a large screen with two people engaged in deep conversation. As the camera of your inner eye focuses on the pair, you begin to realize that both people are you. You are having a conversation with yourself. The person on your right is the conscious part of you. Take a minute to really see this image of yourself. Then look at the other you. This part of you is your unconscious, which knows vastly more than your conscious self. Take a minute and really see this part of you. What do you see that lets you know this part is different?

Now observe your conscious self asking your unconscious self what your father's secrets are or were.

Wait a couple of minutes and really let your unconscious self answer spontaneously. Once your unconscious has replied, question it for clarification. Gradually let yourself fade away from this scene and slowly come to your full working consciousness.

Now write down whatever you got out of observing this dialogue between your conscious and unconscious selves.

Some Final Questions

How are you like your dad? What are your dark secrets? Do you see any connection? How are you different from your dad? Are you sure you are really different? Perhaps you are his exact opposite. He was weak and self-indulgent, you are strong and self-negating. Being opposite is okay if it is a true choice, if it is the way you really want to be. If you must be opposite so that you can be sure of being different from Dad, then it's not really a choice, and you are not free.

This exercise is applicable to both sons and daughters. Richard's daughter, earlier in this chapter, was driven by her secret fear of being ugly. She became an intellectual misfit—just like her dad. A woman can embody her father's character traits just as a man can.

Now you are ready to draw your father's genogram.

CONSTRUCTING YOUR FATHER'S GENOGRAM

Start your dad's genogram by filling in the basic facts about his life. Then begin to explore the four questions I outlined in Chapter 5:

1. What are/were your dad's major problems? What symptoms did he manifest?

2. How do his problems relate to the facts in your three-generational family map? Are there similar patterns in other areas of your family history?

3. What was going on in the emotional climate of the family when your dad was born?

4. What issues arise from your dad's sibling position? How do these issues relate to significant others in the family in the same sibling position?

I will again use the genograms of the Jeder family to illustrate each of these issues. I have deliberately used an example that is very straightforward and obvious. Your family may be more complex.

1. Major Problems (Symptoms)

James Jeder's father, Shane, was an alcoholic and a womanizer. He had a high school education and suffered from asthma as a child. He had a bad heart attack when he was forty-three and continued to smoke and drink after that. He drifted from job to job, but finally settled in a job at the Union Pacific Railroad, where he worked until he retired at sixty. He died three years later of a heart attack related to severe emphysema, caused by smoking and heavy drinking.

2. Problems in Context

The first genogram offers some factual information that puts Shane's problems in the larger context of his mother's and father's families in the year of his birth, 1920. (See Chart 7–1.) Shane is born into the

CHART 7-1

SHANE JEDER: PROBLEMS IN CONTEXT

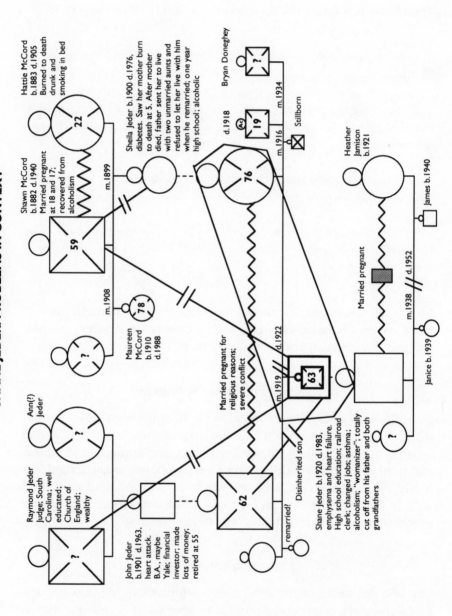

Raymond Jeder
Judge; South
Carolina; well
educated;
Church of
England;
wealthy

Ann(?)
Jeder

Hattie McCord
b.1883 d.1905
Burned to death
drunk and
smoking in bed

Shawn McCord
b.1882 d.1940
Married pregnant
at 18 and 17;
recovered from
alcoholism

m.1899

Sheila Jeder b.1900 d.1976,
diabetes. Saw her mother burn
to death at 5. After mother
died, father sent her to live
with two unmarried aunts and
refused to let her live with him
when he remarried; one year
high school; alcoholic

Bryan Doneghey

d.1918

19

m.1934

m.1916

Stillborn

John Jeder
b.1901 d.1963,
heart attack.
B.A., maybe
Yale; financial
investor; made
lots of money;
retired at 55

m.1908

Maureen
McCord
b.1910
d.1988

78

76

Heather
Jamison
b.1921

Married pregnant for
religious reasons;
severe conflict

d.1922

m.1919

63

Married pregnant

m.1938 // d.1952

remarried?

Disinherited son

Shane Jeder b.1920 d.1983,
emphysema and heart failure.
High school education; railroad
clerk; changed jobs; asthma;
alcoholism; "womanizer"; totally
cut off from his father and both
grandfathers

62

Janice b.1939

James b.1940

anxiety and conflict of John and Sheila Jeder's enforced marriage. He is not wanted. He is the product of sexual impulsivity, religious guilt, and duty. His father will leave within two years, never to have anything to do with him again, and will also disinherit him. Shane's stepfather will be an alcoholic who doesn't like him. In his early teens, when Shane comes home from a date, his stepfather will be sitting up drunk, holding a butcher knife, and threatening to kill him. This family offers Shane very poor male modeling.

Shane's mother, Sheila, is filled with anxiety, knowing her second husband is likely to leave her. By the time she was seventeen, she had already suffered three traumatic losses—the deaths of her mother, her first husband, and her first baby, who was stillborn—and had been abandoned by her father. The theme of abandonment and unresolved grief runs through this family.

Sheila is an alcoholic, as was her own father, Shawn McCord. Shawn has sobered up, but he has nothing to do with Shane or Sheila. Sheila will also model sexual promiscuity for her son.

Shane's problems have been present in his family for two generations. He has been abandoned by all the significant male figures in his family and basically left in bondage to his very wounded and disturbed mother.

3. Family Emotional Climate at Time of Birth

Looking at your family's emotional climate at the time of your father's birth can help you understand factors that predispose him to become symptomatic at a particularly stressful period in the family's life. Or you may clearly see factors that make it likely for him to keep dark secrets and/or act them out.

Shane Jeder's mother, Sheila, suffered severe trauma at age five by seeing her own mother burn to death. (See Chart 7–2.) At seventeen she lost her husband, who was electrocuted accidentally at work. She was already a drinking alcoholic at seventeen. She is a post-traumatic stress disorder victim. These factors strongly dispose her to make Shane the primary object of her projection.

During his childhood Shane's mother clung to him and set up severe enmeshment. She spoke of him as her "little man" and told him things like, "No woman will ever love you like I do." She romanced him and treated him as a surrogate husband. Because of her unboundaried sexuality, she emotionally incested her son.

CHART 7-2

EMOTIONAL CLIMATE AT SHANE JEDER'S BIRTH, 1920

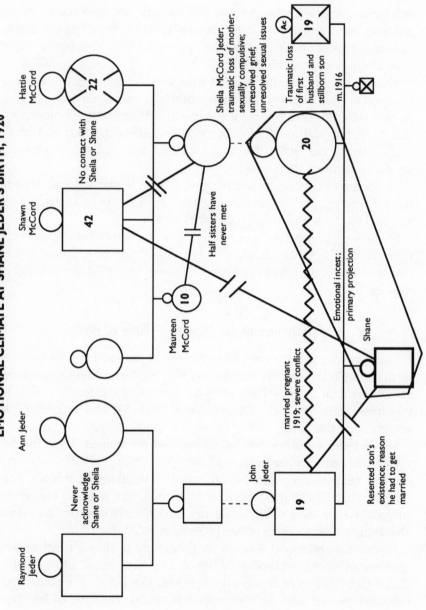

In view of all these factors—his abandonment by his grandfather, his total rejection and scapegoating by his father, his mother's emotional sexual abuse in using him to fill up her unresolved grief and emptiness—we can reasonably guess that Shane will be predisposed to have serious problems with commitment and a hunger for immediate attachment. We can also reasonably predict that he will be predisposed to sexual addiction.

4. Sibling Position Issues

In doing your father's genogram, be aware of the person or persons whose secrets his sibling position would most likely bond him to. When you draw this genogram, look at the issues of emotional cutoff that recur across the generations in your family. Emotional cutoff is indicative of unresolved intensity. Cutoffs tell you that there are secret feelings or resentments that have never been resolved.

Both of Shane's maternal grandparents were only children, and both his mother and father are in only-child sibling positions.

According to Walter Toman in his book *Family Constellation,* the female only child often has a spoiled and egocentric personality in her contacts with men. According to Shane, his mother was extravagant and demanding. At times he described her as a shrew and a hysterical bitch. She was also a compulsive spender and had severe boundary problems.

Sheila indulged Shane incessantly, and he grew up to expect indulgence from others, especially women.

Male only children need to be on center stage. Like Shane's father, John, they are often very successful. Shane, however, went to the other extreme, although he was quite narcissistic when he was drinking.

Shane is really in the number-two sibling position after Sheila's still-born infant. He was, therefore, bonded to her unresolved grief over losing her first baby, which set him up to take care of her pain. The secret message to Shane was, "Your job is to make me happy, to make up for the child I lost." He did not know this consciously. Children are bonded to their parents' unconscious needs.

The only other child in the family in the number-two position is Maureen and too little is known about her to make any comparisons.

What is clear is that the relationships in Shane's family are either cut off, conflictual, or enmeshed. He will act them out and repeat them in his own life.

Dark Secrets

There are a number of dark secrets in this family. Shane's father is ashamed of him and hides the fact that he has a son at all. His mother is out of touch with her unresolved grief and her narcissistic wound and uses alcohol, sex, and spending money to mood-alter her pain. She is loud and garish and covers her vulnerability and deep trauma with grandiosity. A tremendous amount of secret resentment and anger is hiding in the emotional cutoffs in this family. Shane cannot know what is happening to him. He cannot know the dark secret of his childhood, that he is being "used." This is very crazy-making.

James felt that his father's darkest secret was his deep-seated toxic shame.

On one occasion Shane told James that he felt quite inadequate as a man. His own father's abandonment and his enmeshment with his alcoholic mother definitely set Shane up to be an alcoholic and impaired his ability to be intimate in his marriage to Heather and his capacity to be a father to James and his sister, Janice.

Both Janice and James felt like Shane had completely abandoned them as children. He was seldom at home, and when he was, he acted more like another child than like a father. James's fondest memory of Shane was when he was eight years old, living in McAllen, Texas. Heather had to leave for a day because her father was ill. Shane took Janice and James to three movies in one afternoon and evening.

James could remember only one time when Shane disciplined him. James had blatantly disobeyed and sassed his mother. She reported his behavior to Shane and insisted that he discipline James. Shane took James into James's bedroom, locked the door, and told him to pretend he was crying, while Shane pretended to hit him with a belt. This was not a case of Shane challenging the long-held belief in corporal punishment. Shane was simply too immature to discipline his son responsibly.

A few years after James's own son, Jack, was born, James confronted Shane for neglecting his grandson. Shane responded by telling James that he felt he had no right to be around his grandson because he had been such a lousy father to James and Janice.

James once told me that the only advice Shane ever gave him was "to go and buy some new clothes when you get real sad and blue."

A Doomed Marriage

Shane's marriage to Heather seemed doomed from the start. It's doubtful that Shane really loved Heather. Their marriage took place because of the pressure Heather's family put on them to get married because she was pregnant. Getting pregnant out of wedlock was a very dark secret at that time.

By getting married pregnant, Shane was reenacting the pattern in two previous generations of his family history. Both his maternal grandparents and his parents had married pregnant.

The early years of his marriage were awful for Shane. His father-in-law, Donald Jamison, disdained him for getting his "precious" daughter pregnant. And since Donald was incestuously attracted to his daughter, he projected his own sexual shame onto Shane. Shane and Heather lived in Donald's home, and Donald let Shane know that he resented him for it. Although he finally gave Shane a job, it was not an effective way to really help Shane improve himself. Donald could have given Shane financial help to continue his education. But instead he gave him the lowest-paying and most menial job in his company.

Shane had been rejected by every male authority figure in his life. His father-in-law's rejection added to his sense of shame.

Heather felt awkward living in her parents' home and withdrew from Shane sexually. She also began to criticize and pressure him to get a better job.

It took three and a half years for Shane and Heather to be in a position to leave the Jamison home. They struggled for years to make ends meet.

Shane's drinking got progressively worse, and he was barely able to keep his job.

James and I deduced that Shane probably had his first of many affairs when James was four years old. As his drinking and womanizing progressed, his marriage got worse. Shane and Heather separated and reunited five times over the fourteen years they were married. Heather finally had enough of Shane when he spent an entire two-week vacation, which they had planned for a year, drunk and away from home. She filed for divorce shortly after this drinking binge.

Soon after his divorce, Shane's company committed him to a treatment center for alcoholism. He quit drinking, fell in love with the nurse who cared for him, and married her three months later. Six months after he was married, Shane started drinking again.

Shane's new wife was extremely codependent, and she became his enabler as he went through another fifteen years of alcohol addiction.

Shane finally hit bottom in his early fifties, after being fired from his job. He decided to quit drinking, joined AA, and was sober until he died. He and his second wife lived quietly and peacefully for the last years of Shane's life. Shane's alcoholism and heavy smoking took their toll on his body. He died of emphysema and a bad heart at sixty-three.

CHAPTER 8

YOUR MOTHER'S DARK SECRETS

Nothing has a stronger influence psychologically on their
. . . children, than *the unlived life of the parent*.

C. G. Jung

My mother never quite finished the task of creating herself. . . . She rarely told a story about her childhood that
was not a lie. . . . In a thousand days of my childhood, she
offered a thousand different mothers for my inspection.

Pat Conroy, *The Prince of Tides*

Peggy gets pregnant at age fourteen. She has the child, a girl, but gives
her up for adoption. She is ravaged and tormented with guilt. Ten
years later she gets married, and she and her husband have a baby girl.
Peggy still harbors her dark secret. She vows that her daughter, Emily,
will never have to go through what she has endured. She overcontrols
Emily's sexual development, resorting at times to rigid moralizing. She
joins a church where the minister preaches hellfire and damnation
sermons on the evils of lust and carnal pleasure.

Emily grows up terrified about sex. She seriously represses her sexuality during adolescence. She marries as a virgin in her middle twenties
and experiences vaginitis for the first eight months of her marriage.
With the aid of therapy, she is able to start functioning sexually. She
has a daughter and vows to bring her up differently from the way her
mother brought her up.

Emily is quite permissive with her daughter, Jenny, telling her how
wonderful and glorious sex is. Jenny starts experimenting sexually at
an early age, gets pregnant at fourteen, has an abortion with help from

a friend, and suffers horrible guilt feelings. She tells no one of her dark secret, gets married, and vows that *her* daughter will never have to go through what she has had to endure. And the beat goes on!

When a child grows up with a mother who harbors a dark secret, she will be damaged by it. In order to keep her secret the mother has to set up special safeguards. She sends out clear messages that a certain area is off limits. Peggy's area of prohibition is sex. Peggy's daughter, Emily, wanting to please her mother, learns to *perceive* a certain way. She learns *not* to notice anything related to sexuality. At the same time she develops a great sensitivity to morality and is preoccupied with trying to do "the right thing" in any situation. Learning to notice what pleases mother and not to notice what disappoints her has survival value. In fact, because she is rewarded for it, it enhances her self-worth.

Peggy's dark secret shapes her daughter's sense of self-value. But ultimately it causes her problems. In the world of reality, to equate self-value with being antisexual causes pain. Emily's sexual dysfunction is ensconced in shame and pain and becomes her dark secret. In reaction she preaches a one-sided message about the pleasures of sex. For her daughter, Jenny, self-worth equals being very sexual. She acts on her conscious belief, but she also carries the dark secret of sexual shame. She reenacts her grandmother Peggy's dark secret, and now she has another dark secret to impose on her child.

As our lives can be deformed by our mother's dark secrets, we need to discover what they are.

THE DANGEROUS "SECRET" OF NARCISSISTIC DEPRIVATION

I shall begin this chapter with a dark secret that I did not include in Chapter 2. I believe it is the most common dark secret of motherhood. It shapes the behavior of mothers who love their children deeply and have only the best intentions. The secret I'm referring to is a condition known as *narcissistic deprivation*.

All of us are born with narcissistic needs. We need to look into our mothering source figure's face and see ourselves reflected there. We need this because even though we have an innate and unconscious sense of self-value, we can come to know this only by seeing ourselves as totally accepted, valued, and admired in our mother's eyes. The eyes and face are the arena where the primal scene of human life takes place. We also need to have our feelings and needs taken seriously by an attentive, empathetic, and nurturing mother. When we are valued and nurtured in this way, our narcissistic needs are satisfied.

But what if the mothering source was deprived of her own mother's mirroring face and eyes? Suppose her own mother was cold and indifferent? Or suppose she was overburdened by a bad marriage, several other children, or a lingering post-partum depression? Then the child looks and cannot see herself. Rather she sees confusion and maybe even angry rejection and neediness. A child intuitively experiences her parent's neediness and will give up the expression of her own needs and wants to take care of her mother. This is not a conscious decision made out of altruism; it is an unconscious adaptation driven by survival needs.

"It is the specific unconscious need of the mother," writes developmental psychologist Margaret Mahler, "that activates out of the infant's infinite potentialities those in particular that create for each mother 'the child' who reflects her own unique and individual needs." Mother communicates a "mirrored framework" in infinitely varied ways, to which the infant's primitive self accommodates itself.

When a woman has to suppress her own narcissistic needs in infancy, they rise from the depths of her unconscious and seek gratification through her own infant child. This happens *no matter how well educated and well intentioned this mother may be and no matter how much she is aware of what a child needs.*

The mother's original feelings of being deserted are powerful, and they are triggered by the birth of her new child. As parents go through their child's developmental stages, their own developmental deficits—if they have them—are triggered at each stage.

Of course, fathers may have narcissistic deprivation problems also. But culturally men have had many more ways to get their admiration and mirroring needs met. In the traditional family, while Father is out earning his wages, Mother is at home alone with the children. Father gets the paycheck, the fellowship and admiration of other workers, and a life in the larger world. Mother has no mirror beyond her husband and her child.

As Alice Miller writes in *The Drama of the Gifted Child:*

A child is at the mother's disposal. A child cannot run away as the mother's own mother did. . . . A child can be made to show respect, she can impose her own feelings on him, *see herself mir-*

rored in his love and admiration. . . . The mother can feel herself
the *center* of attention for her child's eyes follow her everywhere.

Thus, in a paradoxical and strange way the child becomes the mother's
narcissistic supplier. But the child is left hungry for nurture. Once deprived, the child will grow up looking for him- or herself in substitute
faces.

Men who have been narcissistically deprived (I am one of them)
spend their lives looking for themselves in the admiring faces of others. But finally, as I've had to painfully discover, no substitute will ever
suffice. No fanfare, money, worldly admiration, and acclaim can supply
the missing face, because it is our own face that we seek. Ultimately
we must deeply grieve this original desertion, and the grief has such
intensity and pain that it is clear we could not have survived it in infancy.

No mother, herself deprived, is bad or to blame for using her infant
to get her need for love and admiration met. She cannot help herself
without some outside help. If she is in a good love relationship, the
wound can start to heal. As Eric Berne once said, "Love is nature's
psychotherapy." But if she has never been loved and valued and taken
seriously, if she has never seen herself mirrored in an empathetic,
attentive, and nurturing face, her need is automatic and unconscious.
It is a dark secret of *ignorance,* one that is rooted in a deep multigenerational wound.

This wound will continue as long as we remain in the dark about it.

Your Mother, Yourself

Take your time and think through your responses to these questions:
Have you spent your life trying to make your mother happy? Give
some specific details. Does your mother call you frequently and chide
you for not calling her or coming to see her? Do you feel guilty when
she does this? When you see your mother, do you change your behavior so that she can feel good? (Like going to church with her even
though you no longer go to church.) Have you spent your life trying
to impress others and see admiration for you on their faces?

Every yes answer to these questions increases the likelihood that
you have been narcissistically deprived.

Have you ever been able to tell your mother your real feelings? Have
you ever been able to express anger to her? Are you able to tell her

the ways you disagree with her? Has your mother ever really "listened" to you? Can you go to her for validation?

Every no answer to these questions increases the likelihood that you have been narcissistically deprived.

We all have a natural desire to please the ones we love, but we do not need to be loved, even by our mothers, at the cost of ourselves. After all, a mother's job is to take care of her children. She has done her job well when they can take care of themselves. To have them beholden to her for life, ravaged by duty, obligation, and guilt, is mystified love grounded in narcissistic deprivation.

REMEMBERING YOUR MOTHER

In this chapter I will ask you to gather material for your biological mother's genogram first. Then I will discuss what James Jeder discovered when he explored his mother Heather's life. If you don't know your biological mother and can't find out anything about her, then move on to your adoptive mother or stepmother, or whoever comes closest to being there for you in a motherly way.

The compulsion to protect your parents is usually stronger when it comes to your mother. Stay focused on your mother's behavior, the things she actually said and did.

Your Image of Your Mother

Have someone ask you the following questions, or put them on a tape recorder. Pause a full minute between each question.

When you close your eyes, what image of your mom comes to you? Let the image be as clear as possible. How old is she? What is she wearing? Notice the color of her clothes if you can. Can you see her shoes? How do you feel when you look at her?

Now go to an earlier memory of your mother. Get into the memory as deeply as you can. What is your mother wearing? What is your mother doing? How do you feel when you look at your mother? Go to a memory from childhood. . . . What was it like to be a small child in your home living with your mother? Now let any other memories with your mother come to you. *(Pause for three minutes.)* How did your mother treat you as a

child? How did she discipline you? How did she show you affection? What did you like most about your mother? What did
you dislike about your mother? How did you take care of your
mother? Now slowly open your eyes.

If you have trouble visualizing, try writing out your answers to the
above questions. Be specific and concrete. Don't write, "My mom was
sullen." Rather write what you saw, heard, and felt that led you to
conclude that your mom was sullen. For example: "My mom was looking off into space and hardly answered when I said hello. She didn't
even turn her head to look at me."

After you write your answers, or as you write them, pay attention to
your reactions.

Or find as many pictures of your mom as you can. Try to find them
from various periods of *your* life and from varying periods of her life.

Set aside the ones that somehow call out to you. Now take these
one at a time, and for a period of ten minutes write spontaneously.
Write anything that comes into your mind. After you've done five or six
pictures, look over your writing and see what themes, if any, emerge.

Now take a few minutes to notice:

- Your inner bodily experiences. Do you feel restless, tense, numb,
  peaceful, sick to your stomach? Just notice whatever you experience.
- Any strong emotional reaction—fear, anger, shame, sadness, guilt,
  or anything else.
- Any desires or longings. Did you touch on heartache, disappointment, frustration, happiness?
- Any new awareness or thoughts pertaining to your mom and secrets.
  Did you experience something about your mom you've never quite
  experienced before?

Your Mother's Rules of Life

What were your mom's Ten Commandments? Take your time and
write them out. Try to remember where you first heard her expound
each one. If her ten were the original ten in the Bible, did she add
anything to them? (Like, "Honor thy father and mother, *but especially
thy mother.*") What were the *covert* rules your mother lived by? These
rules may not ever have been spoken, and they may even have *contra-
dicted* the spoken rules. They are best found by looking at behavior.

What did your mom actually do? For example, one covert rule of my mother's was, "Always please the neighbors, then rip them apart when you get home." She was the nicest person you'd ever want to meet in public, but she would take you apart piece by piece in private.

Favorite Sayings and Jokes

Make a list of your mom's favorite sayings. Do they reveal anything to you? Did she abide by those sayings? Imagine your mother doing the exact opposite. For example, one of my mother's favorite sayings was, "Don't be so emotional." In fact, my mother was highly emotional. There was a strident tone in her voice; she was quite fearful and hyper-vigilant. She was also very angry. Her own inner voices shamed her feelings, and she projected her shame onto me. Her parents' voices lived on in her and became my inner voices—which shamed me by saying, "Don't be so emotional."

What were some of your mom's favorite jokes? (Maybe you can only remember one!) Did she have a good sense of humor? Do you see any patterns in her jokes? Are they clustered around certain topics? What might that pattern reveal about her?

Secret Expectations

What did your mom leave unsaid? Tom Wingo in *The Prince of Tides* says, "I learned to fear the things she left unsaid." There may be powerful expectations that are never spoken aloud but that you know you're going to be held accountable for. Feelings of *anger* or resentment often go underground, and yet the air is thick with them.

Character Traits

What were your mom's five best character traits? (She was patient, she was caring, and so on.) Give a concrete specific behavioral example of each.

What were your mom's five worst character flaws? (She was critical, she was judgmental, and so on.) Give a concrete specific behavioral example of each.

Work and Money

What was your mother's attitude toward work and money? Was there congruity between what she said and what she did? Did she, for example, bad-mouth your father for working all the time but demand that you live in the "right" neighborhood and have the "right" kind of car? Did she constantly criticize and shame your dad for not making enough money? If she worked, did she enjoy it, or did she act martyred and overburdened? Can you trace any of your own attitudes about work and money to her?

Religion (Morality)

You may have already covered some of this in the section on your mom's Ten Commandments. What was your mother's religious belief? If she had no belief, did she call herself an agnostic or an atheist? Did she have a carefully thought-out position that she presented with some passion? Or was she simply indifferent? Did she profess to believe in God but act in a way that made money, possessions, or physical beauty into absolutes? Paul Tillich, the Lutheran theologian, said that your real God is your "ultimate concern." When I was a drinking alcoholic, my God was alcohol. I thought about it and organized my life around it. Everything I did was subordinated to alcohol. My addiction was an idolatry.

If your mother practiced a religious faith, was she fervent and committed? Did her behavior match what she believed? Was she fanatical or rigid? Or did she simply attend church or temple because it was the right thing to do socially?

All in all, was your mom an honest believer or nonbeliever?

Sexuality

In my experience dark secrets cluster around the realm of sexuality more than any other area of human life. Sexual issues were likely to be more hidden in your mother's generation. Can you imagine your mother being sexual? Sexual issues were so secret in many families that grown children have a difficult time imagining their parents being sexual. Take your time with the following questions, and be sure to go over the wrap-up exercise (physical sensations, strong feelings, and so on) after you've written your answers. Also be aware of your own ways of covering up sexual secrets. You may have unconsciously learned how to cover up sexual secrets from one or both of your parents.

How sexual was your mother before her marriage? After her marriage? How do you know? Did she have a good sexual relationship with your father? How do you know?

Did she ever talk to you about sex? How did you feel about sex when she told you about it? What did she stress? What did she leave out? Were you your mom's "little man" or "sorority sister"? Were you her sexual confidante? That is, did she tell you about her sex life? How did you feel about that?

What sexual stuff would you never have discussed with your mom?

Friends

Name five of your mother's good friends. Did her friends have anything in common? If so, what? Does her choice in friends tell you anything about her? If she had no close friends, what does that suggest? Did she try to make you her best friend? How do you feel about that?

Hobbies and Recreation

List five things your mother did for fun and recreation. Did she seem to enjoy life? Did she neglect you because she was too busy with her hobbies and other activities? Did she have no hobbies?

Associative Clusters

Try writing about your mom using associative clusters. Start with any phrase related to your mother that comes to mind. For instance, the phrase *angry housekeeper* just popped into my mind. Take the most significant word and circle it. Then begin to link it to associated ideas. My first association was *day off* because my mother used to do a major housecleaning on her day off from work. Other words that came to me were *miserable,* then *rage.* Then a new idea hit me. I was supposed to *help,* and I always felt guilty for not helping enough. It was an awful day. Mother was angry about the state of her life. She was a young woman, raising three children by herself, and having to use her one day off to clean house. It must have been very hard on her. I know it was on me.

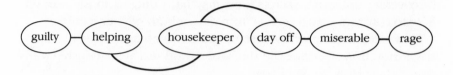

As I think about it, suddenly another idea bursts in on me. Mother was furious because she had us! Her deepest secret may have been that she really didn't want to have three children, not at thirty-four, all alone with no financial help from my father, and with no future because her religious belief forbade remarriage after divorce. This makes sense to me. I could certainly imagine feeling that way about having the responsibility of us three kids. This may have been a big secret my mother carried.

Best Day with Your Mom

Write out the details of the best day you can remember having with your mom. Once you've written about it, read it to someone you trust and let them tell you what they feel as you read your scene.

Worst Day with Your Mom

The same warning I gave you in Chapter 7 applies here: *Do not* write about sexual abuse or severe battering.

If you know that your mom was abusive to you in other ways, have someone with you for support when you do this exercise. After you have written your worst day scene, read it to your friend or support person. Their validation can help you realize that what you went through *was awful.* The focus here is on *your pain and suffering, not on your mother's intention.* As a child, you were prohibited from expressing your protective emotion (anger) and from processing your hurt (grief). When someone you trust validates your pain, it allows you to accept yourself and your experience. What happened to you was awful, and it was about your mom and not about you. The secret you have been keeping about yourself—that Mom treated you that way because you were bad—can be released. You were not bad. You were more than likely a normal child acting in a normal way.

Except in rare cases, Mom was not bad either. She was doing all she knew to do. She was probably acting out what had happened to her in her childhood.

The feeling that "I am bad" or somehow flawed and defective is a secret that all shame-based people carry.

Secret Decisions

Write out several other scenes in which your mother hurt you. Remember to do this with a support person or group. Take your time, and write the scene with as much sensory-based detail as possible. Read it to your support person(s). Get their "feeling" and/or validation. What decision about yourself do you think you made as a result of this experience? Is this decision the source of any dysfunctional behavior in your life right now? That decision was the best one that was available to you then, but you can change it now.

I remember crying because my mother didn't have any money and my sister couldn't go to the school dance. I made the *decision* that I wouldn't be poor when I grew up and that my children wouldn't want for anything. I carried through on that decision.

I also remember a terrible scene at my grandmother's house. My mother and grandmother were having a fight. My mother was closing the door on my grandmother's head! I was terrified! I made the decision that I would never have any children. I didn't want to bring a child into the world and risk that they would suffer as we had to. Thankfully, I later changed that decision.

Your Mom's Addictions

In Chapter 2 I described what Laura Gait Robert calls "the secret" that women carry, their sense of helplessness, anger, and frustration caused by their burdensome role expectations. Instead of expressing these painful feelings, many women turn them against themselves and mood-alter with food and eating disorders. Women have other forms of addictions, of course, but Mom and food somehow go together!

Anything can be used addictively. Common choices are: watching movies, soap operas, or talk shows on TV; going shopping and buying; using prescription drugs, alcohol, or other drugs; being totally obsessed with caretaking her children and/or her spouse; religious addiction; sex addiction (especially affairs); and addiction to fear (worrying).

Did or does your mother have an addiction? How did you take care of her addiction? How did that damage your life?

All addictions cover up a dark secret. The secret is the feelings that are not expressed. What feelings did your mother's addictions hide? How have you taken care of your mother's feelings? How have these feelings expressed themselves in your life?

Dialogue with Your Mother

Either have someone read this to you, or put it on a tape recorder.

Close your eyes, and imagine your mom sitting across from you. She has come to you because she wants to make amends for any harm her secrets have done to you. Ask her, "What is your greatest fear?" Let the image of your mother answer you. Don't try to control what she says. Let her response be as spontaneous as possible. After about five minutes ask your mother, "What must you be sure of?" Once again let her image answer. Then ask, "What would my mother never have done?" Let your imagination run freely until something clicks and your response feels right for you. Why would she never do this?

Now ask yourself, "What ways of life were out of the question for my mother?" Take some time to answer. Why were these ways of life out of the question?

Probing Your Mother's Shadow

What characteristics would your mother strongly deny if you ascribed them to her?

Think of five of the ways you've described your mom. Now imagine that she is just the opposite of those five descriptions. Pretend you are a lawyer arguing that your mother is exactly the opposite of the ways you have described her.

What could you never talk about with your mom? How did you know that you couldn't talk about it? Imagine yourself talking to her about these forbidden topics.

Mom's Enemies

Who were your mother's most passionate enemies? Try to remember who she scorned and criticized. The enemy doesn't have to be a particular person. She may have attacked causes or ideas. List as many persons, institutions, ideas, causes, or whatever that your mother was against. Rank them in terms of the energy (passion) she put into her attack. Maybe she was on an actual crusade! Try to focus on what bothered her the most. If she is still alive, ask her how this hatred started. What happened that caused her to expend such energy on someone or something?

Is her attack congruent with the way she lives her own life? Does she embody values that her enemy violates?

Is this enemy something within herself that she does not want to look at? In other words, is your mother projecting a forbidden part of herself onto her enemy? If she puts down "women who show off their bodies," does she perhaps secretly wish she could wear shorts or a bikini bathing suit, or whatever?

Your Mother's Wound

Look at the following summary of PTSD symptoms. See how many of these apply to your mother. If some of them are applicable, then you might entertain the hypothesis that your mother was traumatized in her childhood or adolescence.

CHECKLIST OF PTSD SYMPTOMS

- Hypervigilance (extreme nervousness or worry)
- Easily upset or startled
- Panic or anxiety attacks
- Chronic irritability
- Fear to the point of terror
- Insomnia (or any sleep disorder)
- Flashbacks (reliving part of a traumatic scene)
- Loss of motivation
- Withdrawal and isolation
- Agoraphobia (complete isolation due to extreme fear)
- Depression
- Chronic feeling of helplessness

- Chronic feeling of hopelessness
- Kindling (being upset by any kind of excitement, good or bad)
- Any form of addiction
- Reenacting a traumatic scene
- Intimacy dysfunction
- Psychosomatic illness (hypochondriasis)

What do you actually know of your mother's childhood? Ask your grandparents about her childhood, if they are alive. Ask your aunts, uncles, and her friends about her childhood. Ask her! Is it possible that she is an abuse victim? This wound may be the root of her addiction or her seemingly irrational fears. Traumatic wounds could also come from adolescence or early adulthood.

Your Mom's Disappointments

Write about your mom's greatest disappointment. Was it your dad? The prison of her marriage? The children to whom she devoted twenty-five years of her life? These issues may have formed the core of what Carl Jung called her "unlived life." In the past many women gave up the beginnings of a career in order to get married, then spent the rest of their lives fantasizing about what they might have been. Or they came to believe they *married the wrong man* and spent years obsessing on what their life would have been like if they had married their other boyfriend or someone else. How have you taken care of her disappointment? Are you an extension of her? Do you feel responsible if she is unhappy? Do you take care of her emptiness and pain? How do you take care of her marriage? Have you excelled so that she can feel good about herself?

Siblings and Others

Interview your brother(s) and sister(s) on any of the areas we have covered so far. Ask them for their perspective on your mom. They are enormously valuable resources in giving you another viewpoint. Each sibling position has its own unique way of perceiving.

Make a list of all the people who might know something about your mother—your grandparents, your aunts and uncles, her old friends, acquaintances, people she worked with, neighbors. Ask them some of the questions you have. Your dad may be an especially valuable resource. He may be very willing to tell you some things about your mother. He may also reveal a great deal by what he *doesn't* want to talk about.

Drawing the Family

Spontaneously draw a picture of your family. You can do it with stick figures or realistic figures or any other way you want. The first time I did this exercise my drawing looked like this:

My mom is the large figure in the center, my dad is the figure over in right field. He is far away, but he casts his shadow over the whole family. My sister is cut off from my mom, and my brother and I are enmeshed with her. When I showed this to the group I was with, someone immediately pointed out that my mother was four times the size of anyone else. She absolutely dominates the picture. I was stunned, because I had not consciously drawn the picture this way! Spontaneous drawings can help you express things that are unconscious. In my childhood we lived to take care of my mother's pain.

In Chapter 7 I had you draw the floor plan of the earliest house you can remember where you lived with your dad. Were your mother and father together at that time? Were there any rooms that were special to mom?

Letter from Your Mom

Imagine that you receive a letter from your mom. It is a letter asking your forgiveness and telling you how much she loves you. You read along until you come to a line that says, "Now I want to tell you my darkest secret." You must finish writing the letter. Write it boldly and without hesitation. Remember, you already know the secret. . . .

Some Final Questions

How are you like your mom?
What are *your* dark secrets?
Do you see any connection? That is, do you think your secrets are the same as hers?
How are you different from your mom?
Are you sure you are really different?

If you are male, you can still be identified with your mother. I was so enmeshed with my mother, I was my mother in my marriage. I fretted and worried and had the exact concerns she had when I was a child.

Take the two most extreme images you have of your mom, and let them coalesce. What emerges out of them? How do you feel about the new image?

Final Dialogue

Look at the last exercise we did on your dad before drawing his genogram. Do this same dialogue in relation to your mom. One part of you knows the secret(s). Let that part of you tell you what you need to know.

Record this exercise or have someone read it to you:

Close your eyes, and take about five minutes to relax. Focus on your breathing . . . just notice the air as you breathe it in and

out. Relax your muscles. . . . As you breathe in, say, "I'm getting," and as you breathe out, say, "Calm." Now imagine that you see a large screen with two people engaged in deep conversation. As the camera of your inner eye focuses on the pair, you begin to realize that both people are you. You are having a conversation with yourself. The person on your right is the conscious part of you. Take a minute to really see this image of yourself. Then look at the other you. This part of you is your unconscious, which knows vastly more than your conscious self.

Take a minute and really see this part of you. What do you see that lets you know this part is different?

Now observe your conscious self asking your unconscious self what your mother's secrets are/were.

Wait a couple of minutes, and really let your unconscious self answer spontaneously. Once your unconscious has replied, question it for clarification. Gradually let yourself fade away from this scene and slowly come to your full working consciousness.

Now write down whatever you got out of observing this dialogue between your conscious and unconscious selves.

CONSTRUCTING YOUR MOTHER'S GENOGRAM

Now you're ready to draw your mother's genograms. Remember our four focus questions:

1. What are/were your mom's major problems? What symptoms did she manifest?

2. What are the family facts that surround your mom's problems or symptoms? In looking at this, you are viewing your mother's emotional issues in the context of three generations of family life. Look at the relational patterns and the parent-child coalitions.

3. What was the emotional climate in your mother's family when

she was born? This helps you to see if she is predisposed to act out the family secrets.

4. What issues arise from your mother's sibling position? How do these issues relate to others in her family who are in the same sibling position? Whose secret would she be most likely to carry?

Now let's look at James Jeder's mother, Heather Jamison Jeder.

1. Major Problem (Symptoms)

Heather was a paradoxical and interesting lady. She had been sick off and on for years. She developed arthritis relatively young, in her early thirties, and was totally immobilized at times. It was as if her body were protesting some deep and mysterious injustice. Almost out of the blue it seemed to come on, and there was no question that she was really in pain. But why? No one seemed to really know. There was no history of rheumatoid arthritis in her family.

Heather Jamison had been quite a brilliant young woman. She started college at sixteen, but dropped out when she got pregnant. She was a voracious reader, and on several occasions in their child-hood, she read whole novels to James and Janice. She always stressed the value of education.

She also embodied a paradox of sexual prudery, contempt for men, and strange seductiveness. At one point during his long psychoanaly-sis, James confronted his mother about her seductiveness. She truly was horrified, as the kind of behavior in question was wholly uncon-scious on her part. While Heather's conscious mind repressed her sexuality, her sexuality did not go away. Instead, it emerged in camou-flaged ways. James remembers his mother coming into the bathroom and urinating while he was bathing. He remembers her asking him to help her remove her bra and girdle on numerous occasions. He also remembers her doing housework in her nightgown with nothing on under it. Her lack of boundaries was far too stimulating for James. He was later attracted to older women, and a core part of his stash of pornography was pictures of older women in girdles.

James angrily recalled his mother's teasing him at the dinner table about the small size of his penis. This caused him great pain.

When she was confronted by James about these things, Heather was horrified. She was clear that she had not done anything with malicious intent. She wanted to help James, so she decided to tell him a dark secret she had learned from her mother, Josephine, during her final illness with cancer.

Josephine's Dark Secret

After Donald Jamison's mother died, he secretly collected her underclothes and demanded that his wife, Josephine, wear them during sex.

When Heather reached her early teens and blossomed sexually, Donald had Josephine wear *her* undergarments during sex and had her pretend that she was Heather. Heather, while knowing nothing of this consciously, seems to have been acting this out sexually. She was quite seductive as a young teenager and once told James that she had fantasized about older men being aroused by her in her underclothes, especially the minister at her church. She also told James that the family doctor had fondled her on two occasions while he examined her. She said she felt very guilty about all this, and that after she got pregnant by Shane, she was convinced she was oversexed and evil.

I mentioned earlier that the secret fantasies of one family member can be acted out by another family member. This situation is the most dangerous when it is a parent's secret fantasy about his child. Donald and Josephine were acting out Donald's fantasies in one bedroom, while Heather slept in another.

Heather rebelled and acted out sexually by having sex with Shane and getting pregnant at a rather early age, but once she divorced Shane, she consciously shut down her sexuality and never went out with or touched another man again. She may have secretly continued to masturbate. This is impossible to verify, but James told me of a strange incident after the divorce, when Heather had to go to the emergency room because she had an object stuck in her vagina. No reasonable explanation was ever given for this; it was simply passed off as if such things happened to every woman once in a while. In the context of this family, a secret life of self-sex would not be an unjustified hypothesis.

James could not understand Heather's sexual isolation after her divorce. He had heard her say on two occasions, "I couldn't start dating—I was too sexual." After this mysterious admission, she added, "I had to be there for you and Janice." James became aware in therapy of how such a statement set him up to carry the burden of his mother's sexuality.

James's sister, Janice, was also severely impacted by her mother. Janice was an unwanted child and a sickly and difficult baby. Later she became defiant and rebellious. Heather was verbally abusive to her, and James reported that Heather and Janice were in a continual power struggle.

Janice left home at seventeen, went to work, and married a verbally abusive man with whom she lived for fifteen years until he died. She remarried an irresponsible man who basically refused to work or support her. She divorced him after ten years.

Janice continually sought her mother's approval, and until she began a recovery program, she stayed emotionally cut off from her father, Shane. Once in recovery, she tried to help her brother, James.

As we have seen, Carl Jung believed that the "unlived lives" of parents are one of the major causes of their children's neuroses. James's mother was setting him up to take care of her unlived sex life, which he did in his masturbation fantasies!

2. Problems in Context

If you look at Heather's genogram in Chart 8–1, it is clear that overt and covert sexual issues dominated her family's life. Her grandfathers, Milton O'Hern and Boyd Jamison, embody this polarization. One was overt in his womanizing and may have incested his daughter; the other kept up the family image as he did incest his daughters.

It is also clear that the women in Heather's family are burdened by what I spoke of in Chapter 2 as "the gender secret" that women carry from their culturally defined role as self-sacrificers.

The women in Heather's family model the repression of anger. All were dutiful and conforming. Her grandmother Elizabeth Jamison set some kind of sexual boundary with her husband, but she turned to the Bible, religion, and her son to mood-alter her pain and loneliness. Her grandmother Patricia O'Hern and her mother Josephine were both seriously overweight and converted their anger into psychosomatic illness. James remembers that his mother's rheumatoid arthritis became so intense, she often had to be carried around their house. The burden she was carrying was too much. Her legs refused to walk. Her body was metaphorically saying, "I can't go on anymore."

CHART 8-1

HEATHER JAMISON JEDER: PROBLEMS IN CONTEXT

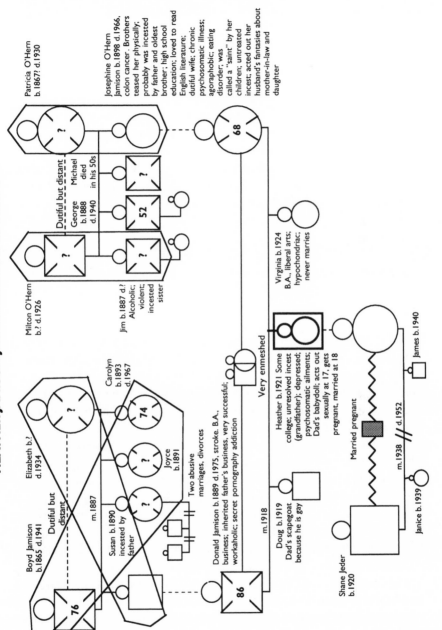

Patricia O'Hern
b.1867? d.1930

Milton O'Hern
b.? d.1926

Dutiful but distant

George
b.1888
d.1940

Michael
died
in his 50s

Jim b.1887 d.?
Alcoholic;
violent;
incested
sister

Josephine O'Hern
Jamison b.1898 d.1966,
colon cancer. Brothers
teased her physically;
probably was incested
by father and oldest
brother; high school
education; loved to read
English literature;
dutiful wife; chronic
psychosomatic illness;
agoraphobic; eating
disorder; was
called a "saint" by her
children; untreated
incest; acted out her
husband's fantasies about
mother-in-law and
daughter

68

Virginia b.1924
B.A. liberal arts;
hypochondriac;
never marries

Very enmeshed

James b.1940

Heather b.1921 Some
college; unresolved incest
(grandfather); depressed;
psychosomatic ailments;
Dad's babydoll; acts out
sexually at 17, gets
pregnant, married at 18

Married pregnant

m.1938 // d.1952

Janice b.1939

Shane Jeder
b.1920

Boyd Jamison
b.1865 d.1941

Dutiful but distant

m.1887

Elizabeth b.?
d.1934

Carolyn
b.1893
d.1967

74

Joyce
b.1891

Susan b.1890
incested by
father

Two abusive
marriages, divorces

Donald Jamison b.1889 d.1975, stroke. B.A.,
business; inherited father's business, very successful;
workaholic; secret pornography addiction

m.1918

Doug b.1919
Dad's scapegoat
because he is gay

76

86

52

In the context of her family history and its many dark secrets, Heather's problems seem quite predictable. Her female role models were covertly telling her:

- Our sex is inferior.
- Sex is a woman's onerous and unpleasant duty.
- Being a woman carries an enormous burden.

Heather openly rebelled against this burden with her early sexual promiscuity, only to confirm her forebears' teachings. Being sexual cost her her life. She eloped with a man because she was pregnant and spent the next twenty-five years raising his two children all alone. The price of rebellion must have been too high for her. She either gave up or went into hiding with her sexuality.

3. Family Emotional Climate at Time of Birth

If you look at Chart 8–2, you can see a number of predisposing factors that make Heather a prime candidate for carrying this family's dark secrets.

She is the fulfillment of her mother's and her father's desires and prayers. Donald has already emotionally cut himself off from his son Doug, saying he doesn't like boys because they are messy and hard to handle. As time passes, it becomes obvious that Doug is gay. Donald cuts him off even more because of this. But it is worth noting that these are just conscious rationalizations to justify the acting out of the deeper family pattern: father-son cutoff.

At the time of her birth, Heather's mom and dad, Donald and Josephine, are happily married and still blissfully in love. Donald has not yet involved Josephine in his secret sexual "acting out." But he makes Heather his "little princess" from the day she is born.

In contrast, Heather's grandparents on both sides exhibit cold and nonintimate marriages. Both grandmothers are in cross-generational bonds with Heather's parents: Elizabeth with Donald, and Patricia with Josephine. Her aunts and uncles are in various interlocking triangles. There is sexual compulsivity in both her mother's and father's families, and both her parents have unresolved sexual issues.

The Jamison family looked very good from the outside. Heather loved to spend Sundays at her grandparents' house. For years she thought that the Jamisons represented what a "happy family" was like.

CHART 8-2

EMOTIONAL CLIMATE AT HEATHER JAMISON'S BIRTH, 1921

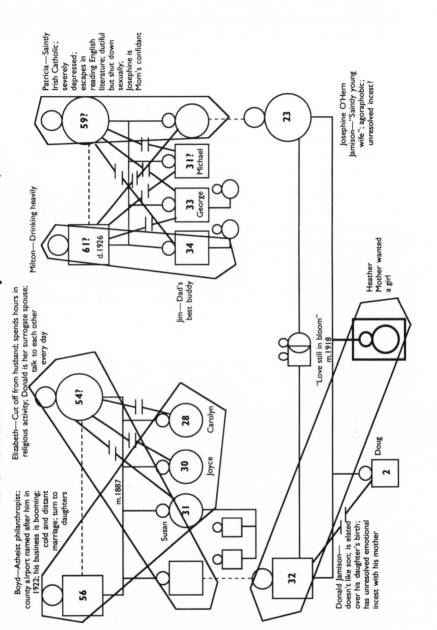

According to James, Heather never spoke much about her experience with the O'Hern family, her mother's parents. When James confronted Heather about her sexual seductiveness with him, she mentioned only that she did not like her grandfather and that he was alcoholic.

A few years later, Heather quite casually referred to her sexual abuse at the hands of her grandfather. James told me that she acted as if he already knew about it and minimized the whole thing. When James questioned her more closely, Heather told him that it had happened twice, once when she was ten and a second time when she was twelve, and that she had always felt that maybe she had "come on to him." On both occasions her grandfather made her sit on his lap. The first time he put her hand on his erect penis and used it to give himself a climax. The second time, as he moved her buttocks over his erect penis, he rubbed her vagina with his finger until he reached a climax. On another occasion Heather casually told the story about Grandfather O'Hern drilling the hole in the bathroom wall.

My own sense of all this was that Heather was quite delusional and dissociated. She looked upon her grandfather's behavior as typical of men and accepted the abuse as part of her lot as a woman. This attitude was fairly common in her day. James also found out from his Aunt Virginia that she had been violated sexually, although she would not talk about any specific incident.

It was clear to me that James's mother, Heather, had been incested by her grandfather, who had been a sex offender and an alcoholic. Heather carries several of this family's dark sexual secrets. She is the most likely child to be the object of her parents' projections during periods of stress and anxiety in their marriage, and she is a probable candidate to act out what is covert in this family system.

4. Sibling Position Issues

Heather is the second child in birth order. Look at her sibling position profile in Chart 8–3.

The child in the second sibling position is the one who most picks up the implicit, unresolved secrets from the whole family and from her mother in particular. Heather is in a precarious position. Her grandmother Patricia O'Hern, who was the second child in her family, is a long-suffering dutiful wife who was victimized by her husband. Her uncle George O'Hern, another second child, was the rebel who ran

CHART 8-3

HEATHER JAMISON: SIBLING POSITION PROFILE

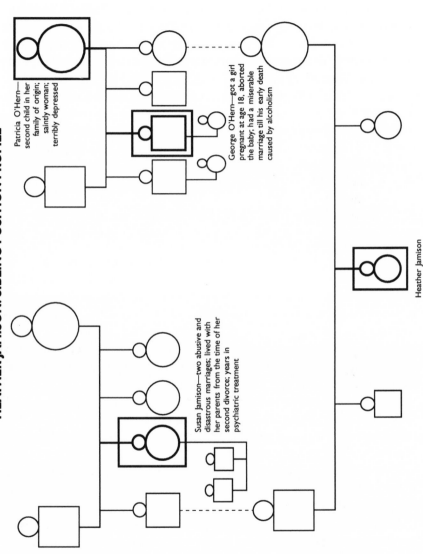

Patricia O'Hern—
second child in her
family of origin;
saintly woman;
terribly depressed

George O'Hern—got a girl
pregnant at age 18, aborted
the baby; had a miserable
marriage till his early death
caused by alcoholism

Susan Jamison—two abusive and
disastrous marriages; lived with
her parents from the time of her
second divorce; years in
psychiatric treatment

Heather Jamison

away from home and got a girl pregnant at eighteen. He paid the mother to have the child aborted, which "almost destroyed" his devout Irish Catholic mother when she found out. He married three years later and had a tumultuous marriage until he died of alcoholism.

Heather's aunt Susan Jamison, the woman in the Jamison family in Heather's birth position, was the aunt she was closest to as a child. Susan was victimized by her father and by two abusive marriages. She spent years in and out of psychiatric treatment. After the second divorce, she lived with her parents until their death.

Heather ultimately chose to follow her Grandmother O'Hern's example of fidelity to her Catholic faith and dutiful, long-suffering enmeshment with her children. Her sibling position choices were rather bleak, and her early rebellion was possibly her strongest push to break the grip of her family bondage.

Effects on James Jeder

James Jeder inherited much of this unresolved family history, particularly his mother's unconscious anger over her sexual abuse. Because James's identity came primarily from his mother, he had to carry the projection of her sexual anger and contempt for men. He internalized this contempt and acted it out in his obsession with pornographic pictures of older women. James's childish and desperate need for attachment, and his lack of a stable male identity, were acted out in his affairs. He frantically wanted to be loved by a woman, and at the same time he feared being devoured by that love.

When I brought his wife Karen into our therapy, she described James as "hanging out of a window in his castle calling desperately for me to come to him, and when I got there, pulling up the drawbridge." She felt she was in a double bind.

Learning how to lower the drawbridge and risk vulnerability was a major step in James's recovery. Karen helped him to do this—but I'm getting ahead of myself.

As bleak as Heather's impact on James was, it is important for you to remember that he was also a brilliant professor of English and a fine poet. All this was certainly stimulated by Heather's desire to learn and by her love of literature. She spent many hours reading to him as a child and always showed great pride in his ability at school.

* * *

At this juncture I hope you've been able to draw your mother's genograms. Don't worry about integrating all the details that I have used
for Heather. Very few genograms come out this neat and tidy. The
important thing is to get a larger view of your family as the context of
your problems and your own dark secrets. We are now ready to see
how all that we have discovered applies to *you.*

PART THREE

GETTING BACK
TO KANSAS

"Where is Kansas?" asked the man in surprise. "I don't know," replied Dorothy sorrowfully, "but it is my home, and I'm sure it's somewhere."

L. FRANK BAUM, *The Wonderful Wizard of Oz*

CHAPTER 9

DISCOVERING YOUR OWN DARK SECRETS

Deprive the average man of his vital lie and you have
robbed him of happiness as well.

HENRIK IBSEN

Every man has matters . . . he would not reveal even to
his friends, but only to himself and that in secret. But
there are other things which a man is afraid to tell even
to himself.

FYODOR DOSTOYEVSKY

When I read the story of the wonderful Wizard of Oz, I could not
understand *why* Dorothy wanted to go back to Kansas. L. Frank
Baum's description made it seem awful. The place she called home
was "nothing but great gray prairie on every side, the grass was not
green, the sun had burned the tops of the long blades until they were
the same gray color to be seen everywhere." Aunt Em "never smiled,"
and Uncle Henry "never laughed and worked from morning to night,
and he looked stern and solemn and rarely spoke." Why would anyone
want to go back there? But Dorothy longs to return.

One way of interpreting these images of barren land, burned grass,
and deadly serious relatives is to view Dorothy's return to Kansas as a
symbol of our own struggle for rigorous self-honesty. To be "at home"
with myself, to be authentic, I have to give up my childhood enchant-
ments and self-delusions and face up to the gray truth about myself.
Challenging our own desire to be innocent is the core of soul work,
and no one ever does it perfectly. Even the best of us create slightly

edited versions of ourselves—and then repress the fact that we are being dishonest. Some self-deception seems to be a hard and fast condition of our human nature. We simply cannot know all there is to know about ourselves—let alone about anyone else in our family.

When we looked for unknown dark secrets in our parents' genograms, we called it their *shadow*. Now, in order to complete your genogram, you need to make a fearless and searching self-examination aimed at finding your own shadow.

To give you a structure for your self-examination, I will use a figure called Johari's window. I first encountered this figure at a group therapy weekend for professional therapists, and I will show you how I used it in my own self-examination.

JOHARI'S WINDOW

Johari's window is based on the assumption that everyone has blind spots in their consciousness and that we cannot fully see ourselves as others see us or even as we are. (See Chart 9–1.) The four-paned window represents your whole self, but only the aspects of yourself in the top two windowpanes are visible to you. These panes house your public and private selves, including your conscious dark secrets. The third and fourth windowpanes represent aspects of yourself that are unknown to you. They house the truths about your identity that others see or that are still unconscious to you. Pane 3 contains the self-delusion that keeps you from knowing who you really are. Self-delusion is the reason a person can slowly self-destruct without any real awareness of how out of control their life has become—even though it is plain to other people. Pane 4 contains the secrets you keep from yourself and that are also unknowable to others. These include repressed memories of trauma and abuse, the repressed parts of yourself that were judged unlovable and unacceptable by your parents or other source figures, and the unconscious dark secrets that are part of your family's group mind. Pane 4 also contains those parts of yourself that are, as yet, your undiscovered potentials.

CHART 9-1

JOHARI'S WINDOW

	KNOWN TO OTHERS	UNKNOWN TO OTHERS
KNOWN TO YOURSELF	**Windowpane 1** YOUR PUBLIC SELF Social roles The face you present to the world (persona) Job, work Pastimes, rituals, games Values	**Windowpane 2** YOUR PRIVATE SELF All areas of privacy Hang-ups (secret fears) Dark secrets held consciously • Resentments • Toxic Shame Uninhibited private behaviors
UNKNOWN TO YOURSELF	**Windowpane 3** YOUR BLIND SPOTS What others observe and know about you that you hide from yourself Clues: • Incongruent behavior • Overreactions	**Windowpane 4** YOUR UNCONSCIOUS The depths of your soul Repressed material Dark secrets in your family's group mind Your undiscovered potentialities Clues: • Repetitive behavior patterns • Denial • Projections • Ego defenses

Windowpane 1: Your Public Self

At the therapists' group therapy weekend, each of us presented ourselves with caution. My own shame voices started blaring the moment
I walked in the room. The other therapists looked and sounded much
smarter, more skillful, and wiser than I. One was dressed in such a
casual way, I felt he couldn't be as anxious as I was. (I had chosen my
green sport jacket with the leather elbow pads and wore a loosened
tie—which fit my image of a smart working therapist.) Two men came
in wearing three-piece suits, claiming to have come to the group
straight from their offices. I felt tension in the room as someone intro-
duced a game of "ain't it awful" about not getting enough insurance
to cover people's emotional health. Someone else was making small
talk about the relative merits of luxury cars. Then the facilitator walked
in. He was a renowned and respected therapist. He looked perfect to
me, lean and trim in a navy blue shirt and form-fitting jeans. He gave
each of us a copy of Johari's window, and showed us how to work
with it.

Windowpane 1 houses your public self. The first three categories it
contains are fairly obvious. You are publicly known by the social roles
you play in life. The face you present to the public includes a lot of
pretense—some of it necessary. Everyone knows the basic rules of
social life, and part of that agenda is benign superficiality rather than
gut-level intimacy. Your modesty warns you to stay guarded till you
feel it is safe to come out. Your work—the third category—forms a
large part of your public identity. We frequently introduce friends (or
ourselves) by saying their occupation right after their name.

Pastimes, Rituals, Games

It is accepted that we will structure public time in certain conventional
ways. Eric Berne, the founder of a mode of therapy called transactional
analysis (TA), outlined several ways of structuring time. These include
solitude (time with yourself) and intimacy (sharing your self and time
with another). In between these two extremes he put things we usually do in groups, including work, pastimes, ritual activities, and games.

Pastimes are things like hobbies and talking about the weather,
sports events, cars, the children, and the spouse. Rituals include things
like salutations and good-byes, rules of etiquette, and standing to sing
the national anthem. Doing your daily job involves starting and finish-

ing rituals. Families have rituals around eating, going to church, and celebrations. Business offices hold various rituals, like planning sessions, weekly meetings, going on breaks, and gossiping.

Berne's exploration of "games people play" is especially important for Windowpane 1. Common social games involve secret strategic moves that put us into one-up positions and give us a feeling of power over others. This happens a lot at work and in the family. An insecure boss, needing to feel more powerful, might be quite vague about a work deadline and then raise holy hell because the work was not done by 5:00 P.M., shaming a worker with a statement like, "You should have known."

Another common game is called "Now I've got you, you SOB." For example, Billy Jones wants his oldest brother, Tom's, attention. One evening the whole Jones family is watching a TV show. At one point everyone except Billy laughs at a certain comic scene. At the end of the program, Tom, who likes to be one-up, asks Billy if he thought the scene was funny (knowing that Billy hadn't laughed).

Billy, who didn't get the jokes in the scene, answers no. Instead of explaining the jokes, Tom tells him he has a lousy sense of humor. Billy feels like there's something wrong with him.

In any game there is always a come-on, a *secret* move that invites the other person to play. Tom's question appears to be a genuine inquiry, but it is really a setup to put Billy down.

A game always has a gimmick. The gimmick is the other person's vulnerability, which sets up their need to play. In the Jones family Billy wants Tom's attention—that's why he answers the question. A game always has a reversal where one is caught off guard and is put in a one-down position. Billy answers Tom in the belief that Tom is interested in him and then finds himself shamed.

Games can have various degrees of toxicity. Some are simply nasty. Others are sadistic and deadly. Parents who have unresolved abuse issues and lack a sense of personal power often engage in abusive games with their children. One of my clients described how her father used to come into the bathroom while she was combing her hair in the mirror. He would ask her if she thought she was pretty. If she answered in any way that implied she did, her father would start slapping her face and quoting Scripture to her, declaring how evil it was to be vain and that the Devil was in her.

Time and Values

Berne suggested that it is worth thinking about how much of our time we spend in each category. For example, let's say your time graph looks like this:

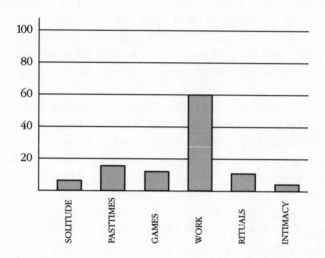

This would indicate that your public and private lives are way out of balance. Ninety percent of the time you are in the public arena. Less than ten percent of your time is devoted to privacy. Social life necessitates a certain amount of deselfing, and you are not allowing yourself enough time to recuperate and nurture yourself. A time graph can help you see where your values lie, since you give time to what is valuable to you. For example, if you spend seventy percent of your waking hours at work, you might want to look at the possibility that you are lying to yourself about your devotion to family life.

Your public life can be a good gauge for clarifying your values in other ways as well. Do you consistently and repeatedly take action about the things that are important to you? Are you willing to publicly proclaim what you believe?

Exercise for Roles and Values

Make a list of all the roles you play in your life (for example, plumber, catcher on the softball team, member of the Presbyterian church, father, good neighbor, comedian in the family of origin, mother's scape-goat). Now imagine giving up these roles one at a time, from the least significant to the most significant. This will give you a sense of how much you are attached to each role and how much value it has for you. The roles that are the most difficult to give up are the ones you value most.

Windowpane 2: Your Private Self

Windowpane 2 is the part of you that is unknown to others and known only to yourself. This area includes all the behaviors of privacy described in Chapter 1. These are things that we should be protected from having to share, like our sexual fantasies and our own special ways of prayer.

Windowpane 2 also houses all of your hang-ups (secret fears), your consciously held dark secrets, your resentments, your areas of toxic shame, and your uninhibited private behaviors.

The therapist who was working with my group explained that when we choose to share what's behind Windowpane 2 in Johari's window, we *level* with each other.

I found that as others in the group leveled about things, it became very easy for me to do the same.

One man leveled about his sense of inadequacy as a therapist. He told us that he often felt confused and unable to help his clients. Another leveled about sleeping with a young female client. He shared that he was nearly crazy with fear that she would sue him and that he "felt rotten, that he was a lousy human being." I leveled about the fact that I was teaching adult theology and having severe doubts about my faith. I told them how much I resented my authoritarian religious upbringing. Another man leveled about his fear of speaking in a group.

Leveling in this way had a deep impact on me. I was touching my feelings and sharing my honest beliefs and desires. I was telling secrets that seemed terrible to me, and yet these guys were totally *accepting me*.

I urge you to level with *yourself*. It's a good place to begin. Maybe you are sick and tired of lying, cheating, and living with toxic shame. Maybe this is the time to get honest with yourself. If you're an addict, start with a 12-step group that deals with your addiction, or find a therapist or a therapy group. You need a nonshaming friend who will hear you without judgment or interpretation.

You need to tell someone your secrets. The only way out of toxic shame and hiding is to embrace the shame and level about it.

The Best Secret

I can tell you that the best secret you have ever discovered lies beyond all your fantasies of rejection resulting from telling your faithfully kept secrets. I wrote about this ultimate secret at the end of my book *Healing the Shame That Binds You:* If toxic shame is revolutionary, shame itself is *revelatory.* Toxic shame not only hides our true self from others, it *hides our true self from ourselves.* Only by embracing the shame and coming out of hiding are we able to see ourselves reflected in another's eyes. Only by seeing ourselves reflected in the eyes of a valued other can the process of self-discovery begin. As our significant others accept us as we are in the act of revealing our secret selves, we can internalize their mirroring eyes and accept ourselves. Leveling is one of the major means of *self-discovery.* To risk leveling is very scary. It is a big step on the way through the Haunted Forest.

As our therapy group moved on to Windowpane 3, I realized that I had told some secrets, but there were others I was still too ashamed to tell. These were secrets about sexual behavior; about my disappointment in my marriage; about my insecurity about money; about how much fear contaminated my life. Some of these secrets began to surface when we looked at Windowpane 3.

Windowpane 3: The Blind Aspect of the Self

Windowpane 3 contains your blind spots—the secrets you don't know but that others know about you. People reveal themselves through their behavior. And no matter how hard they may try to cover up, what they actually *do* gives them away.

You are unaware of how you look in the categories listed in Windowpane 3, but this pane is open to others. That is one reason it is so important to have a trusted friend or support group. We need to let another person tell us how we *appear* to them.

Once we establish trust by leveling, then we can risk confrontation. We all need feedback and, at times, the confrontation of others.

My group confronted me on two issues that led me to discover deeper secrets later on. The first secret was my all-pervading *fear.* One evening while I was leveling to them about my family background, the therapist confronted me with the sensory-based fact that I was talking very fast and in a higher-pitched voice than usual. He said there was a "pleading," almost frantic quality to my disclosure. Others in the group agreed. I sounded like a terrified little boy, they said, who was begging them to validate the pain and terror I grew up with and obviously (to them) still had. I had no idea that I came across as frantic and pleading. As they gave me their feedback, I connected with the raw terror that had dominated my early family life. I suddenly had a memory of clinging to my sister as we walked to school. I remembered being terrified as we passed older and bigger boys. Later I saw that fear dominated the emotional system of my family of origin.

The group also confronted me after I described how happy I was in my marriage. Actually my marriage had been in trouble for twelve years. I was lonely and not getting my needs met. My wife felt the same, although we never actually talked about it. Later, when I did my first genogram, I saw that I had reenacted my relationship with my mother in my marriage. This was due to my secret bond to take care of my mother's happiness.

Confrontation taught me that the most obvious way that people know us is through our *behavior.* The way we look at someone or away from them; whether our voice tone matches our body posture; the way we breathe; the flush and color of our face; the way we hold our hands—all these nonverbal cues tell others whether we are being *congruent* or *incongruent.* Congruence is the match between what we say and how we say it. When we talk to others, we are aware that sometimes the content of their speech doesn't match the process. A man telling us how happy he feels in a slow droning voice makes us wonder about his truthfulness, but it's hard to notice this about *ourselves.*

People often know about our secrets by noticing our defensive overreactions. When a person "protests too much," they often reveal their dishonesty. I look for the amount of energy in a defensive response. If a person is not guilty, they usually say so immediately and matter-of-factly.

Nothing triggers my defenses more than when someone criticizes me in the same way I am secretly criticizing myself, or when I know I am wrong but don't want to admit it. My loud protestations are often a dead giveaway. They reveal to others what I deny in myself or refuse to see.

As my self-awareness has grown through confrontation and feed-back, I have started to learn a lot about Windowpane 4.

Windowpane 4: The Secrets You Keep from Yourself

We had no time to work on Windowpane 4 at my therapy weekend, but this window represents those things you don't consciously know and that others don't know about you but that can be hurting you greatly. It can also represent parts of yourself that are secret strengths and potentials. We come to discover our unconscious over time. Its content emerges in our repetitive patterns of behavior, in our denials, in our projections, and in our ego defenses. We can also discover it by looking at our family patterns in the genogram.

Before I return to your personal genogram, I'll give you some con-crete tools for exploring Windowpane 4 of Johari's window, with exam-ples from James Jeder and other patients.

CLUES TO UNCONSCIOUS DARK SECRETS

Repetitive Behavior Patterns

Freud's greatest insight was that repression leads to repetition. When our needs are unresolved and unmet in childhood, we keep trying to get those needs fulfilled. We unconsciously look for a person or situa-tion that resembles the original situation, and we repeat it. *Since the motivation is unconscious, we forget that we have repeated it, and when a new and similar situation arises, we do it again.* Sometimes it takes a third abusive relationship, a third divorce, or a third lost job to signal us that something is wrong. We begin to see a recurring pattern and suspect that something unconscious is going on.

James Jeder's discovery of his mother's emotional incest forced him to look at a repetitive pattern in his relationships with women, includ-ing both his wives. Chart 9–2 gives you a quick overview of the pattern.

James met his first wife, Sue, while he was in his last year of college. She worked as an assistant at the university library. James fell madly and intensely in love with her. She was economically unable to attend college, quite young (seventeen years old), smart, and totally fasci-nated with James's mind.

CHART 9-2

JAMES JEDER'S CYCLES OF SEX AND LOVE ADDICTION

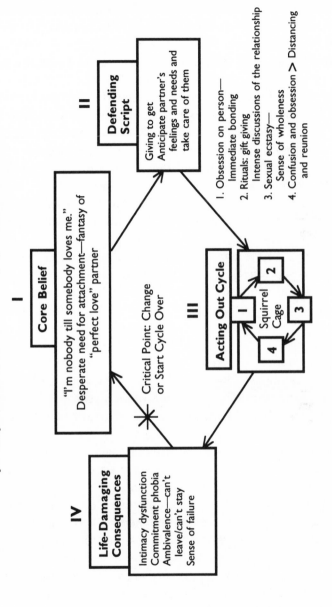

I Core Belief

"I'm nobody till somebody loves me." Desperate need for attachment—fantasy of "perfect love" partner

II Defending Script

Giving to get
Anticipate partner's feelings and needs and take care of them

1. Obsession on person—
   Immediate bonding
2. Rituals: gift giving
   Intense discussions of the relationship
3. Sexual ecstasy—
   Sense of wholeness
4. Confusion and obsession > Distancing and reunion

III Acting Out Cycle

Squirrel Cage

1 2 3 4

Critical Point: Change or Start Cycle Over

IV Life-Damaging Consequences

Intimacy dysfunction
Commitment phobia
Ambivalence—can't leave/can't stay
Sense of failure

James loved how she pampered and admired him. He felt "high" on the narcissistic supplies she gave him. The stage was set for great disappointment, as this luminous reciprocal fantasy was bound to fade. When it died, each became aware of the other's intense neediness and all-too-human foibles. But Sue was already pregnant with Jack. They made their marriage vows with great ambivalence. James always had one foot in and one foot out of the marriage. This remained the pattern in all his affairs and in his second marriage.

James was in graduate school when he began an affair with Karen, a fellow grad student. The affair began with immediate passion and intense emotions. When Karen got pregnant with Hannah, James divorced Sue and married Karen. But they soon became disillusioned and disappointed with each other. Karen had developed strong feelings of distrust for James, which is often the case when a woman marries a man who leaves his wife for her. Karen became all-engulfing, checking on James to know his whereabouts at all times. James soon felt his familiar *ambivalence.* His fantasy of Karen as the "perfect" woman was shattered. He wanted to leave the marriage but felt guilty because of the promises he had made during courtship—promises of everlasting love and adoration. He also felt guilty because of their daughter, Hannah, who was the apple of his eye and soon became his "little princess."

James interspersed periods of trying to work on his marriage with periods of alcoholic drinking, affairs, and self-sex with pornography. Daily life with Karen often consisted of intense late-night discussions that were endlessly repetitious and that usually ended in rageful threats.

These repetitive patterns reflect emotional incest. Emotional incest victims are the "special" child. They are *used* by the parent (most often unconsciously) to fill up his or her desperate hunger for attachment. But in filling up the parent's emptiness, the victim is abandoned emotionally and becomes extremely needy. This was the case with James. His mother Heather's neediness, plus *her* unresolved incest, moved her to seduce her firstborn son. She became the "perfect" mother, whom James sought in every woman he fell in love with. Emotional incest victims create an idealized fantasy parent in order to protect themselves from the pain of knowing that their parent is *using* them. This idealization is unconscious. The fantasy of perfection, plus James's neediness, made it impossible for him to make a relationship choice based on reality. When the illusion died, the struggle with commitment began.

In the beginning of a relationship, James would take care of all his lover's needs (as he had taken care of his mother's) in order to fill his own tremendous needs (which is mother had never done). James was "giving to get" and committing to a fantasy. But his giving and the intensity of his early commitment promises made it hard for him to leave. He felt intense guilt even at the thought. The guilt stemming from the fantasy-bond giving also kept James from identifying his own personal needs and expressing them in a healthy way that would help the relationship. Instead, James mood-altered the ambivalence and uncertainty with alcohol and self-sex.

Discovering all this in his therapy was momentous for James. As we will see in Chapter 10, James was able to demythologize his mother, grieve his abuse, forgive, and stay connected with her and work on his relationship with Karen and his children.

Denial

Denial and its cousin, delusion, hide our secrets from ourselves. *Denial* is defined as "believing in spite of the facts." A woman's thirty-year alcoholic husband stops drinking for a few days, and she says he's not *really* an alcoholic! *Delusion* is sincere denial. Mother *really believes* that all families have problems and that men will be men—that's why Dad gets loaded twice a week.

Denial is usually the end process of a sequence that begins with lies. The lies create secrets. The secrets are maintained through silence, and the secrets lead to denial.

According to Edgar P. Nace, in his book *The Treatment of Alcoholism,* denial has four characteristics:

- It is largely unconscious. It therefore differs from lying.
- It protects the person's option to keep doing what they are denying, which in the case of addiction is believed to be a life-or-death matter.
- It protects the fragile self from being overwhelmed by a sense of hopelessness and despair.
- It keeps the person from knowing their own secrets. Maintaining these secrets feeds their denial.

Exercise for Blind Spots and Denial

Honestly write out a list of character defects or negative behaviors or traits that people have confronted you about. These are painful matters, and you have probably been very defensive about them.

You may be so controlling and rageful that your friends and loved ones fear you. If this is true, you live in ignorance about yourself. Think it over carefully. Be sure you are willing to receive confrontation without retaliation. If so, ask your spouse, children, or best friends to give you honest feedback on how they experience you.

Projection

Projection is another clue that can help us to track down the secrets we keep from ourselves. Projection is a way to handle forbidden feelings, impulses, or thoughts by putting distance between ourselves and whatever we can't bear. What we feel on the inside, we cast outside. The excessively self-righteous, who judge and condemn others, are often avoiding the very things within themselves that they can't bear to look at. The paranoid see dangers and threats everywhere, but the real dangers are the voices within them that condemn and criticize their feelings, desires, and wants.

The feeling, impulse, or idea, once projected, becomes a deep and unconscious secret we keep from our awareness. When we meet a projected part of ourselves, it appears as a strange and foreign experience that we passionately oppose. Carl Jung pointed out that when an inner experience is repressed, it often appears outside of us as fate. We think it is fate, but it really is a disowned part of ourselves that secretly gathers energy and functions like a hungry animal chained in the cellar trying to get out.

Two very famous TV evangelists were ruined because they were unaware of the dynamic power of their own projections. One preached vehemently against sex, even condemning women for wearing shorts; he was twice caught with prostitutes. The other disavowed any personal desire for money, even as he was being indicted for fraudulently cheating his followers out of millions.

We need feedback and confrontation because our earliest defense mechanisms are mostly unconscious. Observers can sometimes see our projections and help us through confrontation. But spotting projections is not as easy as spotting incongruity. You usually have to know a person and their associates for a while before you can spot their projections.

So many of us do not know who we really are because we hang around with people who tell us only what we want to hear, or we live in families that mistake lies and niceness for truth.

Projection Exercise

Make a list of the people you frequently criticize or passionately despise. Next to each write down the character defect or personality trait that you particularly dislike about them.

Next go through the list and ask yourself honestly if you have the same trait and secretly despise it in yourself. Thinking about the people and things you dislike and resent may reveal secrets about yourself that you keep from yourself.

Ego Defenses

Your brain's major task is self-preservation and avoidance of pain. Whenever reality became intolerable to you as a child, you had natural mechanisms of pain reduction called ego defenses available to help you. They were the best choices you had, and once you chose them, they became automatic and unconscious.

Your ego defenses, so necessary for your survival in childhood, are among your secrets today. Since they are still unconscious, you need to make them conscious so that you can use them when appropriate and let them go when they are inappropriate. For example, Elvin's secret was that he had been molested as a child. He had no conscious awareness of his violation till he heard a lecture on incest. During the talk he felt agitated and had a wild desire to scream at the lecturer to shut up. After the lecture he went home and cried for several hours. He thought about himself and his life. He was 120 pounds overweight. His handsome face and body were lost in the rotund layers of flesh that hid all vestiges of his male sexuality. He had rarely dated or been serious about a woman. His two sexual experiences, both with prostitutes, had been painful and humiliating. He vowed to seek help.

During the course of his treatment, he "remembered" performing oral sex on his grandmother several times. Slowly, painful memories began to surface as he felt once again the feelings of his violation. It took several years for him to connect with all his feelings, especially his anger and rage about the violation. He came to see that most of his symptoms of dysfunction—his obesity, agoraphobia, hatred and fear of women, and disdain for sex—*were symptoms of his violation and abuse.* These behaviors were perfectly consistent with the self-preserving ego defenses he had chosen in order to keep himself from further harm. These *very* defenses that had saved his life, he came to see, *were also keeping him from having a life.*

THE DARK SECRET OF AN ABUSIVE CHILDHOOD

The most potent ego defense is what I call "the dark secret of an abusive childhood."

This secret contains two subsecrets:

- Erasing the truth of what happened in our childhood
- The compulsion to protect our parents

Being unaware of the dark secret of an abusive childhood can hurt you worse than any other secret you keep from yourself.

Erasing the Truth of What Happened

Our current awakening about physical, emotional, and sexual abuse has come very slowly because abuse victims either identify with their offenders, repress their memories, or induce autohypnotic states of defense in order to survive the abuse. The victims are set up to lose their sense of self, and therefore they prohibit themselves from knowing what happened to them. But as the Swiss psychiatrist Alice Miller has pointed out, any child raised according to matriarchal/patriarchal parenting rules carries a dark secret to some degree. The secret is *that they cannot know the truth of their own childhood.* Let me explain this statement.

A child in a patriarchal/matriarchal family system is expected to give up his will, mind, and emotions and obey his parents' commands. This is equivalent to being deselfed. This deselfment is achieved through physical punishment, emotional shaming, and the continual violation of modesty, the healthy shame that protects the privacy of the budding individual self. If we have no self to protect, then we accept only those behaviors that our family finds lovable.

Obviously some people are more deselfed than others. Physical abuse dramatically calls for the child's body and psyche to use their defenses. Children internalize their parents' behavior most dramatically when the parents are at their worst—that is, when a child's life is most threatened. Physical discipline is dramatically threatening. The child who is being physically abused must use some form of sensory numbing to survive.

Those who are tortured, threatened, and battered sexually, emotionally, and physically must develop powerful defenses in order to survive. Severe abuse destroys spontaneity, wonder, and what I have described as the realistic imagination. To imagine freely requires an atmosphere free from constant or chronic threat. When there is chronic threat and anxiety, one becomes ruled by fear and lives defensively. One's mind experiences a kind of closure, since spontaneous free association is not possible under conditions of severe threat.

Since imagination is a natural faculty, it does not disappear. But under chronic bodily stress, imagination loses its grounding in the body and becomes fantastic—living in exaggeration and fantasy. A child may create a fantasy parent who is good, so that no matter how cruelly the real parent acts, the child sees them as good. To deny that your father or mother is making you angry or hurting you, you have to make an imaginary picture of them *not* hurting you, *not* doing what they are doing. Out of a child's urgent and basic need to matter and be loved, the rejecting and cruel (real) parent is transformed into the fantasy parent who is all good and loves the child. The child thus *denies* the reality of their parent's actual cruelty.

Since children get their identity from their parents, and since the real parent (now idealized as the good nurturing parent) is beating them and inflicting bodily harm on them, they conclude that they themselves are bad and evil—otherwise the loving parent wouldn't be doing such painful things. Denial *erases history*—that is, a child creating the autohypnotic defense of denial and positive hallucination *erases the experience they are actually having.* Without a self (a will, feelings, needs), and with a fantasy parent, a child no longer knows the truth of their own childhood. This is a very damaging dark secret. It also sets the child up with a *compulsion to protect the parent.*

The Compulsion to Protect Our Parents

When physical, sexual, and severe emotional abuse are added to the normal patriarchal demand to repress a child's will, mind, feelings, needs, and wants, the result is what has been called *soul murder*. The more the child's authentic self is shamed and rejected, the more the child becomes deselfed and bonds to the controlling parent. This deselfment sets up a compulsion to protect the parent.

Dr. Leonard Shengold wrote a book about abuse entitled *Soul Murder*. He took the phrase from a book written in 1832 by Anselm von Feuerbach, a judge and legal scholar. The book was called *Kaspar Hauser: An Instance of Crime Against the Life of the Soul of Man*. It was the story of a boy named Kaspar Hauser who was kept in a dark dungeon separated from all communication from early childhood until the age of seventeen. When he was beaten, Kaspar got an occasional glimpse of his jailer, whom he called "the man who was always there." When Kaspar was found, he had the body of a man but acted like a child of two or three years old. He had great natural intelligence and unusual powers (he could distinguish colors in the dark). He was taught to speak and read and write in a relatively short time. But Kaspar seemed to be devoid of emotion and incapable of anger. Feuerbach was most surprised by the fact that Kaspar's most passionate desire was to return to "the man who was always there."

Kaspar illustrates to us the remarkable fact that the more abused a victim becomes, the more they idealize and protect their abuser. In fact, they may idealize them so much that they identify with them and ultimately become an offender too. Or they remain a victim, seeking out their idealized offender, whether in actuality or in some surrogate form. Thus a child raised by a punishing authoritarian father may seek out a boss or religious authority who is punishing and authoritarian just like Dad.

This autohypnotic sleep that victims of traumatic abuse must create causes them to *erase* their actual history and idealize their parent.

People *can* get into blaming and parent-bashing and downright abuse of their parents, but that is not what the pattern of dark secrets produced by patriarchal/matriarchal parenting is about. It's something far more subtle and difficult to grasp. To truly grasp it is like waking up out of a trance.

When I worked with Lorna, the woman who cut her wrists whom we met in Chapter 2, I was amazed at how she protected her father. I asked her how she felt about her father commanding her to be silent about her grandfather's sexual violation. She told me that she understood that her father had to protect the family image. "But your father's primary responsibility was to protect you, his daughter," I said. "You just don't understand about my family's image and our standing in the community," she replied. "We'd have been thrown out of the Junior League and out of the country club. He had to defend our family's name." It took over two years for Lorna to feel some genuine anger over her father's betrayal. This is quite common among survivors of severe physical, sexual, and emotional abuse. It is also common for anyone who has grown up with patriarchal parenting. Children have an absolute need to idealize their parents. They need to believe their parents are okay because their parents are necessary to their survival.

When a child is violated, their natural response is hurt, pain, and anger. The abusing parent has no tolerance for the child's rage and sees to it that *the slightest manifestation of anger is punished*.

The victim child is under the battering parent's absolute power. The parent can hit at any time for no reason. The parent is the child's only protector, and the child has no option but to turn to his tormentor for relief. This creates an intense need in the child to see his tormentor as good and righteous. The parent thus becomes blameless for the child's feelings of hurt, pain, and anger. This is enhanced when parents profess to be righteous ("I'm doing this for your own good") and religious.

REPRESSED MEMORIES OF SEXUAL ABUSE

Our darkest secrets are our repressed memories of sexual abuse. Such repressed memories are most often the result of being chronically traumatized as a child.

I offer you the information in this section for educational purposes only. It is certainly not intended to replace the expert diagnosis of a mental health professional trained in these matters. The work of recovering sexual abuse memories should be done *only* under the care of such a professional.

Recovering memories of abuse is a very painful process, and it can bring up feelings that frighten and overwhelm you. If strong feelings come up as you read, you may want to consider seeking professional help.

Dr. Renée Fredrickson is one of the pioneers in the field of sexual abuse. Much of what follows has been gleaned from her lectures and tapes and her book *Repressed Memories,* although I take full responsibility for my interpretations of her work.

Sexual abuse is the most secret crime of all. There are no witnesses, and the betrayal, humiliation, and degradation are soul murdering and bewildering. Since toxic shame causes one to want to hide, the natural tendency of the victim is to be silent. The abuse is too horrible for words, and a small child has a limited vocabulary anyway. A victim of sexual abuse wants to be rescued, but the offender and the family let them know that it is not possible. The need to forget is thus powerfully reinforced. Even when all the children in the family are being sexually abused, they seldom, if ever, talk to each other about it.

The sexually abused child has no allies and may be held captive by the offender's threats, seductive attention, and strokes, or by the awful fear of breaking up their family.

Warning Signs or Clues to Repressed Memories of Sexual Abuse

The most common clues that point to repressed memories are various combinations of PTSD symptoms. *However, not everyone who has been abused shows PTSD symptoms, and you need a professionally trained person to accurately determine whether you have PTSD.*

The two most important PTSD characteristics for survivors of sexual abuse with repressed memories are *delayed onset of the disorder* and *amnesia*.

Delay of Onset

A person with PTSD may develop severe depression or start having anxiety attacks without any previous history of either of these.

In one of Dr. Fredrickson's case histories, her client said that she had never been happier. It may seem paradoxical for memories to start to emerge during a period of unprecedented calm and happiness. But, in fact, calm and relaxed safety allow the person to let down the intense psychic guards they have been using to block the horrible memories.

A triggering event usually sets off the delayed onset of PTSD, un-

leashing dormant feelings and memories. Triggering events set off de-
layed-onset PTSD reactions in people who remember their abuse as
well as those who do not remember.

Those who do remember can more easily understand and evaluate
the nightmares, images, fears, and other frightening symptoms. Those
who don't remember are bewildered by the barrage of their emerging
memories.

Dr. Fredrickson lists the following as common triggering events:

- Unknowingly experiencing a situation that is similar in some way to
  the original event.
- The death of a sexually abusive perpetrator, or the death of a parent
  you are unconsciously protecting from the abuse.
- Pregnancy or the birth of a child or grandchild.
- A child you identify with reaching the age at which you were abused.
- Entering a new development stage (puberty, middle age).
- Confronting a known sexual abuser.
- Ending an addiction. With the end of the anesthetizing addiction,
  memories emerge.
- Becoming conscious of the reality of sexual abuse (perhaps by read-
  ing a story about sexual abuse or seeing a TV presentation).
- Feeling safe.
- Feeling strong. Personal growth leaves you strong enough to face
  what could not be faced before.

Amnesia

Nearly all survivors of sexual abuse have some amnesia about their
abuse. The most disturbing aspects of sexual assault are the most sus-
ceptible to amnesia. Survivors frequently remember how an incident
began but have forgotten the most intrusive part (the orgasm of the
perpetrator and how they were treated afterward). What is forgotten
contains the most pain.

As it is currently discussed, PTSD does not adequately describe the
effects of memory repression in cases of chronic child abuse. A new
category has been developed to discuss this called the *repressed memory syndrome*.

Repressed Memory Syndrome

The repressed memory syndrome was developed to describe those who have *no* memory of the abuse, as well as those who remember but have significant amounts of amnesia. Repressed memory syndrome consists of four categories. Dr. Fredrickson lists them as:

1. Attractions, fears, or avoidances unexplained by known history

2. Indications of emerging memory

3. Evidence of dissociation

4. Time loss or memory blanks

These are not absolute criteria. You don't have to have all of these.

1. Attractions, Fears, or Avoidances

Attractions to, fears of, avoidances of, or distress surrounding objects or situations unexplained by your known history are warning signs of repressed memories, especially if they are logically or frequently associated with child sexual abuse. One person may be attracted to an object that was associated with their abuse; another person may fear or want to avoid certain objects altogether. Avoiding sex or anything related to sex is often where the avoidance comes out. Some people may become sexually compulsive. Places may be avoided, such as bathrooms, basements, or closets, which are common places where sexual abuse occurs. Household items that might be vaginally or anally inserted are often used during abuse, like sticks, penis-shaped foods, or bottles.

I once worked with a woman who had terrible problems with her teeth because she refused to go to the dentist. Over the course of several months it became clear that as a child she had been orally raped several times by her uncle.

Extraordinary fear of dental visits is quite often a signal of oral sexual abuse. It reminds the person of having their mouth forced open while something painful is done to them.

2. Indications of Emerging Memories

Memory may begin to emerge in dreams, disturbing images, flash-backs, bodily sensations, or unexplainable emotions.

According to Dr. Fredrickson, violent *nightmares* may be a red flag of emerging memories; so too may dreams where someone is stalking you or trying to murder you.

Images sometimes come in the form of "blips," brief flashes of part of a sexual abuse incident that flit through the mind, usually at odd moments. You may, for example, get a picture of a knife or a penis that is totally unrelated to what you are doing. The images may not be violent, and they may be related only to the beginning or the end of an incident.

Painful *flashbacks* may occur. The person having the flashback feels as if the abuse were occurring in the present.

Our body reacts to everything that happens to us. The more significant the happening, the more impact it has on the body. There are *body memories* even when the abuse caused little physical pain. "Nausea," writes Renée Fredrickson, "is a frequent physical reaction to sexual abuse. Infants will sometimes spontaneously vomit on their perpetrators, even though they are not being physically hurt by the abuse. Genital awareness or arousal may also occur when non-violent body memories take place."

A person's genitals may hurt as certain feelings surface related to sexual abuse. Their legs may shake as they remember the physical strain of uncomfortable sexual positions.

Feeling memory is your emotional response to a particular event or situation. If the event is a repressed memory, you will remember the feeling but not the event. According to Dr. Fredrickson, "a felt sense that something abusive has happened is a common form of a feeling memory."

3. Evidence of Dissociation

Trauma often causes dissociation, which is characterized by the feeling that you are not in your body. The dissociated state is often described as a waking dream. You observe what is going on, but it's as if you were not actually in the experience.

The dissociation state can become a permanent part of a person's life. This chronic state of dissociation is experienced as a feeling of unreality or estrangement. It can also be experienced as numbness.

Many sexual abuse victims feel the dissociation when they are having sex. They are literally "not there" while the sex act is going on.

4. Time Loss or Memory Blanks

It is entirely normal to have very few memories prior to age six. However, if you remember nothing at all about your childhood, or nothing about a particular period, say ages nine to eleven, then you may want to consider the possibility that you were seriously traumatized. (People do not usually block out years of their lives for some minor trauma.)

When the memory of a significant person is blocked, this may be due to some form of traumatic violation by that person.

Repressed memories are the most baffling kind of secrets we keep from ourselves. Perhaps more than anything I've written about, these secrets underscore the statement that what we don't know can hurt us.

COMPLETING YOUR PERSONAL GENOGRAM

Now it's time to finalize your personal genogram. If you've done the work in this chapter, you may have some new awareness about yourself and the dark secrets you've been keeping from yourself.

As the focus person of your genogram, summarize your problematic and symptomatic behavior. Then look at yourself in the context of your three- (or four-) generational genogram. By now, your genogram should contain all the significant facts about your multigenerational family.

James Jeder's Dark Secrets in Four-Generational Context

Chart 9–3 is a completed four-generational map of James Jeder's family. All James's personal problems, including his darkest secret (self-sex with pornography), are presented.

CHART 9-3

FOUR GENERATIONAL FAMILY MAP OF JAMES JEDER, 1994

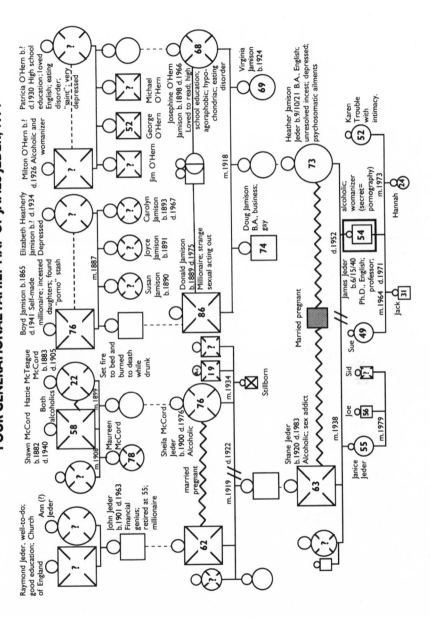

CHART 9-4

RELATIONAL PATTERNS: CROSS-GENERATIONAL COALITIONS

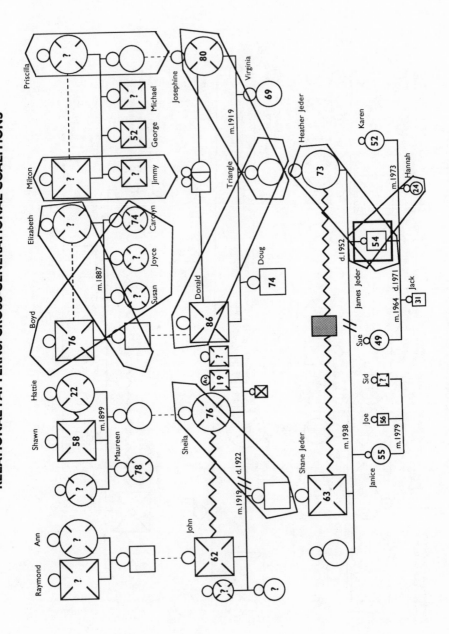

From James's genogram, it is clear that his overt sexual issues (his womanizing and extramarital affairs) and problems with alcoholism are modeled on his father's side of the family. His covert sexual issues come from his mother's side.

Both sides of the family have a history of intimacy dysfunction and repression of feeling, especially intense emotions, as evidenced by the many emotional cutoffs. Feelings are either mood-altered or acted out.

There are also a large number of parent-child coalitions. James's mother and father were both in emotionally incestuous parent-child coalitions. (See Chart 9–4.) The generational boundaries are seriously impaired. Anyone looking at this genogram when James Jeder was born could have predicted the kinds of problems he would have to struggle with.

It is worth noting that both generations of Jamisons present an external image of prosperous, well-adjusted family life. Their sexual addiction is covert and thus more crazy-making. And while the Jamisons may seem rather bizarre to you, I do not find them at all atypical of the many families I dealt with during my twenty-three years of active counseling. Donald Jamison's demand that his wife wear his mother's and daughter's undergarments may be unusual, but the emotional bonding with his mother's unresolved sexual issues and his projection of his sexual desires onto his daughter are *not* unusual.

Freeze-Frame the Family's Emotional Climate at Your Birth

What was going on with your great-grandparents, grandparents, aunts, uncles, and immediate family at the time of your birth? Pay special attention to the historical, social, and economic circumstances that could have been affecting the family. Also look carefully to see if there were any traumatic events or deaths in the family around the time of your birth. Was there any coincidence of life events? For instance, is your birthday the same as that of the great-uncle you are named after, or did someone get sick or die the day you were born?

The genogram in Chart 9–5 shows the emotional climate when James Jeder was born, in 1940. Three of James's great-grandparents are dead. His great-grandfather Shawn McCord died two months ago. His great-grandfather Boyd Jamison is dying of cancer. Grandmother Sheila Jeder is denying her grief and acting quite hysterical—drinking heavily and fighting with her alcoholic husband. She has been abandoned by Shawn and has great bitterness mixed with love for him.

CHART 9-5

EMOTIONAL CLIMATE WHEN JAMES JEDER WAS BORN, 1940

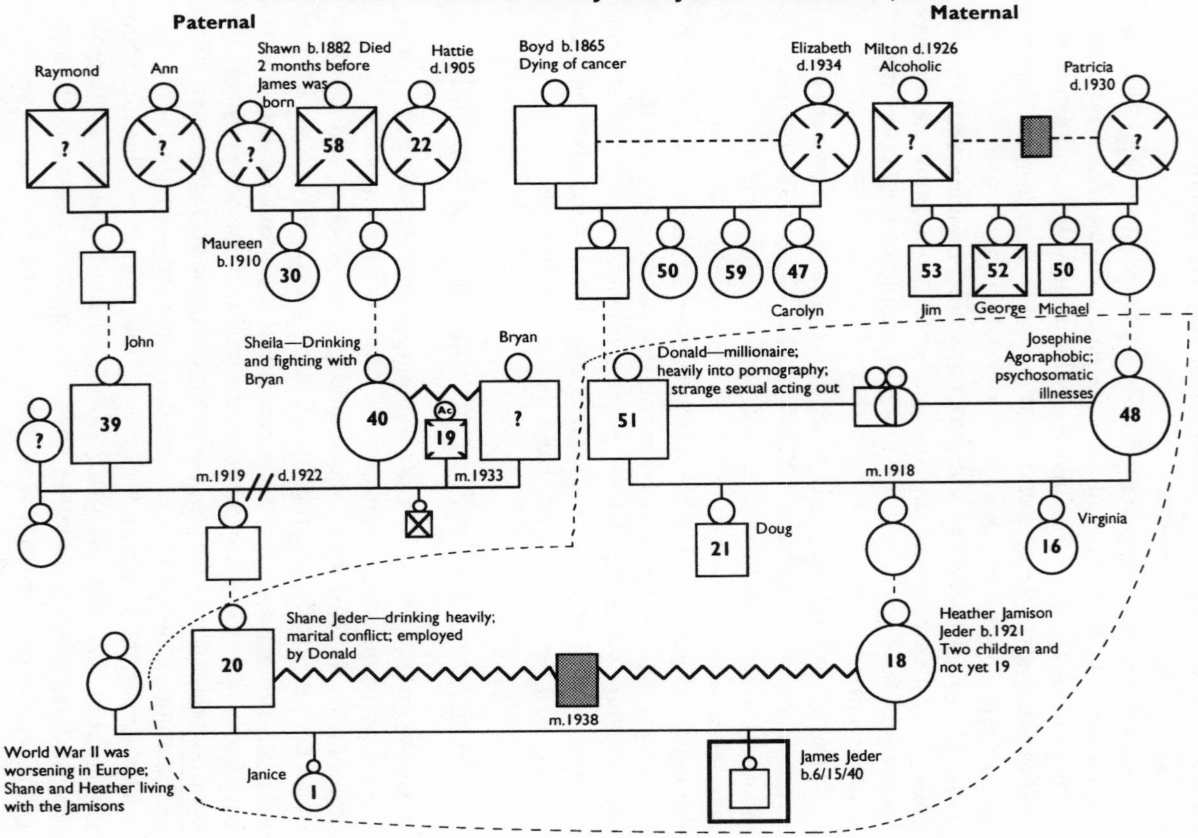

Paternal

Maternal

World War II was
worsening in Europe;
Shane and Heather living
with the Jamisons

James's father, Shane, has just been given a job by Donald Jamison, and the young couple has been living with Heather's family. Shane worked during his early teenage years and has been looking for a permanent job since he graduated from high school. Jobs are hard to come by. At one point Shane actually sold apples on the street to earn money. Enlisting in the army would have solved all his problems, but he had lifelong asthma and that was a deterrent to being accepted. Donald has confronted Shane, calling him a "no-good bum." There is lots of tension between them.

The secret sexual stuff is going on between Josephine and Donald Jamison. Heather is approaching nineteen. She is angry and depressed over Shane's accelerated drinking and irresponsibility. Janice, the reason Heather married Shane, is one year old. Heather projects her anger onto Janice and turns to James to get her own narcissistic needs met. And to look at the widest picture, although the United States had not yet entered the war, World War II was worsening in Europe. The Germans entered Paris the day before James was born. Heather remembered someone telling her, "This is a terrible time to be bringing a baby into the world." All in all, it *is* a very depressing setting for a little boy to be born into.

James Jeder's Sibling Position Profile

James is in the second birth-order position, as are both his mother and father. (See Chart 9–6.) (Shane is considered to be in the second sibling position because his mother, Sheila, had a stillborn child in her runaway teenage marriage.) James's mom and dad are each bonded to their parent of the opposite sex in coalitions of emotional incest.

James's great-aunt Susan and great-uncle George, both second children, are the two most damaged people in the family system. Susan was violated by her father and went through two abusive marriages by the time she was thirty-one years old. She lived with her father for the rest of her life. George was a severe alcoholic who died of liver damage at the age of fifty-two.

A child in the second birth-order position in any new generation would be highly predisposed to carry this family's projections and dark secrets and to act them out.

CHART 9-6

SIBLING SYSTEM PROFILE, JAMES JEDER

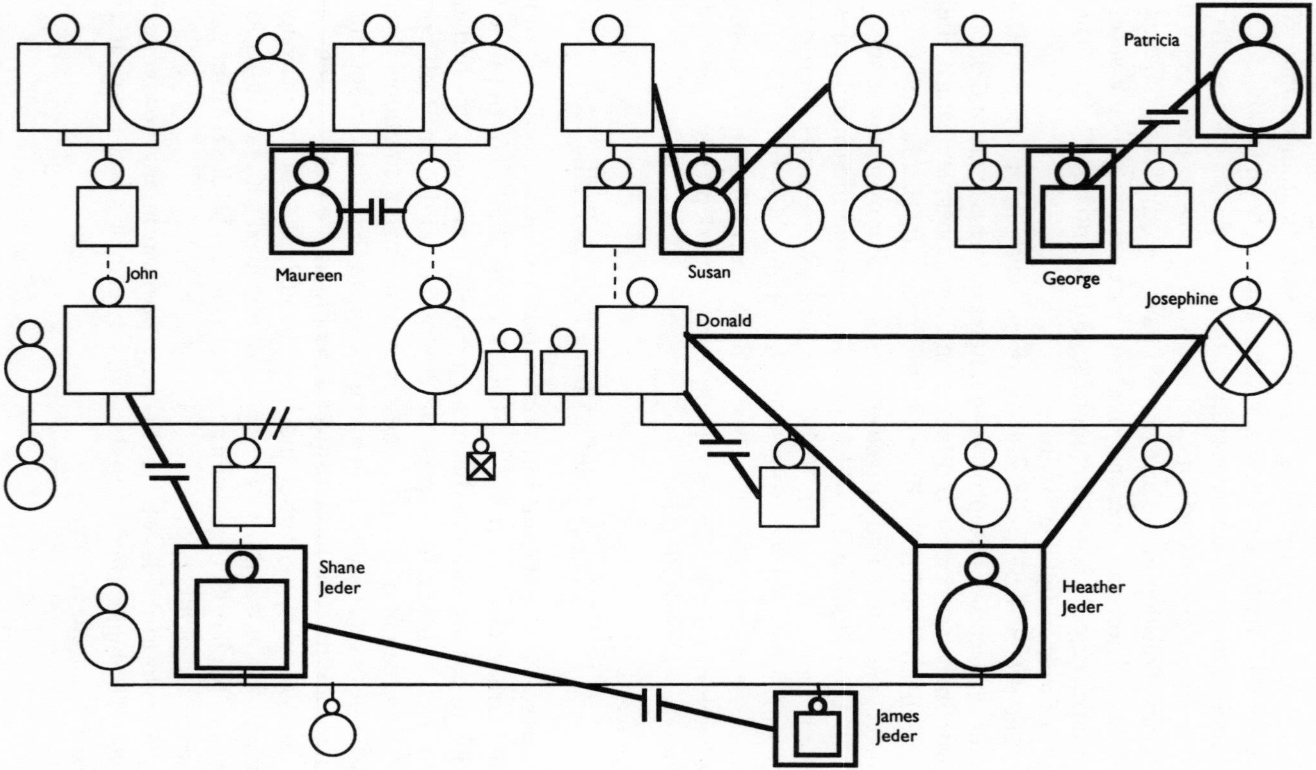

Emotional Cutoff

There are emotional cutoffs in every generation in this family. This means that there are also intense unresolved feelings of love/hate. There are painful abandonments over several generations. John Jeder abandoned Shane, who abandoned James, who abandoned his own son, Jack.

I've not said much about James's son Jack. When Jack was born, James was working part-time and going to graduate school getting his Ph.D. He had very little time for his son. Jack was six when James divorced Sue to marry Karen. Sue was very bitter and did everything she could to make Jack hate his father. As the years went on, the cutoff became more and more intense. James's genogram also reveals that Boyd Jamison cut off Donald, who cut off Doug. What is unresolved in one generation becomes a "hot" issue in the next.

In Chapter 11 we'll discuss the importance of resolving as many issues as possible in our extended family so that they are not carried over into the next generation or into our new relationships. I'll use as an example James Jeder's recovery from his emotional incest with his mother and how that helped his marriage to Karen.

CHAPTER 10

FREEING YOURSELF FROM THE POWER OF DARK FAMILY SECRETS

The truth must dazzle gradually or every man be blind.

EMILY DICKINSON

Honesty without sensitivity can be brutality.

MARILYN MASON

I am my secrets. And you are your secrets. Our secrets are human secrets, and our trusting each other enough to share them with each other has much to do with the secret of what it is to be human.

FREDERICK BUECHNER

For years now in my workshops, I have been using an exercise that originated in the values clarification work of Sidney Simon and his colleagues. Read the following story quickly, without trying to make complete logical sense out of it.

GWENEVIERE'S DILEMMA

Once upon a time a man named Farquhar married a woman named Gweneviere. They made their home in a wilderness outpost in South

America. Farquhar was a lumberjack, and he made his living working for a company that operated in the deepest part of the jungle. To get to work each day, Farquhar had to cross a dangerous mile-wide river teeming with alligators and piranhas. A rickety bridge had been built across the river. One morning after he had left for work and crossed the bridge, a high wind came up and spawned a twister that damaged the bridge beyond repair. Farquhar had no way to return home, and it would take many months to rebuild the bridge. As yet there was no telecommunication system from the lumber camp to the outpost.

Gweneviere had no way to know if Farquhar was safe and no way to get to him. It could be as long as a year before they were reunited.

There was a strange old man in the outpost who hunted alligators and sold their skins. His name was Sinbad, and he owned a boat. Gweneviere asked him how much he would charge to take her across the river. He told her that it was a dangerous trip because of the rapids and that he would have to charge her $250. Gweneviere had about $100, money she needed to live on for the time Farquhar was gone. So she told Sinbad that there was no way she could pay him that amount. He told her there was another way: She could sleep with him as payment. Gweneviere was horrified. With deep grief and anxiety, she went to her friend Ivan, who had a very small boat that he used for recreation. He never ventured out farther than two hundred yards from the shore.

Gweneviere asked Ivan to take her across the river. He was a people-pleaser, but he told her he was too afraid to try to cross the river and that he had a lot of problems of his own and couldn't help her. She was devastated, and one day in the depths of despair, she went to Sinbad and did the dastardly deed!

Sinbad, true to his word, navigated the treacherous waters and got her to the other side. She ran through the woods and found her beloved Farquhar at the lumber camp. Their reunion was passionate and endearing. Farquhar had built a simple but nice log cabin, and the two lived for several months in bliss.

But Gweneviere's guilt was eating her up. She couldn't give herself totally to her beloved, because she felt so dirty and unclean. So one night she told Farquhar her *dark secret*. She felt she had done it so that they could be together and that he would understand. This was a big mistake!

Farquhar went crazy, raging and throwing things around. The next day he kicked her out of his cabin and told her he wanted a divorce.

Gweneviere was devastated. She wandered around the woods not knowing where she was going until she ran into a wilderness man named Ulric. People at the outpost knew about him and a few had seen him, but all considered him very strange and scary. Actually Ulric had dropped out of society because of the cruelty and evil he found in so-called civilized life. Gweneviere told him her story. He felt compassion for her and got her back across the river. He then went and found Farquhar and thrashed him soundly.

That's the end of the story I tell. I then ask the workshop participants to quickly rank in order the five characters in this story in terms of their emotional appeal. Number one is the person they like best, number two is second best, with five being the one they dislike the most. You can stop right now and do this yourself if you want to.

Once they have rank-ordered the people, I ask them to compare notes with a partner.

I have never done this exercise with any group without *every* character getting ranked number one by someone in the group, and I have worked with hundreds of different groups.

I have people reflect on their choice and ask them to see if it relates to any personal life experience they have had, the point being that their choice is most often colored by their own experience. But as diverse as the opinions are, Gweneviere always gets the most number-one votes.

I usually do this exercise to illustrate people's differences and how little our differences are based on objectivity. Recently, however, it occurred to me that this story is also about how Gweneviere handled her dark secret. She feels she must tell Farquhar for the sake of honesty.

But it rarely seems to occur to anyone that maybe Gweneviere's motivation is to rid herself of guilt. It could be argued that she is disclosing her dark secret in order to feel better about herself. Should she tell a dark secret that relieves her of guilt but causes her partner great pain? Is it really crucial that he knows?

IS IT ALWAYS RIGHT TO TELL THE SECRET?

There are those who would answer unequivocally that Gweneviere was right in disclosing her infidelity. Frank Pittman, a psychiatrist and family therapist in Atlanta, in his book *Private Lies: Infidelity and the*

Betrayal of Intimacy, argues that "honesty is the central factor in intimacy" and that "even the smallest lie can be hopelessly disorienting." For Pittman, infidelity should never be lied about, since "there is no truth that is as destructive as any lie."

Pittman probably would have encouraged Gweneviere to understand her own issues, and he might have confronted her with the fact that no good intention could really justify her infidelity. He would probably also have pointed out that if she didn't tell, her guilt would gradually distort and destroy her relationship with Farquhar. He would insist that the dark secret of infidelity always be told.

But not all therapists would agree. An M.S.W. and couples therapist in Switzerland, Rosemarie Welter-Enderlin, sees such a position as a kind of therapeutic "morality," dangerous because it becomes a fixed formula, a *law* concerning the telling of secrets, a mandate for permanently disclosing oneself. Her therapeutic experience suggests that we have to accept the imperfection of *"la condition humaine,"* but without "falling into lethargy." I'm not sure what she means by lethargy, but I assume she means we shouldn't condone infidelity just because it happens a lot. At the other extreme from Pittman are some professionals who believe that the danger of a secret is *always* relative, determined by the social, cultural, ethnic, and religious context, as well as by the unique process of the particular family in question. Some of these schools of thinkers have gone so far as to relativize incest! That is, they say that the family process is more important than confronting a parent who is incesting his child.

DEGREES OF TOXICITY

My own position falls between these two extremes. I've chosen to categorize dark secrets by their degree of severity and toxicity, and to use this as a guideline in disclosing them. (See Chart 10–1.)

Some dark secrets (those listed on the chart as first- and second-degree secrets), are *always* toxic and need to be confronted, disclosed, and dealt with.

Third- and fourth-degree dark secrets are damaging, but decisions about how to handle them are more contextual. In some cases, it may even be difficult to distinguish fourth-degree dark secrets from matters of privacy—except for the distress they cause to the person who owns them.

CHART 10-1

TOXICITY OF DARK SECRETS*

First Degree–Deadly (Lethal)
Always need to be confronted and disclosed

There is always a victim. Violates the rights of others to life, liberty, dignity of self, and personal property. Usually against the law.

Disclosure puts offender at high risk. May also involve physical and emotional risk to person disclosing.

Criminal Activity
Murder
Mutilation/Torture
Arson
Terrorism
Kidnapping
Battering/Assault
Mugging
Münchausen by proxy
Satanic cult
Racial violence
Gay bashing
Drug trafficking
Stalking
Burglary/theft
Shoplifting
Con games

Sexual Crimes
Rape (including marital and date rape)
Incest/molestation
Sexual torture/sadomasochistic sex
Child prostitution/pornography
Sexual abuse
Unprotected sex with AIDS

Victimization
Emotional abuse
Spiritual abuse
Suicide

---

*The lists presented here are not intended to be exhaustive.

Second Degree–Dangerous (Demoralizing)
Always need to be confronted and disclosed

Violates one's sense of personhood. Has life-damaging consequences for self and others. Can lead to legal violations.

Disclosure may involve economic, social, and emotional risk to secret-keeper and to person disclosing.

Substance Abuse
Alcoholism
Drug abuse

Eating Disorders
Anorexia
Bulimia
Binge eating
Thin/fat disorder

Activity Addictions
Sexual addiction
Multiple affairs
Wife-swapping
Chronic masturbation with
    pornography
Voyeurism
Exhibitionism
Love addiction
Work addiction
Gambling addiction

Birth and Identity Issues
Adoption
Surrogacy
In vitro fertilization
Paternity issues
Lost siblings

Third Degree–Damaging
Need for confrontation and disclosure depends on family process and social, cultural, ethnic, and religious context

---

Violates one or more persons' freedom. Violates boundaries. Involves conscious or unconscious dishonesty. Damages good name of others. Blocks family mutuality. Creates distrust. Closes communication.

Disclosure may hurt someone else or violate a confidence. Involves primarily emotional risk to person disclosing.

Family Enmeshment
Triangles
Covert family rules
Cross-generational bonding
Compulsion to protect parents
Rigid family roles
Being scapegoated/labeled the "problem"

Marital Secrets
Closet gay or lesbian marriage
Hidden anger and resentment
Sexual infidelity (some individual cases)
Married pregnant
Unemployment

Suffering-Related
Emotional illness
Mental illness
Physical disability
Denial of death and sickness
Agoraphobia/clinical depression

Intellectual/Spiritual
Homophobia
Racial prejudice

Fourth Degree–Distressful

Need for confrontation and disclosure depends on personal process and social, cultural, ethnic, and religious context

---

Damage to self primarily. Guarding the secret depletes energy and spontaneity.

Disclosure would not put anyone else at risk. Involves primarily emotional risk to secret-keeper.

Toxic Shame
Fear
Guilt
Anxiety
Depression

Contextual/Cultural Shame
Appearance/body
Socioeconomic status
Educational level
Social awkwardness
Ethnic shame
Spiritual/religious crisis

Affairs as Second- or Third-Degree Secrets

To return to Gweneviere, note that affairs can be located on the toxic-ity chart in two places. My belief is that where there are multiple affairs, there is sexual addiction. Multiple affairs, as an addiction, are a second-degree dark secret. I believe that second-degree secrets, like first-de-gree secrets, are dangerous and should be confronted. If you are the one having multiple affairs, you are probably sexually addicted. You are endangering your own life and the life of your spouse and family.

On the other hand, Gweneviere's infidelity was a one-time event and the chances of her acting in this way again are slim. I place her secret in my third-degree category of toxicity. In itself, it does not have to be told. One could argue that the secret was strategic and had an adaptive value for her. Moral theologians and ethicists have always seen intention and circumstance as mitigating factors in deciding the goodness or badness of an act. Much would depend on how she inte-grated this behavior into her life. If her guilt was so strong that it blocked her marital intimacy, then she should do something about it—maybe talk it out with a friend, or go to a clergyman or rabbi to get spiritual advice, and pray for forgiveness if she believed she sinned. She might go to a therapist and talk it out if that were an option for her. Third-degree secrets cannot be dealt with in black and white cate-gories. Very much depends on the full context within which the secret is functioning. A single extramarital affair could also be an attempt at individuation, maybe even a rebellion against the mandate of the "new law of openness" and permanent disclosure that can rob a couple of privacy.

I spoke of the need everyone has for an individual space, "a room of one's own," Virginia Woolf called it, as a foundation for the process of individuation. A lack of privacy can prevent individuation. One may have an affair as a way to individuate. It may be a temporary secretive-ness that precedes a new balance of power and intimacy. Rosemarie Welter-Enderlin writes: "My therapeutic experience with couples in this situation very often follows this pattern: an extramarital affair, which is kept secret, at first seems to fulfill the not yet conscious need of one or the other to demarcate a 'room of one's own.'" She allows that *from a rational point of view there are better ways to achieve this goal.* But people are not always rational. Loyalty is sometimes overwhelmed by passion, and passion is egocentric. Passion is part of the human condition. Welter-Enderlin is certainly not encouraging affairs, nor would I, but she is recognizing the fact that an affair may not *always* be about deep secrets that a couple refuses to look at.

Process and Content

In evaluating third-degree secrets, you must pay attention to the process—the unique family dynamics involved—not just the content of the secret. Consider the case of Susie and Peter.

Susie came to me in April 1975. She presented a bleak picture of her ailing marriage. She was dramatic, gorgeous, and filled with energy, while her husband was nonemotional and absorbed in his work.

Susie told me she had been having a romantic but nonsexual rendezvous with a married man named Peter who was a dynamic man involved in a world hunger project. She was considering having an affair with him. Peter had been married about five years and, like Susie, had never had an affair. In spite of my strong opinion that an affair would only complicate things and create more distance in her marriage, Susie began an affair with Peter that would ultimately last for five years.

At first the thrust of their being together seemed to be intense sex. But as time went on, it became clear that they spent hours in intimate sharing, talking about everything from problems with their children, the beauty of nature, and politics, to their beliefs about God and spirituality. They were both learning how to communicate on a deep intimate level.

One day Susie told me that her husband was seeing a therapist and that they were starting to share feelings for the first time. Although Susie's marriage got better, she continued the affair with Peter.

At the end of the third year, Susie told me she and her husband wanted another child but she was afraid of Peter's response, as she felt that she could not continue to have sexual intercourse with him if she got pregnant by her husband.

As Susie's counselor, I felt absolutely crazy at times. I had no idea how to direct her therapy. I sought consultation from a wise therapist colleague who helped me to see that a dynamic process seemed to be taking place for Susie. Her marriage was actually strengthening as a result of the affair. This was true. She no longer talked of leaving her husband. He had gone into therapy totally on his own. They were communicating more frequently and in a more intimate way. They were considering having another baby.

Peter stood by Susie throughout her pregnancy. When they were together, he held and nurtured her without in any way pressuring her for sex. About a year after her baby was born, Peter started another affair, telling Susie he could see that she was going to end their own affair very soon. Susie spent a year grieving the loss of Peter. But she came to see the process that had taken place over the five years. She had gone from a marriage that was "on the rocks" to a marriage and family that were growing. Peter did not fare so well. I had occasion to counsel Peter and his wife a few years later. The affair had made it clear to him that he needed to get out of a marriage that was ill-fated from the beginning. Peter had married pregnant, and he and his wife had made an unconscious contract to raise their child. Peter's wife was aware that she tolerated his affairs as a way to avoid her own intimacy issues.

I came to see Susie and Peter's five-year affair in the following way: It allowed Susie's husband time to learn about emotions and intimacy. Her triangulation with Peter temporarily fulfilled the intimacy she was not getting in her marriage. It allowed Peter and his wife a way to be nonintimate and still honor their contract to raise the child they had conceived.

Susie and her husband have now had another child, and their family is flourishing.

In this case the content (an extramarital affair), which in itself was a dark secret, was clearly mollified by the process (the way the secret functioned to strengthen Susie's marriage). For another couple, an affair could have been devastating and created a very different process.

Disclosure of Secrets

In my own lifetime attitudes have changed radically on issues that were once considered dark secrets. Think of the prominent American women in the last twenty years who have come out publicly about their abortions in an attempt to support women's reproductive rights. This would have been unheard-of thirty to forty years ago.

Telling about your out-of-wedlock birth would not go over well in certain neighborhoods where the population is conservatively religious. In another neighborhood an out-of-wedlock birth is a common life transition. This shifting cultural and societal context must be kept in mind as we draw up guidelines for secret-telling.

With Betty Ford, Magic Johnson, Jane Fonda, Suzanne Somers, Oprah Winfrey, and many other celebrities speaking of their secrets in public, a norm has evolved for telling the secrets. This has generally been good. The closet doors have been opened wide, and the skeletons are out.

But with every breakthrough, there are drawbacks. I watch people being revictimized daily on many of the lesser-known talk shows, where shoddy behavior and secrets have become the mainstay for commercial success. Simply telling dark secrets is not enough to integrate the impact those secrets have had in the family. Horror stories are growing where incest survivors, pushed by outside pressures, confront the whole family in one fell swoop, causing devastation.

In the early days of my recovery, I was victimized by a therapist who told me to go home and express all my secrets to my wife and twelve-year-old son. He gave me this advice in a group setting, without any regard for my son's age or any real knowledge of the quality of the relationships in my family. And while I have to take the responsibility for choosing to follow his advice, the results were devastating. It's taken some time to undo the damage. Another therapist at that same workshop gave suggestions that caused several people to believe they were incest victims. One woman I knew well left the workshop convinced she was her father's victim and two days later cut off all relationship with him. It took several years before she decided that she had been wrong about her father.

Our current clinical knowledge of what to do with dark secrets is still evolving. No one claims to *know for sure* when, where, how, and to whom secrets should be told. The best we can do is gain as full a grasp as possible of our family's polarities and do our best to be responsible for our own dark secrets and those that we know are hurting us as well as other family members.

In what follows I'll offer you some guidelines for confronting and disclosing first-, second-, third-, and fourth-degree dark secrets.

Keep in mind always that the goal of confronting and disclosing dark secrets is to restore family members' personal dignity, privacy, quality contact, and nurturing love, to set up an emotional climate in which sensitive information can be shared, and to open channels of communication that can be deepened long after the secret has been revealed.

FIRST-DEGREE DARK SECRETS

Look again at the first-degree secrets listed on Chart 10–1. First-degree secrets are lethal and must be dealt with. These secrets violate human rights and destroy people's lives. There is often need for protection for those who tell these secrets and often need for outside intervention. Most first-degree secrets involve violations of the law. If you identify with any of these secrets, proceed slowly and seek out legal counsel. (See Chart 10–2.)

Children are often at a terrible disadvantage in this area of dark secrecy. For example a child being incested by one parent often tries to tell the nonoffending parent. Typically that parent is caught in victimization also. Sometimes they are PTSD victims who are acting out their own childhood traumas and being revictimized by their spouses. Their child's disclosure may cause them to dissociate and become confused. They often do not support their child for the sake of keeping the family together.

Sometimes both parents are involved in the abuse. The child victim is betrayed twice and loses all hope of ever trusting anyone. For such a person to tell their secret to someone else, a solid relationship of trust must first be established. Many incest victims find this with a therapist. Wise therapists will not let a victim disclose too quickly. Trust is a major element in providing a safe place for secret disclosure.

Dusty Miller, a therapist and professor of psychology at Antioch College in Ohio, writes about a twenty-six-year-old incest victim who revealed intimate details of her father's sadistic sexual violation of her in her very first therapy session. Between sessions the woman "acted in" by cutting her wrists. Over the next few sessions, the same pattern took place. Miller came to realize that the woman had ambivalent feelings toward her father. She hated him, and she loved him. Confessing the secret felt like she was betraying him, and she did not have enough trust and a strong enough bond with Miller to compensate for her opening up the secret. Cutting her wrists was a way to act out her guilt. Miller warns therapists to take time and establish a bond of trust and rapport before allowing a client to tell too much. A victim of sexual abuse has had their inviolable privacy completely ruptured and has probably never experienced a zone of protected space and privacy. It is up to the therapist, counselor, or friend to help create that zone of privacy and a bond of trust before letting their client or friend disclose too much.

CHART 10-2

SUGGESTED GUIDELINES FOR CONFRONTING FIRST-DEGREE SECRETS

WHEN YOU OWN THE SECRET AS AN OFFENDER:

- Accept that you need help.
- Shame and self-hate can be healed only by coming out of hiding.
- Find someone to talk to, and look at your options.
- You will have to take legal and moral responsibility for your behavior, but it's the only way to get your life back.
- You can make amends.
- You can be helped with therapy.
- You can be forgiven.

WHEN YOU OWN THE SECRET AS A VICTIM:

- You have been severely violated and you need to find someone to talk to. Find a therapist who has experience in helping people grieve their victimization.
- Go slowly. It will take time to build trust.
- Make the time to work through your hurt and anger.
- Build a support system with other survivors, and seek legal advice about your choices.
- If it's a parent, relative, or sibling, take time to *think* about a plan of confrontation.
- Warn any other person who might be victimized.
- Be sure you have protection when you confront your offender.
- You may also choose to avoid face-to-face confrontation. But do something to honor your own integrity.

WHEN SOMEONE ELSE OWNS THE SECRET:

- The offender, even though they may be a parent, a relative, or a friend, needs help. By saying and doing nothing, you help enable their sickness.
- Go slowly, and seek out as many family members as possible to help you confront.
- Know the full legal issues before you confront.
- You need to protect yourself. If you're a child, find someone you can talk to.
- See your confrontation as an act of caring and love.
- If you are too frightened to do anything, find someone to talk to.
- You honor your parents by talking to someone about their secrets. They need help, and keeping the secret contributes to their toxic shame and degradation.

If you are disclosing a secret about being victimized, go slowly. You will need to digest and reintegrate each part of it. Don't let anyone rush you. Counselors and therapists are learning that we cannot just blast the person with confrontation to open the secret.

I know of no reliable absolutes as to who, when, where, and how the disclosure should be made. There is a sense of urgency about first-degree secrets because they are so damaging, but I believe that a dark secret should be disclosed within a relationship of trust and that it usually takes some *time* and pacing to create such a relationship.

Working Through the Trauma of a First-Degree Secret

If you are the victim of a first-degree offense, you need careful and nurturing help. I recommend finding a therapist who has experience with the severe kind of victimization that occurs in first-degree secretiveness.

Blanche was raped by a blind date that a girlfriend at her office had gotten for her. Blanche had felt uncomfortable dancing with her date because he was pushing himself up against her. But she was a people-pleaser and had trouble saying no. So she had a couple of strong drinks, rationalizing that this would get up her nerve to tell him to stop. Instead, the booze released her inhibitions. This, coupled with months of isolation and skin hunger, let her give in to his rubbing and touching. Blanche knew the situation was dangerous, and she thought she should take a taxi home, but her girlfriend told her to "loosen up and enjoy herself." On the way home the date stopped the car and proceeded to fondle her. She fought him and protested loudly. Holding her down, he forced her to perform fellatio on him. When he finished, he drove her home. She was in a state of dissociation and shock for days afterward. She tried to talk to her friend, but her friend would not take her seriously.

Months passed before she went to a therapist and told her what had happened. The therapist became her "benevolent witness." A benevolent witness is a nonshaming support person who *listens* to your pain, giving you sensory-based feedback that lets you know that your experience is being taken seriously.

Such validation is very important because victims often wonder if they brought the abuse on, or if there is something wrong with them for feeling the way they do. Victims often feel they do not have the right to feel outraged or angry. Blanche felt that she had brought the rape on herself by letting her date rub up against her. She felt that she was guilty because it had felt good.

These ambiguous feelings are typical of the way abuse victims think. Blanche had been victimized as a child. She was never allowed to have her own thoughts and feelings about anything. Her mother was coercive, moralistic, controlling, and narcissistic. Blanche was always trying to please her. Blanche never knew whether what she was doing was right or wrong. She depended on her mother to tell her. She learned to wait for her mother's evaluation. She never trusted her own experience.

Over the months her therapist validated her experience and gave her mirroring and nurturing. Blanche's sadness and pain slowly moved toward anger. She went from inrage turned against herself to outrage turned against her offender.

She became clear that she had been victimized. She looked at her options for taking action. Her offender had moved away, and no one knew his whereabouts. He still frightened her. She expressed her anger symbolically in role-playing and talked to him in an empty chair. Ultimately she filed suit against her offender. Two years had passed, and her lawyer told her realistically how difficult her case would be, but she went ahead with it.

Blanche's assailant was never found, but the important issue here is that Blanche was standing up for herself. She made the decision to take legal action, and she felt very good about herself.

Blanche found it difficult to deal with the hurt and pain of her violation. She hardly knew her offender. It is much more difficult to do the grief work when one has been deeply attached to the offender.

Grief is the healing feeling. You need to go slowly. The more violent the act, the more slowly you should probably go in letting yourself talk about and feel your pain. Grief is a process that goes through predictable stages and takes time. A lot depends on your relationship with the offender and how attached you were to them. The more you cared about them, the more ambivalent you will feel. It is because of the parent's betrayal that incest and battering are such heinous crimes. When a child loves their parent, there is great ambivalence about telling the secret. The betrayal makes it hard for the victim to ever trust again.

If you are considering legal action, you need an attorney's advice. Be sure the attorney understands the nature of trauma. Gather all the data you can about your options, and then make the decision yourself. You are the one who was victimized, and you have the right to decide what you want to do. The only "must" I believe in is that you *must* talk about it to someone who can mirror you and take you seriously. And if you want to resolve your wound, you need to grieve it—feel the shock, hurt, anger, remorse, and loneliness. The process takes time and is sprinkled with denial, minimization, and redoing certain stages. You may be very angry one week and go back to sadness and hurt the next. You may go in and out of denial. Find a therapist with lots of experience. Let them be your ally.

SECOND-DEGREE DARK SECRETS

Second-degree dark secrets also need to be disclosed and confronted. In my model second-degree secrets are mostly about addictions, and secretive denial is the very essence of addiction. Since the whole family is usually involved in the secret, the whole family needs to be involved in the confrontation. A person can admit an addiction and *still remain in denial.* I used to sit in stinking taverns with my friend George (now deceased, a tragic victim of alcoholism) and discuss our dark secret of alcoholism. Drinking one beer after another, we delved deeply into our common problem. I had to reach a terrible bottom before I was willing to take action and stop drinking. George died before he hit his bottom.

The addiction secret often does not come out until the addict hits bottom, and bottom may be different for different people. Getting fired from a job, getting a divorce, getting AIDS, getting arrested for driving while drunk, having your life threatened by your lover's spouse—these are the kinds of things that bring people to their knees and break down their denial.

In most cases a formal confrontation needs to be made.

Formal Confrontation

Over the years a therapeutic method of formally confronting an addict has been developed.

The key is to assemble a group of the *most significant people* in the addict's life as well as his *enabling support system.* In most cases this is the immediate family. It may also include significant members of the extended family and close friends. It is also most effective to have the person who has *control over the addict's economic livelihood* (usually his boss) at the meeting. A person's boss has the power to threaten the loss of employment. This is powerful leverage. A therapist or 12-step-group person also needs to be there, who can take the addict to a meeting or to treatment right away.

Each person in the group tells the addict that they care for him (or love him) and give him a concrete specific instance of the impact of his addiction on their own life. Each one tells him that they think he is an addict and desperately needs help. When it is the therapist's turn, he tells the addict of a 12-step meeting or a therapy group or a treatment center that he will take him to. His boss tells him that he has to go if he wants to keep his job.

Addictions are whole-family illnesses and affect each member of the family in toxic ways. Members of the family are often simply not aware that as the overfunctioning enabling system, they keep the underfunctioning addict from having any chance of getting well. The family is truly delusional—they really believe that what they are trying to do is help the addict. They share the addict's denial.

Any person in the system can initiate the confrontation. But each member needs to be elicited and briefed on the steps and procedures of the confrontation. Children can often be incredibly potent in breaking the addict's denial system. James Jeder's daughter, Hannah, was the major source of transformation in his life.

James Jeder's Confrontation

James had extremely strong intellectual defenses that I had not been able to break through. I urged James's daughter, Hannah—by then in her early twenties—to be the instigator of his confrontation. I knew she was the one person James loved as purely as he knew how to. I was able to get his wife, Karen, one of his good friends who was in AA, the dean of James's department at the university, and his sister, Janice, to be in on the confrontation. I was glad Janice could be there. James had always spoken of her with respect. She had married an alcoholic and had joined Al-Anon. James told me that Janice had offered him help on many occasions.

We did the confrontation in James's office at the university. He had gotten drunk, gone to see a woman he'd had an on-and-off affair with, and then returned to his office to sleep off his drunkenness. Going to his office after an orgiastic night was a pattern that had developed over the last couple of years. Once I set up the intervention, I asked Hannah, whom I had seen earlier in counseling at James's request, to let me know the first night James didn't come home.

The actual confrontation reduced James to tearful admissions that he was in deep torment and wanted help. He went to AA with his good friend. His friend belonged to a group composed of academic people, several of whom James knew. James soon felt at home there.

Once James got a year of sobriety under his belt and his major denial system was dismantled, he became conscious of how his alcohol and sexual mood-altering kept him from dealing with the emotional pain of his parents' abandonment. Through original pain work, he grieved his childhood losses and began emotionally separating from his mother. What was hard for James was to see how he had created the fantasy image of a "perfect woman" in order to avoid the pain of his mother's using him. His mother had to be demythologized—not by the brilliant English professor and writer of poetry but by the wounded and needy inner child who was desperate for attachment to a goddess who would take care of his every need.

I found a men's group working on sexual addiction issues and got James to join it. Part of their process work, called the first step, was to write down the details of their sexual acting out, and then read it to the entire group. James told me it was probably the most painful thing he had ever done in his life, especially when it came to the details of his self-sex with pornography. But he did it. This simple confession of long-held dark secrets to a group of nonshaming people, who had the same or similar problems, is one of the most powerful healing processes that I've ever seen, and I've witnessed it many times.

James destroyed his pornographic stash within a week of reading his first step to his group, and in two years he has never returned to his habit.

Chart 10–3 will give you an overview of suggested guidelines for dealing with second-degree toxic secrets related to addictions.

CHART 10-3

SUGGESTED GUIDELINES FOR CONFRONTING SECOND-DEGREE SECRETS (ADDICTIONS)

IF YOU ARE THE SECRET-BEARER:

- You have a progressive and pervasive dis-ease rooted in denial.
- You are hurting yourself, your spouse, friends, and children.
- The only way out of shame and self-hate is to go through it. You must come out of hiding.
- Your addiction is life-damaging, and you are powerless over it.
- There is help available and many others who have confronted the same problem.
- Talk to someone you know who is in a 12-step program. Reach out, ask for help.

IF YOU LIVE OR WORK WITH SOMEONE
WHO IS IN AN ADDICTION:

- By avoiding confrontation you are letting them get worse.
- If you are a family member, keeping the "no talk" rule makes you part of the dis-ease.
- If only one parent is addicted and you are the child, the nonaddicted parent is also involved in addiction. Talk to someone—a counselor at school, a friend, a minister, a priest, a rabbi.
- If you're a family member and ready to do something to help your loved one:
  1. Decide who should participate in a confrontation, and get their agreement.
  2. Ask each person to think of a specific incident where the addiction has broken trust and hurt them, the family, or the addict.
  3. Plan the time and place for confrontation. The best time is when the addict is feeling ashamed of their behavior or experiencing bad consequences (just lost their job, caught in an affair).
  4. At the meeting each of you tell the addict:
     - that you love them
     - about the incident of hurt (use concrete, specific sensory-based terms)
     - that you think they are an addict and need help
  5. Have someone present who can take the addict to a 12-step meeting or a recovery or treatment center.

Birth Secrets

Secrets around adoption, paternity, and in vitro fertilization are also second-degree secrets. Every human being has the right to know about their origins.

One of the women on my PBS television series, *Family Secrets,* described finding her brother after years of searching for her natural family of origin. As she spoke, I felt the power of her claiming her rights and the joy of her homecoming.

Her name was Madelaine. She was told in childhood that she was from bad stock. She was shamed and humiliated at school. She also learned that she had a brother. At age sixteen she started looking for him as well as for her mother. The adoption agency refused to give her any information, so she took the phone book and wrote to every name corresponding to what she thought was her original name. The results were nil. So she found the priest who baptized her and asked him to help her. He told her she didn't have the right to find her mother and brother. She said, "I told him angrily that it was my right—it was my birthright."

Madelaine continued the search. When she was eighteen, a friend she had made at the adoption agency told her that she had found her brother and that his name was Robert. Madelaine went to see him and described her response in meeting him.

> There was an instant recognition. . . . I felt safe and at last I was going to have some connection. . . . It was a joy to look into someone's eyes and to think there was a little bit of me there.

No one has the right to keep the secret of our identity from us.

THIRD-DEGREE DARK SECRETS

Third-degree secrets are the most difficult to define and therefore the most difficult to give guidelines for. Their toxicity depends on factors like cultural beliefs, ethnicity, family process, and personal morality. The clearest way to grasp the polarity of third-degree secrets is to look at examples where the same content can function in a benign way in one family and cause dysfunction in another.

Earlier in this chapter I discussed Susie and Peter's long-term affair and how it actually gave Susie and her husband the space to work out their marriage and strengthen their family. Susie chose to disclose her affair to her husband. She did it at a time when their love had solidified and grown. I do not believe it was necessary for her to do so, but that was her choice.

Joe Ed's affair was quite another matter. It happened six months after he married Reba. He claims that the sexual encounter took place in a moment of weakness and involved a woman at his office who had been coming on to him for a long time. The actual sex was disappointing, and Joe Ed wound up with a painful case of herpes. Joe Ed's single infidelity caused him severe guilt. He felt terrible about contracting herpes and had to avoid having sex with his wife during several later outbreaks. Reba noticed these uncharacteristic sexual avoidances and wondered about them. Joe Ed became more and more obsessed with the fact that he might give his wife herpes. Over the next year Joe Ed and Reba's spontaneity and intimacy shut down. Joe Ed started arguments as a way to avoid sexual closeness. His secret affair and its aftermath were causing a gradual decline in his marriage.

I counseled Joe Ed to disclose his secret. When he did, Reba was furious. She withdrew from him for a while, but then talked obsessively about the affair, wanting to know every detail. I helped both of them to gather all the information they could about herpes.

A year later things were back to normal, and they were talking about having their first baby.

Chart 10–4 gives you the criteria that I use to decide if third-degree secrets need to be disclosed or confronted. Chart 10–5, while repeating some of the points I've made in relation to first- and second-degree secrets, is aimed specifically at some suggested guidelines for disclosing third-degree secrets.

CHART 10-4

DECIDING WHETHER TO DISCLOSE THIRD-DEGREE DARK SECRETS

LOOK AT THE FAMILY PROCESS

- Does the secret keep family members from separating and forming their own unique identity?
- Does the secret create rigid patterns of family interaction, blocking open communication, especially the expression of feelings and opinions?
- Does the secret breed distrust, dishonesty, and isolation among family members? Does it involve pretense, deceit, or evasion on a daily basis?
- Does the secret violate one or more family members' basic needs?
- Would the secret be especially harmful to a family member who is not in the know, if they were to find out accidentally or through someone else?
- Does the secret create a rigid triangle that costs one family member their autonomy?
- Does the secret create a rigid dyad that excludes all other family members?
- Does the secret cause the excluded family members (especially the children) to make up strange (even bizarre) fantasies relating to themselves?
- Is the secret long past? Does it have any lingering effects on family functionality? Does it really need to be exposed?
- Could someone be hurt more by exposing the secret than by keeping it?

CHART 10-5

SUGGESTED GUIDELINES FOR DISCLOSING OR CONFRONTING A THIRD-DEGREE FAMILY SECRET

WHEN CONFRONTING:

- Decide who should do the confronting. If it's a parent who has the secret, the other parent is preferable to one of the children.
- Decide on the best time and place for confronting.
- Decide on who should be included in the confrontation. General guideline: All those who are directly affected by the secret.
- Children should be included age-appropriately.
- Proceed slowly—no lightning bolts.
- What protection does the person need who is confronting the secret-keeper? Does the secret-keeper need to be protected?

WHEN DISCLOSING:

- If you are disclosing a dark secret to the family, what protection do you need?
- Start with the person you feel the strongest bond of trust with.
- Select a time when the person or family can debrief. Debriefing involves discussing, asking questions, and explaining feelings.
- Select a place where those who do not need to know (usually children) will be safeguarded.
- If family members cannot be present, prepare a letter to be sent to them. Be available for discussion.

Two Abortion Secrets

The following examples of third-degree secrets involve abortions that took place in the past.

Bud got his college sweetheart pregnant during their freshman year. They decided she should have an abortion. Later they broke up.

Bud married Sarah six years later. Sarah is vehemently anti-abortion and has participated in picketing abortion clinics. Bud believes she would be horrified if she knew about his involvement in an abortion. Bud also feels that his earlier decision was wrong. Does he tell his wife about something he wishes he had never done?

Based on the criteria in Chart 10–4, my belief is that Bud's secret is a matter involving his own conscience and does not need to be disclosed. Bud feels that he made a mistake, but he does not obsess about it. He now supports his wife's anti-abortion activities. The secret does not block open communication and love between Bud and his wife.

Bud does not engage in pretense, deceit, or lies on a daily basis.

Ned, on the other hand, was involved in an abortion during his senior year in high school. He and his father took Ned's girlfriend to a doctor in another city and paid to have the abortion performed. Ned's mother later found out about it and went into a righteous hysterical attack, condemning Ned and his father. The attacks continued off and on throughout Ned's early adult life.

Ned married a moderately religious woman who believes that abortion is wrong. Ned lives in fear that his mother will tell his wife about his girlfriend's abortion.

Ned has also become very vocal about a woman's right to abortion. This has created numerous conflicts with his wife.

Ned's secret causes him to avoid visiting his mother or inviting her over. Ned's wife believes their children should be allowed to see their grandmother and has frequent fights with Ned over this.

Ned's secret is clearly causing dysfunction in his marital intimacy, and this dysfunction will only get worse as time goes on. According to the criteria in Chart 10–4, Ned needs to disclose his secret.

I counseled Ned to pick a time when he and his wife would have ample space to discuss his disclosure. He agreed not to be defensive and to let her talk about her feelings.

Ned disclosed the secret by writing out a simple narrative of the event and reading it aloud to his wife. He tried to describe his frame of mind and his feelings at the time he and his girlfriend decided on the abortion. As he read the narrative to his wife, he started to weep. This surprised him, as he had never allowed himself to know how he really felt about it.

Ned told his wife that although he had vocally defended abortion, he didn't honestly know what he believed about it. He confessed that he wished it had never happened.

Ned's wife was silent for several minutes. Then she quietly and tearfully told him that she had aborted a child when she was fifteen. Ned was dumbstruck. He embraced his wife, and they held each other for a long, long time.

These examples focus on the relativity of third-degree secrets and show how the same *content* can result in a very different relationship *process.* This is why the process must be looked at in order to determine whether the secret needs to be disclosed.

Secrets Involving Children

The children's ages and the degree to which the secret is affecting their lives are important considerations. This is what the therapist who told me to go home and discuss all my secrets failed to take into account.

It is not always an easy matter to sort out. If the children are *into unusual behaviors of self-blaming or self-destruction,* that would be a big reason to include them. Children often engage in self-blaming fantasies in order to fill in the missing pieces. Consider the case of Jay, who was featured on my PBS television series *Family Secrets.*

Jay's father was paranoid and violent. He lived in the cellar of the house, shut off by a steel door. He often went on drug-fueled rampages in which he shot off his guns and screamed obscenities at imaginary enemies. On one occasion when he was eight years old, Jay hid under a table to watch his father, and like many young children who cannot grasp what is going on, Jay created a bizarre fantasy. He believed that his father was going to kill him.

Jay's mother and grandmother refused to explain to him that his father was mentally ill. After this incident Jay went days without sleep and was finally taken to a psychiatrist who gave him Seconal, a strong sleeping pill. Jay began a long bout with drug addiction, ending with his own attempted suicide.

It is clear that Jay should have been told that his father was mentally ill and drug-addicted and that some protection was needed to help him make sense out of his chaotic family life.

Another such secret involving a child could be a coalition between a parent and child. (Mom and Daughter refuse to tell Dad and the rest of the family that the daughter is pregnant and is going to have an abortion.) This secret needs to be disclosed. In a situation like this, you have to be careful of lightning bolts. Go slowly. The right time for Mom to tell Dad would not be just before the relatives come over. *Think* about it, and make a plan.

Another reason to disclose a secret is that it would be devastating if the unaware person found out about the secret accidentally or through someone else.

Secrets that involve a person's identity have often been disclosed by outsiders in traumatic and derogatory ways. I remember a girl in my elementary school who was shamed for being adopted by the older brother of her best friend. He had overheard his mother and father talking about it. The girl had never been told.

Another point to consider is this: The greater the intensity and the longer the secret has been kept, the slower one needs to go in disclosing it to those it affects.

If you are emotionally cut off from one of your children or from your parents, some effort should be made to reestablish contact before you tell them your secret. Suppose a parent or a child is gay or lesbian and wants to tell the secret, but the relationship has been highly conflictual in many ways. Small manageable steps at establishing contact may need to be taken before the secret is disclosed. Harriet Lerner suggests that gay and lesbian secrets may take a homophobic family more than one generation to integrate. Chunking down and moving slowly is a good principle in approaching any conflicted family relationship, whether there is a secret involved or not. The more cut off the relationship is, the more intense it is. We often put geographical distance between our parents, siblings, and ourselves when we do not know how to work out our relationships with them.

FOURTH-DEGREE DARK SECRETS

Fourth-degree secrets are individual secrets that hurt the secret-keeper. My secret fear of dancing anything but the slow dance two-step has curtailed my freedom and spontaneity. When I see people energetically dancing and having a great time, I'm envious. I really want to get out there and dance the way they're dancing. Maybe disclosing this secret here will move me to *do* something about it. Fourth-degree secrets are not fourth merely because they are individual. Individual secrets can be first-degree (murder), second (secret addiction), or third (had an affair and got herpes). Fourth-degree secrets are fourth because they primarily hurt the ones who hold them.

Fourth-degree dark secrets are dark because they impair freedom. They are not just matters of personal taste. Fear of being laughed at may have curtailed your involvement in sports. Being ashamed because you are fat may have caused you to avoid beaches and swimming pools. I have had many clients whose freedom and social life were severely impaired because of secret phobias and fear of panic attacks. Some had their whole lives shut down because of agoraphobia.

If you have a fourth-degree dark secret, it's worth thinking about who you could tell it to. Imagine what their response would be and how you would feel if you got the secret off your chest. The following group exercise can help you move toward disclosure.

Trying Out Disclosure

Ask everyone in the group to write out a fourth-degree secret. Remind them that this is a secret that only hurts yourself. It doesn't have to be huge to be hurtful. I once knew a man who chewed gum all the time because it stopped his lips from quivering when he spoke. Small as this cover-up was, the amount of energy it took cost some of his spontaneity and awareness.

Now have everyone fold up the paper with the secret and put it into a hat. The secrets are jumbled, and then each person reaches in and draws one.

Take turns reading the secrets. After each secret is read, the other people in the group—including the real secret-keeper—say what they think and feel about it. The secret-keeper gets a preview of how people would respond if they knew. Usually they're far less negative than the secret-keeper has imagined.

Of course, some fourth-degree secrets are too serious for games. They may require a therapist's help. Chart 10–6 gives you my suggested guidelines for disclosing fourth-degree secrets.

CHART 10-6

DISCLOSING FOURTH-DEGREE DARK SECRETS

THE COST

- Your secret hurts you by diminishing your freedom and blocking your spontaneity.
- Your secret wastes your creative energy in cover-up behaviors.
- Your secret blocks significant others from knowing you completely.
- Your secret keeps you from being accepted exactly as you are.
- Your secret may keep you from getting the help you need.

SUGGESTED ACTION

- Start with someone outside the family whom you feel you can trust (a therapist, counselor, minister, best friend). Make a pact with them that protects your boundaries about secret-keeping. Be sure they are willing to keep your secret.
- See how it feels to have someone know your secret.
- If it feels safe enough, risk telling your spouse or the family member you feel the closest to.
- Once you've told your secret, it will seem far less potent.
- If your secret is about panic attacks, bizarre fears, or secret phobias, be assured that you can be helped with therapy.

Confronting a Fourth-Degree Secret

You may suspect that someone you care about has a fourth-degree secret. Risk questioning the person about the behavior that seems to cover up a secret. Give them an opportunity to talk about it.

For example, Judy's boyfriend, Ian, was a Vietnam veteran. Every time she asked him to go to a party or to socialize in other ways, he declined.

One day Judy said to him, "Ian, I know you had a terrible experience in Vietnam. I know a little about PTSD and how any kind of excitement can trigger the anxiety and fear. I've been your girlfriend for eighteen months now, and you've avoided every social event I've asked you to take me to. It's taking a toll on our relationship. I know of a PTSD group that could help you, if your fear of social activities is related to PTSD. I'd stand by you all the way, if you decide to go."

Two weeks later Ian joined the group.

CHAPTER 11

STAYING CONNECTED WITH YOUR FAMILY

It can take years to figure out how to reconnect with a particular family member, but if we can slowly move in this direction rather than the direction of more cutoff, there are benefits to the self and the generations to come.

HARRIET GOLDHOR LERNER, *The Dance of Intimacy*

I learned that I needed to love my mother and father in all their flawed, outrageous humanity, and, in families, there are no crimes beyond forgiveness.

PAT CONROY, *The Prince of Tides*

Many people believe that the price they have to pay for staying connected to their families is to continue to be abused. In this chapter, I'll show you that it is possible both to stay connected *and* to refuse to be abused. Abuse is always prohibited.

A soulful approach to the family also demands that we give up our pretense at innocence. That is why we delved into our own shadow in Chapter 9. Even if my family is abusive, I need to look at my own crookedness, phoniness, and selfishness. When I acknowledge my own dark secrets and my own mysterious depths, it is far easier to accept the ultimate unfathomability of my family and the individuals in it.

 I recommend that you work hard to build your personal boundaries in such a way that while truly separating from a violating family member, you stay connected with them. We need to remember that even when someone acts inhuman and appears dehumanized, they are in fact human. *But for the grace of God, there go I.* We all share in the dark side of life, and while you may not have any first-degree dark secrets, I'll bet you can think of someone in your family that you have really hurt! To paraphrase W. H. Auden, we have to "love our crooked family with our crooked heart."

We need to sort out our families' dark secrets as best we can. Working through the secrets can help you separate from your family. But paradoxically, we cannot truly separate unless we stay connected.

One of the reasons it is difficult to separate from our families' emotional field is our powerful need to belong. Another reason is that very few families have broken away from the patriarchal/matriarchal model. This model wants members who conform to the group mind and abhors strong independent people who think for themselves and have passionately held values that differ from the family's party line.

Dark secrets also keep family members bound to the family system out of loyalty. In *The Prince of Tides,* Tom Wingo describes how his mother demanded the whole family's silence about his father's physical battering:

> My mother forbade us to tell anyone outside the family that my father hit any of us. . . . We were not allowed to criticize my father or to complain about his treatment of us. . . . He knocked my brother Luke unconscious three times before he was ten.

The Wingo family's type of loyalty is the rule in abusing families. No one can get out as long as they are ensconced in this kind of bondage to the family's emotional system.

Hopefully reading a book like this can give you a cognitive life raft, as you work on getting free.

SEPARATION IS NOT CUTOFF

Separating from the family's emotional field does not mean physically leaving the family. Many people are confused about this issue. They believe that if they have moved to another state or another country, they have left the family. Or they believe that having no verbal contact or interaction with the family means they are free of the family's emotional field. Quite the contrary, physical distance and refusal to talk or interact are forms of emotional cutoff, and emotional cutoff very often signifies greater-than-average intensity and love. Family members who are cut off emotionally are still embroiled in the nuclear family's emotional system! Harriet Goldhor Lerner writes:

> Distance or cutoff from family members is always a trade off. The plus is that we avoid uncomfortable feelings that contact with certain family members inevitably invokes. The costs are less tangible but no less dear.

What are the costs? The costs are paid in other relationships, usually relationships with our current family members—our spouses and children. The intensity we avoid with someone in our first family we bring to someone in our second—more often than not, to our children. I pointed out that Donald Jamison's cutoff with his son Doug was rooted in his unconscious grief over his father Donald cutting him off. Whatever excessive anxiety and reactivity we carry over from our family of origin gets played out in our subsequent intimate relationships.

Lisa's "Hot Issues"

On my PBS television series *Family Secrets,* a woman named Lisa vividly described how unresolved issues from her first family were triggered by the birth of her daughter and dumped on her husband.

During her childhood Lisa was molested by a neighbor and sexually abused by both her grandparents. Her family had a rigid "no talk" rule, and these matters were not discussed. Neither was her parents' divorce; she was told about it the day her father left the house.

Lisa learned to numb her feelings, and she developed an "everything is fine" false self. She married a man who was the baby in his family and needed to be dependent. Their marriage looked perfect, and Lisa liked the strokes she received for being the overfunctioning caretaker.

Then her daughter was born. Lisa said, "My daughter's birth triggered things I had tried to keep secret, even from myself."

Experiencing the baby's innocence and healthy dependency unleashed a flood of unfelt feelings. Lisa raged over the abuse that had been done to her. She raged over her own unmet needs and at being "trapped" into taking care of her husband's unhealthy dependency.

Lisa raged mostly at her husband. "Everything he said and every-thing he did was wrong. The poor guy didn't have a chance."

Lisa dumped all the unresolved "hot issues" from her childhood onto her husband. This is the danger of carrying unresolved issues from the past.

Irma's Fear of Making a Mistake

Irma came to see me because of her growing anxiety about "making small talk" at social functions. She needed to socialize a lot because of her husband's real estate business interests. She said that when she tried to talk to people, she became so fearful of *making a mistake* about her husband's business that she would just clam up and find an excuse to go to the bathroom or to the hors d'oeuvre table. This was a completely unrealistic fear, because her husband did not expect her to talk business at these affairs at all.

Irma also had a severe sexual shutdown that had started right after her husband expressed a desire to have a baby. She had seen a sex therapist and was able to function enough to have her first child, a boy. Once her son was born, she shut down sexually for a period of five months, and then she spontaneously began to function again.

A year and a half later, she had a second child, a girl. Right after her daughter's birth, her social problem started.

Because of her two pregnancies in two and a half years, Irma's husband had pulled away from her, and she feared he was having an affair. He drank heavily and was seldom home. She was afraid to talk to him.

When we did her genogram together, I found a secret that seemed at first to carry no big emotional energy for her. When Irma was eight years old, her mother confided to her that she had had a baby brother who had died two years before Irma was born. She had made "a terri-ble mistake," she said, and her family had sent her away to have the baby. After the child was born, she and the baby were sent to live in the country with an aunt and uncle. The baby died of "crib death" three months later.

It wasn't until later that I learned how Irma had first heard this. Irma had misbehaved at school the day before, and her teacher had sent her mother a note regarding her misbehavior. This was the reason her mother was telling her the secret! When the baby died, she said she felt that God was punishing her for her mistake. But then she met Irma's father, and they had gotten married, and God had sent Irma to *bring her joy*! She told Irma that her bad behavior at school made her very sad, just like when her brother died. She also told Irma that she was never to tell anyone this secret, especially her father, as he had a bad heart and "something like this might kill him."

Irma told me this after I had confronted her for a glaring incongruity: When she talked about painful things, she always smiled. After she told me about the secret, her smiling made more sense. Her mother had put an awful burden on her. Her reason for living was to keep her mother from having any more sadness or pain. From that day forward, Irma had been a "perfect" little girl and had not told her mother a single thing that would upset her.

Like any child her age, Irma was also confused by what her mother told her. Her mother's secret triggered lots of questions. Who was the father of her brother? Where was her brother buried? What was his name? Did her real father know the man? When she tried to ask a question about her brother's death, her mother told her never to talk about it again.

A child in such a situation creates *unconscious fantasies* and myths that cannot be put to rest as long as the necessary information is unavailable.

When Irma's husband announced that he wanted to have a baby, her unconscious fear of having a child who might die like her brother was triggered. So she shut down sexually—a way of trying to avoid the "big mistake" her mother had made. After her son was born, she was frigid until enough time passed to assure her he would not die.

Her daughter's birth triggered another aspect of the secret. Her anxiety about talking was an acting out of her unconscious fear that if she let down her guard, she might make a mistake and say the wrong thing, betraying her mother.

The end of this story is not a happy one. Irma would not confront her mother and get her questions answered. The secret was like a curse that bound her to her mother and forced her to distance herself from her father and her husband. This secret truly made her miserable.

James Jeder's Rage

We can see the same kind of dynamics in James Jeder's problems. Being set up to take care of his mother's emptiness and unresolved sexual abuse created layers of unresolved primitive rage in James. He acted that rage out in every female relationship. His first wife complained that he was angry all the time. His second wife stated, "No matter what I do, he seems to be angry about it."

James's chronic use of pornography in self-sex was also an act of anger. He viewed picture after picture of women in immodest and demeaning positions. He exercised total control over them as he masturbated to their lifeless pictures. This seemingly innocent "objectification" of women is an act of unresolved rage. This rage was the core of his sexual compulsivity and the major block to his ability to be sexually intimate. He carried his unresolved mother issue like a "hot wire," and it burned a lot of innocent women, including all the "women in the pictures" who were in his collection of pornography.

The common therapy slogans, "You either pass it back or you pass it on," and, "You either work it out or you act it out," are based on the fact that healthy separation from the family requires staying connected enough to "work through" the issues that are unresolved. Often these issues may not or cannot be fully resolved with a certain family member. But we can almost always take some small step in the direction of resolution.

James Jeder's original pain work made him conscious of these issues and allowed him to grieve the past. He was able to symbolically divorce his mother, Heather. He was also able to develop a good relationship with her later on. His wife, Karen, claimed that his rage was gone.

No matter how difficult, family connectedness is a prerequisite for being deeply intimate in the present without contamination from the past.

HOW DO WE SEPARATE AND STAY CONNECTED?

We have to separate and stay connected to our family of origin. What does that really mean? How do we do it?

It means that we develop a strong sense of self with solid but flexible boundaries, and that unless we are in danger of being abused, we do everything in our power to work out conflicts and resentments with family members, no matter how anxious and difficult they may be. Staying connected means that we have as little unfinished business with any family members as possible and that we make a real effort to value them without unrealistic expectations about what we will get in return.

The following test will give you a rough idea about your current ability to separate while staying connected.

Strength of Self Test

Think about each of the following statements. Then give yourself a 4 if the statement is *almost always* true about you and your behavior. Give yourself a 3 if the statement is *very often* true about you and your behavior. Give yourself a 2 if the statement is *seldom* true, and a 1 if the statement is *never true.*

1. I enjoy solitude. I like to spend periods of time with myself. _____

2. Although I've chosen to be in a committed one-to-one relationship, I do not feel I *have* to be in a committed relationship to be happy. _____

3. I am in touch with my feelings and express them to family members when it is appropriate to do so. _____

4. I know what my needs and priorities are, and I work hard to get them met. _____

5. I think about my alternatives and the consequences before I make a choice. _____

6. I can be spontaneous, but I do not make impulsive choices. I am able to respond rather than react. _____

7. I have bottom-line boundaries in my family of origin relationships. _____

8. I act according to well-thought-out values. _____

9. I express my opinion when I disagree with someone else's position. I can do this with my mother and father. _____

10. I don't run away or cut family members off when we are having conflicts. _____

This test is based on my own beliefs about what it means to have a strong sense of self. There are many other aspects of a strong sense of selfhood. I have tried to highlight the most essential ones.

Add up your score. If you scored between 35 and 40, you have reached a new level of psychic evolution! People who have done a lot of work on themselves usually score between 25 and 35. If you scored between 15 and 25, you still have some real work to do. If you scored below 15, you are either very vulnerable or you are putting yourself down—or both.

Let's look at some examples of people who have separated from their families but are still connected.

Bob and His Father

Bob's dad, a staunch Roman Catholic, calls him on the telephone. He asks Bob if his four-month-old son has been baptized yet. Bob was raised in the Catholic Church, but he has a lot of questions about his childhood faith and especially about infant baptism. Bob believes a child should reach the age of reason and have some choice in becoming a Catholic. Bob and his wife have decided to wait before they baptize their son. Bob had thought he could keep this a secret from his father, but now that he has been asked directly about it, he tells him the truth. Bob's father begins to give him a sermon, escalating into a rage after a few minutes. When Bob tells him he's raging, his father yells that he is not. Bob listens for a few more minutes and then warns his dad that he is going to hang up if he continues his diatribe. This infuriates his father, who starts a new sermon about honoring and respecting parents. Bob hangs up!

Two days later Bob calls his father, and his father won't speak to him. So Bob writes him a brief letter making several points in a nondefensive way. He states that it is his (Bob's) responsibility to raise his own child. That he appreciates how his father always taught him what he truly believed, and that he wants to follow that model with his own son. Bob repeats that after several discussions he and his wife had decided to wait till their son is old enough to better understand what he is doing by joining the Catholic Church. Bob ends by saying how much he wants his father in his and his son's life and that he loves him.

In this exchange Bob has exhibited a strong sense of self. He has a bottom-line boundary with his father. He refuses to be abused by his father's yelling. Bob also has his own well-thought-out beliefs and priorities. He states them clearly to his father. When his father becomes rageful and abusive, Bob puts an end to the conversation, but he calls his father a few days later. When his father refuses to talk (cuts Bob off), Bob stays connected by writing his father a letter. He acknowledges his father for his passionate beliefs and for modeling the teaching of those beliefs to him. Bob asserts his own desire to passionately teach *his* son what he believes. Bob ends by telling his father that he wants him in his life and his grandson's life and that he loves him.

Although he greatly feared this exchange and hoped he could keep his son's baptism a private decision, Bob is willing to stand his ground. He stays centered, expressing his own priorities and values and acting on his bottom-line boundary. In this transaction he shows great strength of self, while acknowledging his honest respect for his father's faith and expressing his love for his father.

Bernice and Her Mother

Another mark of separating from the family's emotional system and expressing strength of self is refusing to enter into conversations that triangulate other family members. When we triangulate others in conversation, we are usually avoiding covert, unresolved issues with the family member we are talking to. Talking about other family members allows us to avoid dealing with our own issues.

Consider what happens when Bernice goes to visit her mother. She has lots of love for her mother, who is getting old and has been sick recently. As the conversation begins, an old pattern immediately emerges. Bernice's mother starts talking about her own sister, Bernice's Aunt Mary. As usual it is a critical review of Aunt Mary's behavior over the last ten days. Bernice lets her mother talk until there is a pause, usually indicated by her gasping for air, because she talks so fast. Bernice quietly says, "I don't want to talk about Aunt Mary. I want to talk to you, Mother. I've been wanting to tell you how much I appreciate you and all the kindnesses you have done for me. I especially appreciate your help with the children."

Bernice's mother then begins to talk about Bernice's brother's children, her daughter-in-law, and what a rotten job *they* are doing raising their children! Once again Bernice waits for a pause and tells her mother that she feels it might do more good for her to tell her daughter-in-law directly. There is a long silence. Bernice says, "Mother, when

I talk to you, I want to talk to *you*, to hear how you are feeling, and I want to share my feelings with you. There's a lot I don't know about you and things I want to tell you. I want to be closer to you." Her mother seems uncomfortable, breaks eye contact, and says, "That's nice, but I have to go and get dressed right now. Ruth is taking me shopping this afternoon."

What Bernice has done for the first time in her life is refuse to be triangulated in her mother's conversation about other family members. This is a secret ritual that has gone on in this family for a long time. Bernice maintains her strong self-boundary by not taking her mother's bait and gossiping about her aunt and sister-in-law. She *does not lecture her mother* or *violate her mother's boundaries.* She is straightforward and stays within her own boundaries. Her mother avoids the invitation to greater closeness. There's nothing Bernice can do about this except to make her own intentions as clear as possible.

One week later Bernice writes her mother a card, thanking her for listening to her and again stating her desire to achieve greater closeness. She ends by expressing some specific feelings of appreciation for her mother.

Bernice is separate from her mom. She makes her boundaries very clear. She tells her mom what she needs and wants and stays connected by following up with a tender card.

Bryan's Confrontation

Bryan was twenty-seven and working for his father's law firm. One day as he opened his dad's desk looking for some papers that his father had asked him to find, he saw a letter signed, "Your son, Ralph." Bryan was stunned. He felt disoriented and dismayed. He couldn't believe that his father had another son and that *he* had a half-brother. A week later he called his mother, who had divorced his father when Bryan was fifteen. She had remarried and was living in another city. Bryan's mother told him that his father had had a son when he was in the army. He had gotten a woman pregnant and was going to marry her when he was suddenly shipped overseas. When he returned, she was nowhere to be found. He never knew whether she had had his child or not. Twelve years later she called, saying she needed money for his son, Ralph. Bryan's father went to see her and was convinced that Ralph was indeed his son.

Bryan was still overwhelmed by this news when he came to see me.

He wanted to confront his father right away, but I suggested that he take some time to think through what he wanted to accomplish. He then invited his father to a session with me, saying that they needed to discuss a very serious matter. His father agreed to come.

Bryan began by recounting the many things he liked about his father. He described some of the things he was very grateful to his father for. Then he said, "Dad, you have never told me I had a half-brother. I found out about Ralph accidentally. I feel shocked and betrayed. I have a right to know about my brother. I feel that if you would not tell me something this important, maybe there are other things you have not told me. The discovery of my brother has been a blow to my sense of trust in you."

Bryan's father was silent for some time. Then he said that he had sincerely believed it was best not to tell him about Ralph when he was a child. Over the years the secret had grown darker. Ralph was now an alcoholic and basically a drifter.

Bryan looked his dad squarely in the eyes. "Dad," he said, "Ralph is your son and my brother. I see you looking down and away as you talk to me, and I see lots of shame and guilt on your face. I want to go and meet my brother, and I'm going to do what I can for him." Bryan's dad was again silent. Bryan got up and left my office. His dad appealed to me for advice. I told him I thought Bryan had a right to know about his brother.

Bryan did establish a relationship with Ralph. He kept his father informed about what he was doing. On our last visit together, he told his dad he loved him very much and wanted his help in doing an intervention on Ralph. His dad agreed to be involved. I got a note three weeks later saying that Ralph was in a treatment center in Minnesota. That's the last I heard of them.

Because of Bryan's strong sense of self, he was able to express his love for his father while refusing to sweep the issue of his brother away. While he could understand his father's conscious desire to protect him, he also saw his covert guilt and shame. Bryan did not blame or judge his father, but he did express his strong feelings of betrayal and his strong desire to connect with and help his brother.

Because of his strength of self, Bryan actually helped his father resolve an issue that had haunted him for years. I have no doubt that working together to help Ralph also restored a sense of trust between Bryan and his father.

Giving Up Overfunctioning

My final example is from my own life. My darkest secret was narcissistic deprivation. I learned early on that I got love and admiration in my family by taking care of people's pain. Initially overfunctioning felt very good. It allowed me to feel in control of most situations, and I liked to fix people's problems. I gave a lot of unsolicited advice and was often told I was "patronizing" by members of my extended family. I was so delusional that I dismissed their comments as jealousy. I also had the habit of cutting people off if, after all my efforts to "help" them, they would not follow my advice.

I came to realize that we overfunctioners may look like we've got it all together, but we really need help ourselves. I also learned—much to my chagrin—that the more I overfunctioned, the more the person I was trying to help underfunctioned. I could mood-alter my own pain and emptiness by overfunctioning, but I wasn't really helping anyone.

I have gradually learned not to offer unsolicited help or try to fix my relatives' problems. Instead of trying to "have all the answers," I have deliberately shared my deep vulnerabilities with family members. When asked for help, I do what I can, but I do not try to do more than I am asked to do. When I *really* don't know what to do, I say so. I don't fantasize solutions that sound good but are not based on my own experience. I try to honestly admit that I have my own problems, some of which I don't know how to solve.

The outcome is that I have developed a much stronger sense of self, and my relationships have improved as well. I no longer have the chronic feeling that no one gives as much to me as I give to them. And I know that if I am obsessing on another's problems, I need to look at my own.

I hope that these examples, plus the statements on the test, give you a fairly good sense of what it means to have a strong sense of self. Let me sum up by saying you have a strong sense of self when you can:

- Express disagreement with your father and stay calm.
- Refuse to go to church services with your mother just to make her feel good.
- Set a bottom-line boundary that you will not talk to your alcoholic mother when she's been drinking.
- Tell your brother or sister that you feel upset by their jokes about gays and lesbians or people of color.

- Have a fight with your wife and stay connected with her. Staying connected means that both partners agree to work toward some negotiated compromise. Staying connected also means *refusing to exit,* whether by physically leaving, refusing to talk, using mind-changing drugs, or distracting with TV shows or discussions of off-the-subject topics.
- Have a set of beliefs and values that you live by.

You stay connected to your family when you:

- Send your father a subscription to *Golf Digest,* even though he has condemned you for leaving the family religion.
- Buy your mom a new prayerbook as a special Easter gift.
- Call your mother and tell her you love her when you know she hasn't been drinking.
- Send your brother or sister a humorous card and tell them you love them and *do* have a sense of humor about other things.
- Send your wife her favorite flowers with a note telling her you love her twenty-four hours after the fight.
- Live your beliefs and practice your values to the fullest without trying to convert your family. Send them a sincere statement that honors their values, while acknowledging if you don't share them.

I probably never learned the lesson of separation and staying connected any better than from a woman who was on a TV show with me in New Jersey. The program was on incest, and I was the supposed expert. This woman had been incested by both her parents for the first thirteen years of her life. As a result of this, she had been in some form of therapy for over sixteen years. At one point she spoke of her current relationship with her parents. The host of the program was visibly shocked and interrupted her, asking her *why* on earth she still had anything to do with her parents. She responded clearly and with a softness in her voice, "They are the only parents I have. It's important that I work out a relationship with them." Her parents had also been in therapy and were working on themselves and on having a decent relationship with their daughter.

ABUSE IS ALWAYS PROHIBITED

Please do not misunderstand what I'm saying here. Staying connected to your family never means allowing yourself to continue to be abused. In the examples I have given, people with a strong sense of self set bottom-line boundaries. If your family member is a substance abuser, staying connected does not mean you must be burdened by the consequence of their dark secret. Stating clearly that you will not stay around or talk to them when they are using is a bottom-line boundary, a refusal to share in their secret. Calling when you are reasonably sure they are sober or sending a card expressing love is a way to stay connected.

SOME UNEXPECTED REWARDS

Now that you have delved deeply into your family's secrets, I hope you have found the sources of behaviors that have confused you in the past. I hope you have found some secrets that can be exposed, and I hope their exposure will alleviate some burdensome shame and offer you some solid choices.

My soul-searching journey brought me some very rich rewards. Let me share one of them with you.

My male model as a child was my grandfather. He was a warm sweet man, and I loved and admired him. My family called him a saint and put him on a pedestal. He had a very rigid philosophy of work. He believed that you get an honest job and work as hard as you can, and success will come. He started as an office boy with the Southern Pacific Railroad and ended up fifty years later as an executive. The family considered him to be very successful financially.

The fact is that it never occurred to him to look for another job with a much larger potential. His motto was, "Be satisfied with what God has given you."

As a child of a large family and a survivor of the Depression, he had some good reasons for his beliefs. But his message that "once you've got a job never leave it" also had some unexpressed and secret elements. It contained the almost paranoid fear that had run through my family for generations. This raw fear was a dangerous family secret. My grandfather was too frightened to take any risks, and he was my role model for success. Because he was a "saint," he was unchallengeable.

What he taught me helped me immensely, but it also held me back. He taught me to save money, stay out of debt, and work hard. As long as I stayed bound to my family's emotional system, I settled for very little. I stayed where I was, never asked for a raise, and was grateful to have a job. I had to be fired from two jobs to wake up from the family trance.

Once I emotionally left the family, I challenged the destructive and secret fear that fueled his philosophy of work. I looked around for new opportunities and new levels of financial reward. I changed jobs often. I've gone far beyond what he would have considered financial success.

I had to bring my grandfather's covert message into conscious awareness. I had to *think* about it and understand it in the light of his history. Then I could make my own choices. My life would have been very different had I not emotionally separated from his secret message.

I do not mean to imply that I'm happy because I've made more money than my grandfather. My happiness really comes from a new self-definition: one that says you're worthy of whatever you honestly want and can create. The joy in my life right now stems from the creative risks I've taken because I believed in myself. My grandfather loved me and believed in me. That certainly helped me a lot.

I'm not putting him down for his fears. He was indoctrinated with fear and insecurity by *his* family of origin. He did better than the limits of their fear, and I've done better than the limits of his fear. I believe that this is what each of us is called to do. And I believe that my grandfather would be very proud of me.

I hope you have found some unexpected richness in your family. Whether we like it or not, some of the dark secrets are not just the source of our hang-ups, reenactments, and idiosyncrasies; they are also the source of our genius and our strengths. Our families, with all their dark secrets, are still the ground of our lives and, as Thomas Moore puts it, "the chief abode of our soul."

Once we have deciphered our dark family secrets, we are free to embrace our families with a new sense of freedom and love.

Exercise for Rewards

Make a list of five useful patterns of behavior that you learned in your family. These can be character strengths, positive habits, special ways that you learned to survive, and special ways someone nurtured you. Be as specific as possible about how these have helped you.

FORGIVENESS

I believe that forgiveness is essential to full human happiness. This includes forgiving ourselves as well as all the members of our extended family.

Forgiveness is an excellent way to achieve solid selfhood. It frees us from the endless cycles of resentment toward our parents and the bondage that hate creates.

Fritz Perls, the founder of Gestalt psychology, wrote that as long as we hold on to our resentments, we never really grow up! We remain stuck, powerless, and dependent children, unable to separate from our parents. In expending the obsessive energy and resentment, we are held in bondage to the past and lose our ability to be fully present in the now.

Forgiveness helps the one who forgives. When you forgive, the energy that formerly held the resentment in place can be used creatively. *Forgiveness* literally means "to give as before."

If you are the survivor of a first-degree toxic secret, I'm not suggesting that you in any way condone what was done to you. I'm also not suggesting that you have to spend time with the family member who was your offender. Above all I'm not suggesting that you ever risk being abused by this person. You can stay connected through cards, letters, or phone calls if you don't want to see them in person. Forgiving them doesn't excuse their behavior. It simply frees you from their power over you.

If you have trouble forgiving, you may want to consider some or all of the following:

Certain kinds of abuse are more damaging than others—sexual and physical abuse leave deep emotional scars. When the abuse is chronic, the impact is usually more devastating than a single instance. The kind of abuse and the chronicity of the abuse are two indicators of the time it will take to work through the hurt and pain. In such cases forgiveness often takes longer.

It has helped me greatly to realize that it is impossible to fully understand another person. When I take a soulful approach to parental abuse, I'm forced to look at my own shadow. How many people have

I hurt? If I can be mindful of my own part in hurting others (especially my own children), I can lose my attachment to my own victimization and my readiness to condemn my parents.

I remember a crucial moment in my own therapy. I had been talking again about my dad's abandonment of me, and how we had to move in with relatives, and how we moved ten times in fourteen years. My therapist interrupted me in the middle of my story. He looked me in the eyes and said, "I want you to spend the time between now and our next visit saying to yourself, 'My suffering is ordinary.'" The request seemed strange, but I told him that I would do it.

When I left his office, I found myself getting angry. What does he mean—my suffering is ordinary? I was almost orphaned by my father—he never gave a cent of child support! I went on and on in my head, until I was screaming at my therapist and vowing I'd never go back to him. I stayed angry for several days. Slowly it began to dawn on me that I was enormously attached to my victimization. It had become part of my identity.

Then I remembered my experience with the third windowpane in Johari's window. The other therapists in the group had confronted me with the "pleading," almost "frantic" style of my speech when I was telling them about my childhood abuse and abandonment. It was as if I were begging them to see how wounded I had been! Was this a way to protect myself from people's expectations? After all, anyone as abused as I was should be excused their faults and mistakes. I came to realize that victimization was also a way for me to be accepted. It became a kind of reverse grandiosity. I was the *most* wounded of the group. I was *special*.

Later my therapist helped me to see that by making my suffering "special" and becoming attached to it, I could avoid doing the grief work I needed to do in order to get to forgiveness. As a theologian and a former Dominican priest, he reminded me that most theologians and philosophers see suffering as a *fact* and mystery of human existence. It is as normal as pleasure and joy. And as the biblical character Job discovered, there is no rational consolation for it. "Just accept your suffering, do your grief work, forgive your offender, and move on," he told me. It will take some time, but the important thing is to do it. Making victimization your "special identity" will keep you from actually *feeling* the pain and emptiness you are carrying around with you. Mood-altering by trying to figure out your suffering will keep you from actually grieving it. And unless you do your grief work, you cannot forgive.

Dark secrets are part of my soulful fate. They challenged me to delve deeper into my history. I hope yours have done the same for you. Life is ambiguous to the core. Accepting my family's dark secrets as the shaper of my destiny tempers the terrible moralism of either/or thinking. I am learning tolerance for imperfect human nature. I can begin to love my family's complexities and ambiguity.

I said earlier that along with their dark secrets, we also carry our parents' unconscious desires and their noblest dreams. James Jeder's love of English literature came partly from sitting at his grandmother's bedside and listening to her read to him. His books of poetry embodied his mother's, grandmother's, and great-grandmother's dreams!

James had also learned from his grandfather Donald Jamison. He was shrewd with his finances and had an unusual amount of property for an academic.

James and his father, Shane, reconciled ten years before Shane died. James spent several sessions talking to me about his father's rather tragic life. On one occasion he wept profusely as he recalled that his father had taken several correspondence courses in an attempt to better his education. James felt that his father had had some big dreams that he could never fulfill. His most recent book of poetry is dedicated to his father, with love.

EPILOGUE

One of the dictionary definitions of *secret* is "something that is still to be discovered." In this sense, secrecy is the core of soulfulness.

Our soul's full potential is always being discovered. There is always more than we can know and more than we can define. Your soul is utterly unique and unrepeatable. There has never been anyone like you and will never be again. Because of this uniqueness we can never fully understand ourselves. I have survived things I didn't know I could survive. I have come to see strengths in myself I didn't know I had. I have borne dark family secrets and transformed them in a positive way. And I feel sure that you have done the same.

All of us have a depth of power, a deeper reality that I am calling soul. It is the mysterious source of many of our achievements as well as the ground of our imagination. When we lose touch with our imagination, our soul is stifled. That is why the phrase "What you don't know won't hurt you" is especially deadly. By killing curiosity, which is imagination's lifeblood, it destroys our freedom and creativity.

But soul can never be taken away. I know of no greater miracle than to work with someone, helping them embrace their pain, and then watching their deeper resources and talents emerge. Once they are safe enough to give up their defenses, their soul's power can reveal itself.

At the beginning of this book I asked you to question everything, to embrace beginner's mind. Now at the end I'll remind you that there comes a time when it's valuable to stop questioning. Like life itself, our families cannot be totally figured out. They need to be embraced as a mystery to be lived.

APPENDIX

THE PARADOX OF MEMORY

> Memory is indispensable to our personal and communal lives . . . in order to use it and preserve its value to us, we have to acknowledge its limitations and protect against them.
>
> WALTER REICH

It was November 1989. A woman phoned the police and reported that her father had killed her best friend. The woman's name was Eileen Franklin Lipsker; her best friend was named Susan Nason.

Eileen said she had been standing on a spot in the woods a little above the place where Susan was sitting, when she saw Susan twist her head—Susan had red hair—and look up at her, trying to catch her eye. She said Susan's clear blue eyes were pleading with her. Then she saw something move to the side of Susan, and she recognized the silhouette of her father, George Franklin, outlined against the sun. Both his hands were raised high above his head. He was gripping a rock. He steadied himself and then brought the rock down on Susan's head. Eileen saw Susan put her right hand up to try to stop the blow. She heard a thwack like the sound of a baseball bat swatting an egg. Another thwack, and then she saw blood everywhere on Susan's head, some hair that was no longer attached to her scalp, her blood-covered face, her smashed hand.

Eileen told the police that she felt intense guilt about Susan's death. She told them that it had been afternoon when she and her father encountered Susan alone, and that it had been she—Eileen—who persuaded Susan to go for a ride with them. Her father drove them to a place outside the city, where he first raped Susan and then killed her. He threatened to kill Eileen if she told anyone what she had seen.

Eileen also reported that she had been sexually abused as a child by her father, and that on one occasion he had forcibly held her down while his friend raped her. She had learned not to talk about what her father did to her. She said she loved him dearly.

There is one more key fact about this case: Eileen Franklin Lipsker had been eight years old when her friend Susan was murdered. That was in 1969. *It took her twenty years to report the murder!* She claimed to have forgotten everything about it until one crucial day in January 1989. How could that be possible? And if she had forgotten every detail of it, how did she remember it?

These questions take us to the heart of the current debate about the nature of memory. Are all memories to be trusted? Can memories be repressed for years, and if so, how can we determine their accuracy? Are there false memories, and can they be implanted in a person's mind? What do we know for sure about memory? Is there a clinical reality called "false memory syndrome"?

In Eileen Franklin Lipsker's case, a jury believed that repressed memories are possible and believable. In 1990 her father, George Franklin, was sent to prison for life, guilty of murder in the first degree. In 1993 the California Court of Appeals upheld the conviction, and the California Supreme Court declined to hear George Franklin's appeal.

The question of whether repressed memories are true or false is not only a pressing legal problem but a clinical one. In another recent case, a father was awarded $500,000 in damages by a jury that felt his daughter had been unduly influenced by a psychotherapist to accuse him of molesting her as a child. In this case the jury believed that the therapist was responsible for the patient's "confabulated" memories.

FALSE MEMORY SYNDROME?

To "confabulate" is to replace facts with fantasy. The majority of those accused of confabulating memories are women, and the memories are about incest. In March 1992 an advocacy organization was formed called the False Memory Syndrome Foundation (FMSF). At last count it comprised some four thousand families who say they have been falsely accused of sexually abusing their children. Because of these charges, many parents have lost all contact with their accusing children and grandchildren. Furthermore, when these charges become publicly known, parents find themselves socially ostracized. Some find themselves embroiled in legal battles as their children take them to court. Some women who originally believed they were incested have joined the organization—they now claim that their therapists made direct suggestions to elicit memories of sexual abuse. Finding these memories precipitated confrontations with the alleged offenders (often their fathers), which led to the breakup of their families and to excruciating emotional pain.

In the debate that still rages, the therapeutic community argues that while there are isolated cases of therapists leading their clients with suggestions about incest, the vast majority are extremely responsible when it comes to delicate matters like repressed incest memories. They are concerned that FMSF has started a reactionary public campaign based solely on anecdotal, unverified reports, without bona fide research. While the foundation claims to want to disseminate scientific information concerning false memory, as yet no one has presented clear evidence of the existence of a clinical *syndrome* involving false memory. Yet the public reaction has been substantial enough to put therapists in a kind of double bind.

Therapists feel trapped. There are times when symptomatic behavior in their clients demands questioning them about the possibility of sexual abuse; not to ask questions in such cases is a disservice to their clients.

The entire debate was brilliantly presented by Mary Sykes Wylie, the senior editor of *The Family Therapy Networker,* in the September/ October 1993 issue of that magazine.

At the center of this controversy are three important points that have relevance for this book and for the subject of dark secrets. They are: the power of suggestibility, the nature of memory, and the difference between traumatic memories and ordinary memories.

THE POWER OF SUGGESTION

Michael Yapko, a clinical psychologist in San Diego, did a survey of nearly a thousand therapists. He concluded that some of them—"too many" (he gave no numbers)—were misinformed about vital aspects of the roles of suggestibility and memory in treatment.

Many adults whose developmental dependency needs were

thwarted by abuse, especially during the early toddler stage, tend to *take others' suggestions as orders to be obeyed.* Anyone raised in a strict authoritarian family, where conformity is ensured by means of physical punishment and emotional abandonment, loses the ability to think for themselves. Such a child learns to obey and to conform their will and mind to their family's authority. This conformity becomes a lifelong pattern, which is easily rekindled by another authority figure, especially a therapist. If your childhood developmental dependency needs were frustrated through physical, sexual, or emotional abuse, your suggestibility is exacerbated, and you may be a prime target for those who present themselves as authorities.

Suppose you were raised in a strict authoritarian family that used physical or emotional punishment to keep you in line. Let's further suppose that later in life you begin to experience symptoms of physical illness that have no biological basis—what is often referred to as psychosomatic illness—and that your doctor advises you to see a therapist.

You got to a therapist, who immediately suggests that many survivors of incest have psychosomatic illness as a symptom of their abuse. The therapist further tells you that survivors of sexual abuse numb out emotionally while they are being abused. They no longer feel the rage, hurt, and betrayal of their abuse. So they convert these numbed-out feelings into psychosomatic sickness, which allows them to feel as bad as they *really* feel.

Then suppose the therapist asks you, "Do you have any memories of incest in your childhood?" Suppose you answer, "Not that I'm aware of." And the therapist says, "You don't have to be consciously aware of the symptoms for incest to have taken place. In fact, many people who have been incested are not aware of it at a conscious level." This exchange could easily set up a situation in which the developmentally deprived child in you, eager to please your new parental figure, is ready to follow any suggestion your therapist gives you.

Let's say, in a worst-case scenario, that the therapist gives you a list of other common symptoms associated with incest. Now you are combing through your childhood memories, both dreading and hoping that something will fit together. This imaginary example is a blatant case of an overeager therapist leading a client with suggestions.

As a rule of thumb, the client should always provide the primary data from which questions are asked. Psychosomatic illness can be a symptom of any form of trauma. To immediately select a question about incest clearly reflects the therapist's issues, not the patient's.

THE NATURE OF MEMORY

What do we actually know about the nature of memory? The human brain is extremely complex, and no one yet has claimed mastery over it. We tend to describe the operations of the mind on the basis of what technology our minds have created. When machines were invented, the brain was viewed as a machine. When the movie camera appeared, the brain was compared to a camera. Today, the brain is often considered to be like a computer.

Obviously our brains do have some of the qualities of these inventions, but the brain is more complex and all-embracing than any of these models can portray. Oversimplification is especially misleading when we consider the question of how memory works.

If we think of our brain as a camera, or tape recorder, or computer, then we see memory is a vast data bank of exact neurological impressions. In this view every experience we have ever had is recorded and filed away. Memory is a fixed container of all past experience.

While sometimes we experience memory in this way, most modern psychological research sees memory as more of a dynamic, creative process. The brain has a capacity to invent and create reality from the information it processes, and our intentions shape our memories. In this model, memory is a process that is constantly in flux, updating past experiences in the light of current beliefs. Our current beliefs about the *meaning* of past events, especially as they relate to the present, actually shape our memories of those events.

In Chapter 3 I talked about how perception is selective and tends to trade off full awareness of reality for safety and security. Memory does the same. Normal memory tends to support our current sense of our own identity. The past is being continually remade, and it is strongly reconstructed in the interests of the present.

How We Remember

Dr. Lenore Terr is one of the leading researchers on trauma and memory, and she became a key witness for the prosecution in the Eileen

Lipsker trial. In her book *Unchained Memories* she discusses two primary categories of *how* we remember and six kinds of memories.

The two primary categories of *how we remember* are: explicit, sometimes called declarative memory, and implicit, sometimes called nondeclarative memory. Explicit memory is the result of conscious thinking. You read something, find it interesting, *think* about it, and lay it down in "speech code" as a memory. With some mental practice or rehearsal, the memory can be prolonged forever. When thought and rehearsal are blocked, most memories are lost in about thirty seconds.

The only exception to this is traumatic memory. "An alert traumatized child does not have to rehearse in order to remember," writes Dr. Terr. Traumatic memories behave like memories that are entirely implicit.

Implicit memories require no conscious thought. They are the result of habit. We humans learn in this way when we learn to walk or talk. Once we have learned certain skills, such as reciting the alphabet, or swinging on a swing, or riding a bicycle, we don't have to think about them anymore. We always remember how to do them—unless we suffer brain damage.

Terr also discusses six basic kinds of memories. The first is called *immediate.* Do you remember what your relationship to a co-worker is when you meet them? When you begin a sentence, can you finish it? Immediate memory involves quick association with what is remembered.

The second type of memory is *short-term.* What did you eat for lunch yesterday? Who did you phone yesterday? Where did you go last weekend? Short-term memory loss is a first sign of organic disorder. It is also a common symptom for people who are using drugs or are depressed or chronically stressed.

The next four kinds of memory are all *long-term memories.* The third kind of memory is "knowledge and skills." Much knowledge is firmly entrenched and is entirely semantic. Skill memory carries very few verbal instructions and is implicit and habitual. Once you learn to type, ride a bicycle, hit a golf ball, or tell time, you never forget.

The fourth type of memory is called *priming.* I had never left the country to go abroad until I was in my early thirties. Once I went on a holiday to Jamaica, I felt like going on more trips. The fantasies of danger I had had about the unknown were now replaced with *memories* of fun and excitement. That's the result of priming. A person who knows how to water ski is more primed to try snow skiing than one who does not.

The fifth kind of memory is *associated memory*. This type of memory requires no thinking. I was conditioned by my southern mother and grandmother to say, "yes sir, no sir, yes ma'am, no ma'am," to older men and women. I find myself still doing this at the age of sixty. Good manners, standing up to sing the national anthem, putting your hand over your heart as you say the Pledge of Allegiance, are all associated memories.

The sixth type of memory is *episodic memory*. This is the remembrance of things that happened in your life: the happy episodes, the sad ones, the miserable times, the scary times, the wonderful times, the great times. Episodic memories make up the stories of your life. These episodic memories may include traumatic memories. Traumatic memories are at the center of the debate concerning false memories.

WHY TRAUMATIC MEMORIES ARE DIFFERENT

Some traumatic memories are vividly remembered by the survivor of the trauma. Some trauma victims have flashbacks and experience hypermnesia, a state in which they remember some or all the details involved in their abuse. It is also very clear that many sexual abuse victims repress their memories and enter a state of amnesia. According to Dr. Terr, "memory does not go bad or vague just because it is repressed, and traumatic memories, in particular, do not deteriorate much at all." She goes on to say that episodic memories that are the opposite of trauma—peak moments from childhood—are also remembered in some detail: "Both kinds of memories stay more alive than other kinds of memories."

Type I and Type II Trauma

Dr. Terr spent considerable time studying the memories of twenty-six children in Chowchilla, California, who were kidnapped on July 15, 1976, from their school bus and were returned twenty-seven hours later, physically unharmed. Their abductors had driven them around in darkened vans and then buried them alive in a truck trailer lowered below ground level in a rock quarry. Dr. Terr interviewed a group of the children seven to thirteen months after the event and then again four to five years later. She also interviewed children five weeks and fourteen months after they had seen the space shuttle *Challenger* blow up on television. According to her account, "every single child in both groups [Chowchilla and Challenger] remembered what had happened."

On the other hand, when Dr. Terr studied some four hundred separate childhood tales of trauma in her clinical practice, she found that some children do forget traumatic experiences.

In 1988 Dr. Terr published a clinical study of twenty very young trauma victims whose ordeals had been verified by police or eyewitness documentation. She found that the children who had been repeatedly traumatized had more amnesia than those who had been traumatized only once.

This, along with her work with the children in the Chowchilla group, led her to define a Type I trauma victim as one who has suffered a single traumatic event, and a Type II trauma victim as a repeatedly traumatized person. Type II trauma victims are much more likely to repress their memories.

Eileen Lipsker's violent alcoholic father had beaten her mother and siblings. The first time he violated her sexually, she was three years old. A repeatedly violated child, Eileen learned early in life to suppress her memories. By age eight, suppression was no longer a temporary maneuver. Without any thinking or planning she put her memories out of consciousness.

Mistaken Memories

Dr. Elizabeth Loftus, an expert on memory from the University of Washington, testified for the defense at the Lipsker trial. Dr. Loftus's work studies the "wrong things" that people can be made to perceive and later remember. In experiments she has successfully implanted false memories that her subjects were quite convinced were accurate.

She managed to implant a memory of a minor trauma into a young teenager, who was led to believe he had been lost in a mall when he was five years old. The youngster confabulated details of his own and added them to the original story. This proves that emotion-laden memories can be confabulated. It does not, however, prove that traumatic memories like incest are confabulated.

In spite of the interesting points in the Loftus research, no laboratory-induced memory with a teenage volunteer or graduate student *could remotely approximate an actual incident of traumatic child-hood sexual abuse.* It would be grossly unethical to try and stage a traumatic event with a human subject in order to prove that memories can be confabulated.

Cognitive psychologists point out that the profound terror, grief, and isolation that come from trauma, especially when the trauma involves betrayal by a parent or other survival figure, have a tremendous impact on long-term emotional, cognitive, and even physiological functioning.

"Trauma sets up new rules for memory," writes Dr. Terr. For example, Eileen Lipsker made several perceptual mistakes about her father's murder of Susan Nason—among them, she confused the time of day when it occurred. But despite her perceptual mistakes, the jury believed the central theme of her retrieved memories: that she had actually seen her father kill Susan Nason. They believed she had accurately retrieved the *central subject matter* of the memory.

In fairness to Dr. Loftus, she has spent twenty years trying to dispel the myth that human memory is infallible and immune to distortion. She has argued convincingly that repressed memories of childhood sexual abuse, when they are the sole source of criminal and civil charges against parents, can be the product of a therapist's suggestion and the client's imagination. At this point in our knowledge, we must do all we can to find external corroboration for repressed memories. Dr. Loftus argues that if therapists accept *all accounts* of repressed memories as literally true, they may be increasing the likelihood that society in general will reject the *genuine* cases of childhood sexual abuse.

Traumatic Memories Can Be "Right" *and* "Wrong"

A myriad of vivid details and a few mistakes are not mutually exclusive and do not in and of themselves prove a memory true or false. Both amnesia—the partial, temporary, or complete forgetting of an event—and hypermnesia—the capacity to relive over and over via flashbacks every minute detail of an occurrence—are considered symptoms of post-traumatic stress disorder.

Trauma victims are known to retain both correct and incorrect perceptions in impressive detail. The memory may be both "right" and "wrong" at the same time. Some parts are correct; other parts are incorrect.

The Chowchilla children could recall many aspects of their experience in precise, brilliant detail. Yet eight of them misdescribed something about their kidnapper. The Chowchilla victims were Type I trauma victims.

According to Dr. Terr, once Type II victims recover their memories, they tend to remember more precisely than Type I victims. She writes, "Repeatedly traumatized children are less likely than singly traumatized ones to make perceptual mistakes about their abuse."

A Type I or Type II trauma memory can be precise and detailed and, at the same time, wrong because of the terrible stress and surprise that are involved in every single trauma. At the first moments of an unanticipated shock, a child easily perceives things incorrectly.

REPRESSION IS MORE THAN FORGETTING

Repression is the act of setting a memory aside. It probably starts with suppression. *Suppression* is a deliberate and conscious move. We all do it. We don't say what we feel to our boss about what he does or says. We stop thinking about a painful issue for a while, although we can return to thinking about it if we need to. Suppression is the most common defense against our conflicts.

As one is traumatized repeatedly, suppression leads to repression. With repeated victimization the act of setting the memory aside leads to its permanent removal from consciousness. Freud viewed repression as an ego defense. Ego defenses are the attentional strategies we use to avoid pain that is so great that it threatens our core sense of self. According to Daniel Goleman, repression has come to mean "the defense wherein one forgets, then forgets one has forgotten." R. D. Laing, the British psychiatrist, wrote about catching himself in the act of forgetting a very embarrassing situation. "I had already more than half forgotten it," he wrote. "To be more precise, I was in the process of sealing off the whole operation by forgetting that I had forgotten it." When we repress a memory, there is no trace that we have done so. The fact that the information has been repressed is forgotten, and so we have no motivation to try and remember it.

One study conducted by Linda Moyer Williams of the University of New Hampshire followed a sample of a hundred women eighteen to twenty years after they had been brought as children to large urban emergency rooms following sexual abuse. Interviewing these women without indicating that she knew of their abusive backgrounds, she asked whether they had ever been sexually abused. Thirty-eight percent of the sample reported they had not been abused, in spite of their hospital records.

One could object and argue that the thirty-eight percent were simply guarding their privacy. The problem with that objection is that these women were answering other questions involving areas of great privacy.

Triggers for Repressed Memories

Since we have no conscious motivation to discover what is repressed, how do repressed memories surface and come to a Type II trauma victim's attention?

Bessel Van Der Kolk, a research psychiatrist at Harvard Medical School, has done extensive research on trauma of all kinds, especially trauma associated with sexual violation. He contends that when a child is chronically violated, the brain is so overwhelmed by the negative stress that it cannot accommodate and integrate all the information it is receiving. The person's limbic system, which filters and integrates emotion, experience, and memory, is disrupted. Memory and emotion are in effect severed. This may be the explanation for flashbacks. It may also explain another phenomenon, the "body memories" that sexual abuse victims often experience. Van Der Kolk says that "the emotional sensations related to trauma are remembered through a different memory, either as bodily sensations or visual images."

There are really no adequate words to describe traumatic experiences. The more horrible the trauma, the fewer words there are for it. Likewise the earlier the trauma, the more difficult it is for the victim to express what had happened. When any new experience resembling the original scene occurs, an arousal is triggered and is experienced as a memory fragment blip, a flashback, a visual image, or a nightmare. The person experiences it in a nonverbal way. There are no words for it, because it has never been integrated into the person's full experience.

Eileen Lipsker's memories of her father's murder of Susan Nason were triggered by looking at her own daughter from a certain angle. One January day in 1989, her five-year-old daughter Jessica, whom she called Sica, had just come home from kindergarten with two friends. The three girls sat on the floor to play, and Eileen sat on the couch.

At one moment Eileen caught Sica glancing up at her, twisting her head to ask a question, her clear blue eyes shimmering in the afternoon light. At exactly that moment Eileen remembered her friend Susan Nason looking up, twisting her head, and trying to catch her eye. Eileen then saw her father gripping a rock above his head, and she saw Susan put her right hand up to try to stop the blow. And then she heard a thwack like the sound of a baseball bat swatting an egg.

Eileen said later that she tried to stop the memory and stop the chill that ran up her spine. She felt intense fear that if she told anyone, her life and her children's lives would be in danger. Eileen had always known that Susan had been murdered. But she did not consciously know that she had been there when it happened. Over the next ten months, additional memories emerged, until she felt she had to go to the police.

In this case the repressed episodic memory returned because of a visual cue and because Eileen was in a general emotional state of security. Because she was feeling relaxed, her mind on idle, the memory could bypass the powerful inhibitions that blocked the memory. But usually emotional security is not enough. For traumatic-memory retrieval, there needs to be a perceptual stimulus—a sight, sound, smell, touch, or taste—or the experience of a state, mood, or feeling originally connected with the repressed memory. Sometimes the memory comes back via a dream. Vision seems to be the strongest immediate stimulus to lost memory. When the Franklin jury saw photographic blowups of five-and-a-half-year-old Jessica and Susan Nason side by side, their similarity brought on involuntary gasps. Any or all the senses can be the trigger for a repressed memory.

Conflictual Feelings

Conflict is a key to repression. Eileen was torn between images of her father as a monster and images of the father she loved. When her memories began to return, she tried to stop them because they brought back the conflicted feelings of love and hate that were part of the reason she repressed them in the first place. She did not want to deal with the memories because to do so she would have to see her father (whom she loved) as evil.

Most victims of abusive parental trauma have repressed their memories partly because of their conflictual feelings of love and hate for their parent. Most do *not* want to deal with the memories once they are triggered.

Symptoms of Repressed Trauma

Trauma causes injury and leaves a scar. There are often clusters of subjective feelings and symptoms that offer confirmation of terrible episodic repressed memories.

There were some powerful clues in Eileen Franklin Lipsker's life. Eileen had adored her father. She had *perpetuated her father-daughter relationship* by marrying a man much older than she, who was extremely controlling.

Other symptoms were there from the time the memory was first repressed. Soon after Susan's murder, Eileen became withdrawn at school. She began pulling out the hair on one side of her head, creating a big bleeding bald spot near the crown. This was Eileen's unconscious attempt to duplicate the horrible wound she had seen on Susan Nason's head.

Eileen became promiscuous after leaving high school. She tried prostitution for a period of six weeks. This could have been an acting out of her sexual abuse. As a child her father had forced her into sex. Prostitution may have given her the belated chance to control sex and choose it.

Eileen had another habit that seemed connected to her childhood trauma. Susan Nason had been playing alone when George and Eileen spotted her. Eileen had talked her into going for the drive with her and her dad. As an adult, whenever Eileen found a child playing alone in her Canoga Park neighborhood (where Susan had been playing), she took the child home.

When Eileen was fourteen, her mother and father divorced. The sexual abuse ended, and she stopped pulling out her hair.

Such symptoms and signs—in addition to those I mentioned in Chapter 9—are easier to see in hindsight, once the repressed memories have resurfaced. But they often vividly tell the story of a Type II trauma victim's early childhood.

A FINAL WORD OF CAUTION

It is a fact that the traumatic abuse of children by their caretakers occurs with some frequency and has enormously damaging effects on the abused child. It is also a fact that these memories can be forgotten as a result of psychological processes whose nature is not fully understood. It is a further fact that these unconscious memories may emerge later, sometimes decades later, with power and clarity.

But not all recovered memories are true, although many surely are, and not all those accused of abuse are guilty, although many surely are.

The bottom line for this book is that I want to warn you to be very careful and thorough in probing your family's secrets. Recovering traumatic memories is a very delicate matter. If you feel like you are uncovering such memories, you should seek out a reputable person who has some expertise in these matters. Leave no stone unturned in finding another family member who might be able to verify the abuse, and use all other objective means available to verify your memories.

BIBLIOGRAPHY

I'm grateful to the following authors for helping me to grasp the meaning of family secrets. I recommend your reading their books as a way to deepen your understanding of family secrets.

Adams, Kenneth. *Silently Seduced: Understanding Covert Incest.* Deerfield Beach, FL: Health Communications, 1991. This is an excellent presentation of how love addiction is rooted in covert incest.

Baum, L. Frank. *The Wonderful Wizard of Oz.* Berkeley and Los Angeles: University of California Press, 1986. This is a reprint of original version of *Dorothy and the Wizard of Oz.*

Birdwhistell, Ray L. *Kinesics and Context.* Philadelphia: University of Pennsylvania Press, 1970. This fascinating book on nonverbal communications and patterned covert behavior in families is a great resource in understanding how we first learn the family secrets.

Bok, Sissela. *Secrets.* New York: Pantheon Books, 1982. This is a difficult book, because it is so scholarly. I found it quite profound, especially on the issue of why some secrecy is essential for personal liberty.

Bowen, Murray, M.D. *Family Therapy in Clinical Practice.* New York: Jason Aronson, 1978, 1985. This is a collection of Murray Bowen's collected papers. See especially chapter 16, "Theory in the Practice of Psychotherapy," and chapter 22, on separating from your family of origin.

Bradshaw, John. *Bradshaw On: The Family.* Deerfield Beach, FL: Health Communications, 1988. This book outlines the theory of family systems in depth and describes several types of dysfunctional families.

————. *Bradshaw On: Healing the Shame That Binds You.* Deerfield Beach, FL: Health Communications, 1988. This is my extensive treatment of healing toxic shame.

————. *Homecoming: Reclaiming and Championing Your Inner Child.* New York: Bantam Books, 1990. This book gives you a checklist for each developmental stage of childhood and offers several ways to work on grieving your unmet needs. In *Homecoming* I offer you a way to know the secret of your childhood abuse.

————. *Creating Love: The Next Great Stage in Growth.* This is my work on the secret or covert beliefs about love that each of us carries from our family of origin. This belief needs to be made conscious and critically evaluated.

Buechner, Frederick. *Telling Secrets.* San Francisco: Harper, 1991. This is an intriguing autobiographical piece in which Buechner candidly shares the secret of his father's drinking and suicide and the impact this secret had on him as a father, husband, and writer.

Conroy, Pat. *The Prince of Tides.* Boston: Houghton Mifflin, 1986. A brilliant novel about one family's dark secrets. Reading it gave me an experiential awareness of the power of dark secrets to impact lives.

Covitz, Joel. *Emotional Child Abuse.* Boston: Sigo Press, 1986. I'm indebted to Covitz for a number of Jungian quotes. I think that this book is the best presentation of emotional abuse that I have read.

Flannery, Raymond J. *Post-Traumatic Stress Disorder.* New York: Crossroad Publishing Co., 1992. Flannery is a clinical psychologist and an assistant professor of psychology at the Harvard Medical School. This book offers an excellent discussion of PTSD and is especially good in explaining the phenomenon of kindling.

Foster, Carolyn. *The Family Patterns Workbook.* New York: Jeremy P. Tarcher/Perigee, 1993. A good resource for helping you discover family patterns.

Fredrickson, Renée. *Repressed Memories.* New York: Simon & Schuster, 1992. This book, written by a psychologist with many years of experience, is an excellent presentation of material relevant to traumatic memory and repression. I consider Dr. Fredrickson to be one of the leading authorities in the area of sexual trauma.

Goleman, Daniel. *Vital Lies, Simple Truths.* New York: Simon and Schuster, 1985. The subtitle of this book is *The Psychology of Self-Deception.* I found it to be very helpful, especially the parts that pertain to group psychology and the power of the group mind to distract individual group members' perceptions and distort their ability to think critically.

Guerin, Philip J., ed. *Family Therapy.* New York: Gardner Press, 1976. This book brings together original contributions from the leading family system thinkers in the field of family therapy. There are several good articles by Murray Bowen in this book.

Harper, James M., with Margaret H. Hoopes. *Birth Order and Sibling Patterns in Individual and Family Therapy.* Gaithersburg, MD: Aspen Publications, 1987. This is the most current material on birth-order positions that

I know of. Both authors worked with Jerry Bach and Alan Anderson and have their endorsement in this book.

Imber-Black, Evan. *Secrets in Families and Family Therapy.* New York: W. W. Norton & Co., 1993. This book was published a year after I began working on my book. Its appearance was like manna from heaven for me. It gives the reader scholarly articles from expert clinicians on various family secrets. Although I take full responsibility for what I've written, I used this work as a primary resource.

Lerner, Harriet G. *The Dance of Intimacy.* New York: Harper & Row, 1989. No one presents the Bowen material with any greater clarity than Harriet Lerner. I encourage you to read this book if you're interested in *experiencing* the Bowen Theory rather than just reading about it. Also see her fine book *The Dance of Deception* (New York: HarperCollins, 1993).

McGoldrick, Monica, and Randy Gerson. *Genograms in Family Assessment.* New York: W. W. Norton & Co., 1985. This is the best book available to help you understand the power of the genogram and to guide you in constructing one for your own family.

Miller, Alice. *The Drama of the Gifted Child.* Translated by Ruth Ward. New York: Basic Books, 1981. Miller describes the wound of narcissistic deprivation in this book. Also see her *The Untouched Key,* translated by Hildegarde and Hunter Hannun (New York: Anchor, 1990). Miller uses the story of the emperor's new clothes to help us grasp the secret that we cannot know—the real truth of our childhood—once we've been victimized by normal patriarchal parenting! The boy in the story has not yet become a victim of patriarchal pedagogy.

Pittman, Frank. *Private Lies: Infidelity and the Betrayal of Intimacy.* New York: W. W. Norton Co., 1989. Pittman focuses on the secrecy and dishonesty involved in an affair and makes a strong case for disclosure.

Schneider, Carl D. *Shame, Exposure and Privacy.* Boston: Beacon Press, 1977. I'm indebted to Schneider for all the research on healthy shame that he did for this book. I recommend it to all, especially to those who read my book on shame. This book will stretch and expand your understanding of shame.

Sheldrake, Rupert. *The Presence of the Past.* New York: Random House, 1988. This is the best book for the lay reader on the subject of formative causation (how forms are passed from one generation to the next). If you want to probe deeper, start with *A New Science of Life,* Sheldrake's first book (Los Angeles: J. P. Tarcher, 1981).

Shengold, Leonard, M.D. *Soul Murder.* New York: Fawcett Columbine, 1989. In this book Dr. Shengold describes two unconscious secrets that are created by severe childhood abuse and deprivation—the erasure of the abuse experience so that the victim cannot know the truth of their childhood, and "double think"—the phenomenon of simultaneously holding two contradictory concepts in mind without seeing that they cancel each other out.

Taub-Bynum, E. Bruce. *The Family Unconscious.* Wheaton, IL: Theosophical Publishing House, 1984. Taub-Bynum writes about the power of the family as an enfolding energy field. He offers a number of other ways to understand the mysterious fact that everyone in the family knows the dark secrets at some unconscious level.

Terr, Lenore, M.D. *Unchained Memories.* New York: Basic Books, 1994. This book is very helpful in understanding traumatic memory. I took much of my discussion in the Appendix from Dr. Terr.

Toman, Walter. *Family Constellation.* 3rd ed. New York: Springer Publishing Co., 1976. This book contains Toman's work on sibling positions and other relationships. Some of this material is quite helpful.

Webster, Harriet. *Family Secrets.* Reading, MA: Addison-Wesley, 1991. This book offers some in-depth stories about several different family secrets and how they impacted family members' lives.

ACKNOWLEDGMENTS

I want to express my thanks to all the people who have had the courage to share their family secrets with me.

I'm very grateful to my editor, Toni Burbank, for her patience, organizational skills, and creative brilliance.

This book would not be possible without the pioneering work of Murray Bowen. I take full responsibility for my interpretations of Dr. Bowen's ideas.

The 1980 article on "Family Secrecy" in *Family Process* by M. Karpel was an invaluable resource for helping me to clarify the difference between constructive and destructive secrets and for suggesting guidelines for confronting destructive secrets.

I thank Dr. Evan Imber-Black and all the clinicians who contributed articles to her book *Secrets in Families and Family Therapy*.

Carl D. Schneider's work on *Shame, Exposure and Privacy* helped me expand my own understanding of natural shame as modesty—the emotion that protects privacy. Schneider's work led me to the central thesis of this book, the view that dark secrecy is a defense against violations of modesty.

There are many other family system thinkers, too numerous to mention, who paved the way to my writing this book. I thank them all.

I'm most thankful to my sister, Barbara, who painstakingly labored through three revisions of this book. Barbara often added useful comments of her own, which enriched the text in many ways.

I thank Maggie Rees for lovingly keeping my secrets.

I thank my higher power for all the secret blessings bestowed on my life.

For information on John Bradshaw's audio and video cassette tapes, write:

Bradshaw Cassettes
8383 Commerce Park Drive, Suite 600
Houston, TX 77036

or call (800) 627-2374.

For information about workshops and lectures, write:

John Bradshaw
2412 South Boulevard
Houston, TX 77098

Please send a stamped, self-addressed envelope.